VERY SPECIAL PLACES

A Lovers' Guide
to America

VERY

A guide to the most romantic inns, hotels, resorts, and other hideaways in America

Additional material by Bob Scanlon

Illustrations by Claude Martinot

(Former title: *Lovers' Guide to America*)

SPECIAL PLACES

A Lovers' Guide to America

IAN KEOWN
with Linda Burnham

COLLIER BOOKS
A DIVISION OF MACMILLAN PUBLISHING CO., INC.
NEW YORK

COLLIER MACMILLAN PUBLISHERS
LONDON

OTHER BOOKS BY THE AUTHOR:
Lovers' Guide to the Caribbean & Mexico
KLM's Holland
Arthur Frommer Guide to Athens
KLM/ALM Guide to the Dutch Caribbean
Guide to France for Loving Couples (co-author)

Macmillan Publishing Co., Inc.
866 Third Avenue, New York, N.Y. 10022
Collier Macmillan Canada, Ltd.

Library of Congress Cataloging in Publication Data
Keown, Ian.
  Very special places.
  Edition of 1974 published under title: Lovers' guide to America.
  1. Hotels, taverns, etc.—United States.   I. Title.
TX 909.K46   1978   647'.9473   78-7716
ISBN 0-02-077230-0

SECOND PRINTING 1979

Printed in the United States of America

CONTENTS

GREEN MOUNTAINS, WHITE MOUNTAINS

IN AND AROUND THE
BOSKY BERKSHIRES

FROM THE SHAWANGUNKS
TO THE ALLEGHENIES

IN AND AROUND THE
CHESAPEAKE BAY

THE SHENANDOAH VALLEY
—UP HILL AND DOWN DALE

FROM THE CAROLINAS
TO THE KEYS

FROM THE GREAT LAKES
TO THE GULF

IN AND AROUND
THE ROCKIES

THE DESERT RESORTS
OF THE GREAT SOUTHWEST

SUNNY SOUTHERN CALIFORNIA

SAN FRANCISCO AND ITS NEIGHBORS

THE PACIFIC NORTHWEST

PREFACE

The title has changed, the credo is the same. Apparently the word "lovers" confused some people. There were those for whom it meant honeymooners only (what, one wonders, are newlyweds supposed to be before and after?); for others it connotes "shacking up." You might almost get the impression that America is a nation of closet lovers.

To avoid confusion, therefore, and reach a wider audience, the guide will now be known as *Very Special Places.* For very special people. Because one of the most encouraging results of the original guide was the number of readers who took the time and trouble to write and comment, corroborate or criticize. This correspondence is extremely useful in keeping track of the performance of each hotel, and I hope it will continue. Many readers also sent me suggestions for places that they thought should be included in future editions. Many of these suggestions have, indeed, been incorporated into this edition. There are, in all, about fifty new inns, hotels, and resorts in this edition; it also covers new parts of the country, and it includes a supplementary list of places that for one reason or another did not quite make it into the main body of the text. Several hotels have been dropped; some have gone out of business, one or two asked to be left out (presumably the "shack-up" syndrome), others just cannot be recommended any longer. Some just did not bother to answer my preliminary questionnaires, perhaps because they were afraid that putting something down on paper might commit them to spending money—but the fact is, *no hotel pays to be in this guide.* It's completely independent. The selection of hotels and the ratings are entirely my responsibility. If I've left out one of your favorites, I apologize; if I've overpraised or underrated, I hope I will get it right next time.

THANK-YOUS

This guide could never have been produced without the help
and encouragement of countless people—friends, readers,
colleagues in the travel business, total strangers in chance
encounters. I thank them all, and ask that they will forgive
me for not naming them one by one. However, I would like to
single out a few colleagues for a special vote of thanks:
Lynda Bernard, who relieved me of the chores of preliminary
research; Susan Hannah, for invaluable critiques of work-
in-progress; my copy editor at Macmillan, for thoroughness
and erudition. Above all, a thank-you for three fellow writers
who researched and wrote about several of the hotels: Linda
Burnham (L.E.B.), Bob Scanlon (R.E.S.), and Maria Shaw
(M.S.); I assume they did it for friendship because the pay
certainly didn't justify the effort, and I'm deeply grateful to
all three.

INTRODUCTION

*"O for a seat in some poetic nook,
Just hid with trees and sparkling with a brook."*

This is a book of nice places.

Old inns. Hideaways. Resorts. Trysting places. Shangri-las. Places to nip off to for a few days to be together and alone.

These are special places for people who enjoy the finer things in life. Not necessarily expensive, just simple things—watching sandpipers at sunset, munching freshly picked apples, scrambling over rocks, sipping mulled cider in front of a log fire, bicycling through lanes of moss-covered oaks, trudging through the snow, listening to Mozart under the stars, riding desert trails among saguaro, cholla, and cottonwoods.

It's primarily for lovers—of all ages and inclinations. Man/woman, boy/girl, boy/woman, roué/Lolita, boy/boy, girl/girl, rich lovers, poor lovers. Couples whose children have grown up and fled the fold, and who now have an opportunity to enjoy each other once more.

This guide is *not* for swingers.

It's *not* for people who'd rather see a floor show than the moonlight, who'd rather hear the action at a crap table than the sound of surf in a rocky cove.

It's *not* for people who want heart-shaped bathtubs, or mirrors on the ceilings, walls, and headboards, or tiger-skin bedspreads and tiger-skin rugs in rooms with fountains dribbling down purple walls (don't snicker, these places exist). Swingers will be bored out of their bejoggled skulls by most of the places in this guide.

SETTING THE GROUND RULES. All the inns, resorts and hotels in this guide have something special going for them. The something special could be antiquity (Longfellow's Wayside Inn in Massachusetts or the Wayside Inn in Virginia), location (Skyland Lodge in Virginia's Shenandoah National Park, Highlands Inn in Carmel, California), charm (the Inn at Sawmill Farm in Vermont, Greyfield Inn on Cumberland Island), nostalgia (Wentworth-by-the-Sea in New Hampshire, La Valencia in California), unabashed luxury (The Stanford Court in San Francisco, The Breakers in Palm Beach), seclusion (Sundance in Utah, Timberline in Oregon), sports facilities (Sun Valley Lodge in Idaho, Hilton Head Inn in South Carolina)—or more often than not, a combination of several of these special "somethings." A few are included mainly because they combine charm with relatively low prices.

They're places where you won't be embarrassed if you forget to write Mr. and Mrs. when you sign in, where bellhops won't wink if the initials on your luggage don't match, where chambermaids won't come barging in on you in the morning, where you won't have to sit down to breakfast with snoopy old ladies who'd just love to know what you were really doing up there. They're places where you can escape neon, piped music, television and jukeboxes, formula decor, conventions, coach-loads of tourists and irruptions of children. (Well, more or less, because the advantage to writing an independent guidebook is that you not only make your own rules; you can then break them. Some of the places listed in these pages *do* have piped music and television and conventions, but they're included because they have other qualities that compensate for these drawbacks.)

PET PEEVES. You'll notice occasional references through-out this guide to irritants like piped music and television. They're among my pet peeves, and even if I end up sounding like a curmudgeon, here's why. You go away for a quiet weekend together, and you deliberately pick out a spot where you think you'll be allowed to enjoy the blissful environment, so you do *not* want to sit down in the bar or dining room and have to listen to what someone else has decided you ought to listen to. It just doesn't make sense to search out a Colonial tavern in New England, order lobster or pumpkin pie, and have to listen to "Down Argentina Way" or some hack's or-chestral arrangement of the love duet from *La Bohème* (I've had to listen to both during *one* piece of pumpkin pie). Like-wise TV. You drive around country lanes, lapping up the sce-nery and the solitude, and you arrive full of the joys and glories of nature at a lovely old inn, go into the lounge ex-pecting to find a welcoming fire, and instead find gunslingers going full tilt on the telly. (This is not to say that inns and hotels should not have any television sets for guests who want them; I just feel that TV should be in places where peo-ple can watch without interfering with other guests who *don't* want to watch.) If you feel the same way about TV and piped music (and I'm delighted to discover from readers' let-ters that many of you do), ask the innkeepers to turn the bloody things off. Tell them you came to the coun-try/beach/mountains to listen to the birds and crickets, not hectoring commercials or piped marshmallow music.

Live entertainment is another matter. You can't very well ask the innkeeper to send his musicians packing, so the best you can do here is to ask him to throttle back the ampli-fication. In this guide, I've tried to alert you to places with live entertainment so that you will not be surprised; many of them are large enough to allow you to slip off to someplace where even the boomingest amplification can't penetrate.

Now, about children. They can be, at times, a combina-tion of piped music, television and amplification in a few tiny bodies. But not always. And it may not be the children who are the problem; more likely it's the parents, trying to have a vacation themselves, who allow family discipline to deteriorate to the point where order can be restored only by a public slanging match. This is no fun for other *parents* who are trying to get away from children for a few days, and quite shattering to people seeking a romantic atmosphere. A few of the smaller hotels in this guide flatly refuse to have children under, say, ten; many of the large resorts have separate play areas, dining rooms, and dining hours for children, which should help to keep them out of your hair. In a few of the hotels, children (and their transistor radios) are likely to be present during the vacation periods, which is only fair, and these hotels should be avoided at those times. (Some readers have, apparently, come to the conclusion that these comments indicate some form of kidophobia. Tsk, tsk. Some of my best friends are children, and I herewith apologize for any misunderstandings to Karen and Mandy, Jay-Jay and Susan, Jaimie and Kate, and other young ladies and gentlemen who know how to eat with a knife and fork.)

CONVENTIONS. Throwing out hotels that hold conventions would mean eliminating every other hotel in the guide. However, there are conventions and there are conventions—groups, seminars, annual meetings, workshops, and a score of other assemblages. These days, any excuse to get away from the office is reason enough to hold a meeting in a hotel or, better still, resort; and even the smallest hotels rely on groups of some kind to keep themselves alive during the slow months. However, very very few of the hotels and resorts in this guide are able or willing to handle mob conventions of beer salesmen or placard-waving politicians; when they do host meetings, their groups usually consist of high-level executives, professors, governors, company directors, and others who can usually be relied upon to conduct themselves in an unobtrusive manner. Most of the larger hotels and resorts in this guide can be enjoyed by a loving twosome even when there's a group or seminar in the house (some-times even more so, if the group in question is closeted all day in meetings, leaving you with the tennis courts and beaches all to yourselves). *However, to be on the safe side, when you make your reservation, ask if a large group is scheduled for that period.* Most hotels will understand your concern; indeed, some will warn you automatically without having to be asked. You can also do some preliminary re-search yourselves by reading the "P.S." category in the indi-vidual hotel listings, where you'll find a rough guide to the convention/group situation in each hotel.

CHECKING IN. In these liberated times, nobody seems to bother to check credentials. Even nice little old ladies at re-ception desks in Maine don't care (*unless* one of the partners looks very, very young, or one or both partners look down-right disreputable). If you sign Mr. and Mrs., chances are no one will question it. If you balk at anything so specific, sign the accurate if unromantic "Mr. Blank and party." If both parties prefer to list individual names (for business reasons, for phone calls), most hotels will understand, especially since many *married* couples now check in by listing their indi-vidual names. The simplest solution, for guests and ho-tels, is the noncommittal M/M. Bear in mind that many hotels will add your name and address to their mailing list, for newsletters, brochures, and updated rates; if you're not supposed to be wherever you are, and you don't want anyone to find out months later, ask the manager to keep your name off his list.

SIGNING CHECKS. If, for some reason, you must check in under an assumed name (you are, say, a very famous film star), there's no point in flashing a credit card in your own name; in such cases, have a quiet word with the innkeeper or credit manager *before* you sign any checks in the bar or res-taurant. Also, even if you have registered as Mr. and Mrs., the young lady, for example, may instinctively sign her own name, causing minor palpitations in the bookeepers' cubicle; just remind each other occasionally who you are. Also, if the signing partner has a quaint name, like Keown, make sure the other knows how to spell it. And pronounce it.

RESERVATIONS. There's a lot to be said for just driving around in a pleasant carefree way, then stopping for the night where and when you like. But that's not always possible, and there's nothing more frustrating than being all ready to tumble into bed only to discover that there's no bed available in the inn where you wanted to tumble, nor in the other inn down the road, and you waste hours driving around looking for *something,* only to end up in an unromantic motel. Don't take chances: *always make a reservation in advance,* even if only a few hours in advance. (And always doublecheck the rate when you do so, just in case an innkeeper has had to jack up his rates since he published his 1978 figures.) Moreover, if you want to specify a particular room or type of bed, it's essential that you reserve as far in advance as possible.

Most inns, hotels, and resorts will hold your room until 6 p.m. If you plan to arrive later than that, ask them to hold the room (and to be sure they do, send a deposit). This is particularly important in small inns that cannot run the risk of having an empty room. Conversely, if you make a reservation and later decide to cancel, call the inn to tell them, so that another couple will not be turned away needlessly.

RATES AND RATINGS. Hotels have different ways, often unfathomable, of establishing their rates, and what you're going to pay depends on such variables as twin beds versus double beds, with bath, without bath, facing the front, facing the rear, lower floor, upper floor, on beach, off beach. And so on. I wish I could spell out all the variations for each hotel, but if I were to try, the seasons would be over before I managed to get halfway through. In any case, I assume that you like each other so much that tiresome trivia and a few dollars won't come between you. Some guides, of course, do not give you *any* rates, on the theory that the subject is too complex and unpredictable. I think this is unfair to you: if you are paying for a guide, you deserve as much information as possible, and you should not have to make dozens of phone calls just to find out which inns you can afford. Granted the published rates may not be 100 per cent accurate, but at least they give you an opportunity to *compare* one hotel with another.

A lot of letter writing, telephone calls, interrogations, and other travail have gone into acquiring accurate and up-to-date rates for this edition. The bulk of this research took place in the fall of 1977, and, to the best of my knowledge, the rates printed in these pages are correct for the period through the fall of 1978. I emphasize these dates because some readers complain about inaccurate rates in guidebooks two or three *years* after the guidebook is published. Also, it's not always possible for innkeepers (especially in smaller inns without computers and economists) to forecast their costs accurately, and they may have to make additional alterations as the seasons progress.

Therefore, as innkeepers always stress: *All rates in this guidebook are subject to change without notice, due to matters beyond the innkeepers' control, and, in some cases, anyone's control.* Forgive me for echoing this reminder here and there throughout the guide.

THE CATEGORIES OF RATES. Before we go any further, *all rates in this guidebook are for two people sharing a room.* To avoid repetition, I have used the standard abbreviations for categories of rates:

EP	European Plan	You pay for the room only, no meals, not even breakfast (except when noted in the text)

MAP	Modified American Plan	Room with breakfast plus one other meal, usually dinner
AP	American Plan	Room, breakfast, lunch, afternoon tea (when served) and dinner

AP and MAP allow you to order your meals from a fixed menu, usually with a choice of dishes, and often with additional dishes available for a small surcharge (usually the dishes you really want—like lobster in Maine). Some hotels give you no choice and you have to go along with AP or MAP rates, especially during their peak season. However, whenever possible I have tried to indicate that EP rates may be available if you insist, so that you don't have to eat in the same dining room every evening. It's much better to have the option of dining where *you* choose to dine.

Meals that are served *family style,* standard practice in a few small inns, do not involve dining with the family (although that *may* be the case, and often is a real pleasure); it simply means that dinner will be served at a fixed hour, with little or no choice of menu (unless you have a word with the cook in advance and have sound dietary or religious reasons for wanting a change).

HOW TO CUT COSTS. Many of the rates quoted in this guide may seem steep. One reviewer of the first edition made the profound observation that "none is in the $5-a-day category," which is indeed true—what these hotels are offering is something out of the ordinary, solitude, charm, style, quality, and these commodities don't come cheap. It costs a fortune to convert and furnish an inn like the Sawmill Farm in Vermont or to maintain the palatial splendor of a Greenbrier. Low rates come from standardization, and that means the type of accommodations you get in motels. And have you checked out motel rates recently?

However, there *are* ways of containing costs. The most obvious is to *avoid peak seasons and weekends*. Obviously, this is not always possible, and there are times when you'll want to go away on weekends in peak season, to catch the music festival at Tanglewood in Massachusetts, for example, or candlelight tours of the mansions in Charleston, South Carolina. However, there are so many advantages of the off-season that it's worthwhile making the effort to go somewhere when most other people have left. If what you're looking for is peace and solitude, the advantages are immediately obvious; if you're counting pennies, the rewards are greater still (see, for example, the listings for The Breakers in Palm Beach or Marriott's Camelback Inn in Arizona). Think anew about the weather, too: the idea of Nantucket in summer is very appealing, but for many people the months of May, June, October, and November are the best times for beach-combing and moor walking. Other benefits: in the off-season you get a better choice of rooms, and you probably won't have to stand in line for a table or wait for service at mealtimes.

The peak and nonpeak seasons vary, of course, from region to region, but sometimes they also differ between hotels in the same locale. In Vermont, for example, the Inn at Sawmill Farm in West Dover is usually busy during winter weekends because it's a five-minute drive from the ski slopes, whereas the Old Tavern Inn at Grafton, only an hour away, is less crowded because it doesn't have a ski slope right on its doorstep. The basic seasons for each hotel are listed in the following pages. Note them carefully: they can make a big difference when you're trying to get reservations—and in determining how much value you get for your money.

Remember, too, to *check out exactly what you get for your dollars.* A first glance at the rates for, say, Jenny Lake Lodge in Wyoming may seem prohibitive, but when you read that this includes your own log cabin, all your meals (gourmet meals to boot), *and* unlimited horseback riding, then calculate what all that would cost you at an average resort, you realize it's not so expensive after all. Go through the listings for "Diversions" with a keen eye; note the rates for things like tennis, golf, and horseback riding—sometimes they're included in the rate, sometimes they cost only two or three dollars, sometimes they cost almost enough to pay for a room. Choose your inn, hotel, or resort carefully and you can save yourselves quite a lot of money.

Some hotels put together special packages for weekends or honeymoons, for tennis or golf buffs; they're not explored in detail here, but some of them are worth looking into. Another way to save on expenses is to choose hotels with refrigerators, wet bars (alias sinks), or kitchens in the rooms; a refrigerator can cut out costly room service, and even facilities for making an occasional cup of coffee can save money, if you don't eat an elaborate breakfast. Finally, go Dutch. In these enlightened days, there's no reason why both parties should not pay their own way—in which case they often can afford places they probably thought were beyond their means.

I have included a few inns and hotels in these pages mainly for their rates, because they have some of the qualities you are looking for and they are relatively inexpensive. They are identified with the sign: ¢. This means that in these hotels you can have a room for two, without meals, for less than $30—if not in the peak season, at least in the off-season.

THE RATINGS. All the inns, hotels, and resorts in this guide are, in one way or another, above average; but some are obviously better than others, and to try to make life easier for you, I've rated the individual establishments. Unlike other guides, such as the Mobil guides, which seem to rate hotels by a formula relying heavily on the number of elevators and coin-operated laundries, this guide's ratings are personal and subjective. Fortunately, the ratings seem to coincide with the views of most readers, too, judging from their letters and reports. Here's a short explanation of each rating.

Cupids represent *romantic* qualities—that is, personality or charm, decor and ambiance, the attitude of the staff, the setting, and what the hotel does with its environment. Please note: a cupid is not the equivalent of a star in other guides; it's more concerned with trees than elevators, with good taste than good plumbing. However, you *can* assume that every inn, hotel, and resort in this guide does have good plumbing (maybe not the most modern, but certainly functional), good beds, good housekeeping. That goes without saying.

Champagne bottles evaluate the wining and dining aspects of your stay; this includes the overall *attitude* to food and wine, and the competence of the staff, as well as the quality of the wine cellar and the food that's actually placed before you. It takes into consideration the ambiance of the dining facilities, the way a table is laid, the way a busboy removes empty dishes, the reception you get from a maitre d', and so on. In other words, a hotel that rates only two champagne bottles might deserve three for the actual food but loses out because the waiters are sloppy and noisy.

Tennis rackets give you a guide to the availability (and accessibility) of diversions other than the one you really came for. The individual diversions are listed at the end of each hotel entry; wherever possible, I have tried to give you information on which facilities are *free,* and, in the case of tennis, golf, horseback riding, and other sports, how much you pay.

Here are the ratings:

 For a one-night stand or stopover

 For a weekend

 For a week or longer

 Happily ever after

 Sustenance

 Good food

 Cuisine

 Haute cuisine

 A few diversions

 Lots of things to keep your mind off sex

 More diversions than you'll ever have time or energy for unless you have a spat

¢ Inns, hotels, or resorts which charge less than $30 a night for a double room, without meals

Remember, please: The cupids are an evaluation of "romantic" qualities, *not* of facilities or luxury; rates are, of course, subject to change, for reasons beyond the control of author or publisher.

DOUBLE OR SINGLE BEDS? Hotels nowadays have more twin beds than double beds. The reasons are that a surprising number of American couples prefer solitary slumbers; also, with so much convention and business traffic, hotels have to be able to accommodate a couple of executives in one room (apparently American corporate team spirit hasn't yet reached the point where executives want to bunk down in the same bed). However, most of the hotels, inns, and resorts in this guide have both twin and double beds. Always specify which you prefer when you make your reservation; if all the doubles have gone and you really must have one, most hotels will bully their maids or handymen into pushing the twins together and making a double. (This may not be true in smaller inns where the manpower situation is more critical.)

THE INN THING. You'll find many old-time inns listed in these pages. They are not everyone's cup of tea, and several innkeepers tell me they're concerned that people sometimes arrive on their doorsteps and are disappointed with what they find.

Here are some of the *nonfeatures* that may disappoint: You usually won't find a porter to carry your luggage; occasionally the innkeeper himself will help, but you should try to keep your luggage manageable because one of you may have to carry it up two or three flights of stairs.

You usually won't get room service in an inn. No breakfast in bed—unless one of you goes and fetches it. Also, don't expect the sort of service you'd get at the Beverly Hills Hotel or the Greenbrier; these places just don't have the staff to cope. They can offer you friendly personal service—but not night and day, and not in matters beyond the call of duty.

You may not find phones, radios, TV or wall-to-wall carpet in your room. Or even a bathroom.

The plumbing may be rebellious; the floors may creak, and if you get back late you have to remember that other guests have come for peace and quiet. Tiptoe.

Also try not to *arrive* late at night, because the innkeeper is probably in bed since he has to be up early the next morning; if you must arrive late, call ahead and say so.

Most of these inns are operated on precarious budgets, and survive on love rather than cash flow. We should all be grateful to all those innkeepers who get up at the crack of dawn to prepare breakfast, do the marketing, organize the staff, greet the guests, stick around the bar until after dinner, and probably get only a couple of weeks' vacation themselves in a year. Play the game. If you make a reservation, keep it; if you can't don't just shrug it off, but call the innkeeper or drop a line and cancel it, as far in advance as possible. One empty room in a twelve-room inn can be the difference between an inn's profit and its plot of land being bought up by a motel chain.

Who wants to stay in an inn, in that case? A lot of people—because inns offer other attractions that more than compensate for occasional drawbacks, as you'll see in the following pages.

GETTING THERE. Most couples will immediately think of hopping into a car and driving off, and undoubtedly that's the coziest, most convenient, least expensive way to go off together for a few days; but when you read through this guide you'll probably discover some places you'd like to try which are just beyond your customary driving distance. Question is, should you skip the place, or drive like crazy to get there and then drive like crazy to get back? Few things in this world are less conducive to love than long taxing drives on highways with lots of traffic. For those special places, consider the other possibilities of getting there.

Flying is the obvious one. Now that most of the domestic air carriers have developed the habit of introducing special low fares for off-peak periods, think of flying somewhere for a few days—say, with after-dinner or nightcoach flights between New York or Chicago and New Orleans, or with special eight-day tickets between New York and Los Angeles or San Francisco. Unfortunately, the airlines (and the C.A.B.) never seem to be able to resolve their fares far enough in advance to be able to supply information for a guide such as this, so you'll have to check out the possibilities with your local travel agent when the time comes.

Also, don't overlook the possibilities of commuter airlines like Air New England, which can speed your travel time between New York or Boston and places like Nantucket, Vermont, and Maine; or from Atlanta, Air South, which will get you sooner to bed in Hilton Head.

Air travel is something of a hassle these days, however, with security checks, so you may want to consider another way of getting around the country—train. By *train?* Who's he kidding?

The best way to get through Iowa and Ohio is in bed, tangled together in your sleeping compartment, watching the scenery, such as it is, roll by (but remember to lower the shades before the train pulls into a station—Ohio and Iowa are not ready for that sort of thing yet). Just think of it—you can love your way clear across the continent; and you can even arrange for your conductor or waiter to bring your meals to your berth.

Amtrak is slowly perking up America's trains; it's a struggle, because on many long-distance routes they have to make do with existing equipment, and some of the cars are a mite grubby, depending on which route you're on. If it's any consolation, your berth may once have been pressed into service by movie stars and moguls shuttling to and from Hollywood in what the Amtrak crews refer to, rather unloyally, as the good old days. Give the train a try; at least wander round to your local Amtrak office and pick up a schedule.

Please note: The initials at the end of several sections identify the following writers who have collaborated on the research and text:

L.E.B.   Linda Burnham
R.E.S.   Bob Scanlon
M.S.   Maria Shaw

VERY SPECIAL PLACES

A Lovers' Guide to America

THE
NEW ENGLAND
COAST
AND
LONG ISLAND

One day I wrote her name upon the strand,
But came the waves and washed it away . . .
SPENSER

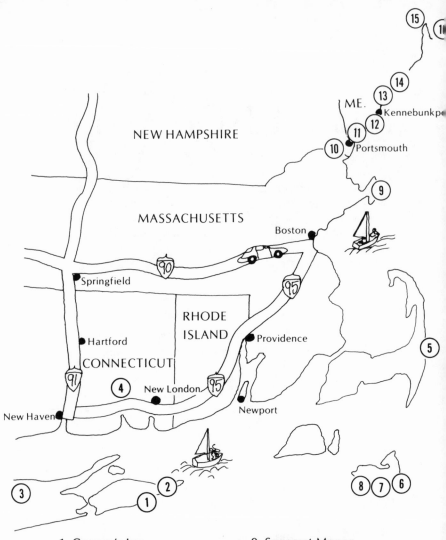

1. Gurney's Inn
2. Montauk Yacht Club & Inn
3. Three Village Inn
4. The Griswold Inn
5. Ship's Knees Inn
6. Jared Coffin House
7. The White Elephant Hotel
8. Ships Inn

9. Seacrest Manor
10. Wentworth-by-the-Sea
11. Stage Neck Inn
12. Dockside Guest Quarters
13. The Captain Lord Mansion
14. Seacrest Inn
15. The Squire Tarbox Inn
16. Spruce Point Inn and Lodges

Gurney's Inn
Montauk, Long Island, N.Y.

You can't get much closer to the beach than this without living in a sand castle. And what a beach! Mile after mile of baby powder. You can jog on it from here to forever. It's almost the end of the world. The Atlantic comes rolling in on one side, hundred-foot-high hills shut out the world on the other, and 120 miles of Long Island separate you from New York.

The inn is actually a collection of cottages and motel-like units by the edge of the beach or up on the hill, spread comfortably over eleven acres, brightened with bushes, trees, and nooks of flowers.

It's an everything-or-nothing place. You can lie on the sand in front of the inn all day, or you can jog off together to a secluded corner of the dunes. You can drive over to Montauk and sniff around the fish market, or continue to Montauk Lighthouse and scramble among the rocks at the very tip of Long Island. In the evening, get involved with combos and dancing in the inn or go to the John Drew Theatre in East Hampton. Best of all, kick off your shoes and chase the moon along the beach.

Montauk is sensational in the fall and winter, when you have the beach to yourselves, and you have to huddle up in sweaters and scarves, and the spray comes whipping across the sand. Then after you walk you come back to a warm room, a warm shower, a warm bed. You can even have your dinner shipped over from the dining room—lobsters or roast beef or a thick steak.

You have quite a choice of accommodations at Gurney's. Make your days together a special event and have the inn's best love nest—the Crow's Nest (a self-contained cottage right by the edge of the beach, with a living room, fireplace, hostess pantry, patio, and bedroom), or a room in the Foredeck (a three-story lodge unit with pine-paneled walls, armchairs, individually controlled heat and air conditioning, telephone, television, tile bathrooms, his and her vanities, and a patio).

The new Forward Watch wing is totally out of synch with the rest of the resort, inside and out, and a new conference center hasn't helped matters from the point of view of lovers. More diners seem to be arriving from the surrounding resorts and highways, and house guests may have to wait up to an hour for a table. Grrrrr, Gurney's! But maybe you won't even notice if you spend all your days on the beach, your evenings in your room.

NAME: Gurney's Inn
OWNERS/INNKEEPERS: Joyce and Nick Monte
ADDRESS: Old Montauk Highway, Montauk, L.I., N.Y. 11954
DIRECTIONS: Just keep driving; when you hear a splash you've gone too far.
TELEPHONE: (516) 668-2345
ROOMS: 128, including 10 suites and 5 villas
RATES 1978: MAP only, from $70 to $96 in spring and fall, from $82 to $116 in summer; plus 7% tax on total bill.
MEALS AND ENTERTAINMENT: Breakfast 7:30–10, lunch noon–3, dinner 6–10 weekdays, 1–10 Sunday; room service 7 a.m. to 11 p.m.; jacket and tie for dinner; live music, dancing in the lounge, free movies in your room; theater nearby.
DIVERSIONS: Heated saltwater pool, therapy pool, sauna, exercise room, parlor games, table tennis, billiards; bird watching, scuba diving, flying, fishing, boating, sailing, golf, tennis, hiking, horseback riding nearby.
P.S. Summer, of course, is the busy season, and there may be groups in the house at other times; if not, fall and winter are wonderful.

Montauk Yacht Club & Inn
Star Island, Montauk, N.Y

It's more inn than yacht club, in case you were about to reach for your blazer and white ducks. The original club was, in fact, "the first chartered yacht club in America," but the Inn is a new cedar-shingle structure built around what remains of the old clubhouse and a sixty-foot-high lighthouse. Built, fitted out, and decorated very lavishly, too. The guest rooms have walls of barn-siding for a rustic-nautical look, but they're fitted out like the QE2—closets designed to hold steamer trunks, fitted dressing rooms with big fluffy towels and complimentary suntan lotion, coffee tables with marble tops, bedside hanging lamps with long cylindrical wool-tapestry shades. In winter, you can curl up on a king-size bed and watch color TV; in summer, you can lounge on your patio or balcony and watch the boats puttering around on the lake.

The public rooms are decorated with great care and taste. Corridors are hung with tapestries of wool and sisal; the dining room is dominated by an enormous stained-glass floating ceiling, vaguely whale-shaped; and the main Club Room focuses on a huge fireplace with a glove-leather sofa curving around the hearth. There are plants and fresh flowers everywhere, and "not a single artificial leaf anywhere—even in the health spa." Subdued, romantic lighting is supplied by an array of antique hurricane lamps and avant-garde spots that make the Inn look almost like a museum of lighting.

In summer, you might find it a mite busy—what with people dropping in for lunch or dinner (Inn guests have priority reservations for tables), and all the power yachts moored in the marina. In winter, it's exactly the kind of atmosphere you want for a snuggly escape: have a drink on the sofa before the fire, or in the softly lit circular lounge at the base of the lighthouse. Have a swim and a sauna in the indoor pool, a game of backgammon in the Club Room; or muffle up in sweaters and scarves, drive to the Atlantic, and take a long tingly walk on the beach.

The Inn is expensive (what do you expect with all that luxury?), but it has the advantage over hostelries in the neighborhood that you can stay there on the European Plan, and if you don't want to eat in the main dining room you can dine well, at moderate prices, in the Café Potpourri, among the blue tiles, natural woods, and potted plants.

NAME: Montauk Yacht Club & Inn

INNKEEPER: Ralph Hitz, Jr.

ADDRESS: Star Island, Montauk, N.Y. 11954

DIRECTIONS: On Lake Montauk. Drive through Montauk to West Lake Drive, go left on the drive until you come to Star Island Causeway (on the right, beside the Coast Guard signs). By air, Montauk Caribbean Airways; by rail, Long Island Railroad.

TELEPHONE: (516) 668-3100

ROOMS: 84

RATES 1978: EP, $55 lakeview and $70 lakefront weekdays, $65 and $80 Friday and Saturday, through June 30; $70 and $110 weekdays, $90 and $110 weekends, from July 1 through October; plus 15% service charge, and 7% tax on total bill.

MEALS AND ENTERTAINMENT: Breakfast 7–11:30, lunch 12–3, dinner 6–11 (approx. $25 to $30 for two), Café Potpourri open 7 a.m. to 2 a.m.; room service (limited menu) 7 a.m. to midnight; jackets after 6 in the dining room; trio six nights a week in summer (in the dining room), Hugh Shannon, pianist/singer (in the Club Room) nightly in summer.

DIVERSIONS: Heated outdoor freshwater pool, immaculate indoor spa with pool, saunas, and 16-foot-diameter whirlpool, small lakeside beach (for sunning, but you may not

to want to swim from it with so many power boats glop-
ping around), courtesy bus to Atlantic beaches or window permits for your own car for beach parking lots;
billiard room, table tennis, backgammon, waterskiing
(ski rentals in town, power boat provided free of charge);
tennis across the street (6 lighted courts, $7 per court
per hour weekdays, $10 weekends); golf 1½ miles away
($11 a round weekdays, $13 weekends); bicycles and
bareback riding nearby.

P.S. Some business seminars in winter. "The Inn functions
primarily as an adult resort and has no facilities for in-
fants or small children."

Three Village Inn
Stony Brook, Long Island, N.Y.

The inn is best known as a restaurant, an hour-and-a-half
drive from Manhattan, but you can stretch the evening into a
night because there are a few guest rooms upstairs. Story-
book Stony Brook is one of the oldest settlements on Long
Island (it was founded sometime in the 1660s), a seafaring
town where men built ships and then put to sea in them. The
inn was built in 1785 by one of these versatile seafarers,
Jonas Smith, who also happened to be Long Island's first
millionaire; it stands at the end of the village green, down by
the harbor, a white clapboard building sheltered by locust
trees and surrounded by shrubbery.

Drive out here and stuff yourself on Stony Brook Harbor
clams on the half shell, New England codfish cakes, sautéed
Long Island bay scallops, or roast turkey with chestnut dressing; but it's the inn's dessert list that will make you thankful
you had the foresight to book a room for the night—Colonial
nut layer cake, steamed fruit pudding with rum hard sauce,
ginger sundae, fresh persimmon with cream, Concord grape

fluff with soft custard sauce, New England mince pie. Etcetera.

The alternatives to the Long Island Expressway turn out to be seven pretty little Colonial-style rooms above the Tap Room, all with private bath, air conditioning, wall-to-wall carpeting, and television.

There are also a few motel rooms in cottages around the corner, overlooking the yacht marina and a few yards from a stretch of sandy beach where you can rest up before dinner.

NAME: Three Village Inn
INNKEEPER: Nelson M. Roberts
ADDRESS: Stony Brook, L.I., N.Y. 11790
DIRECTIONS: Sixty miles from New York City, by L.I. Expressway to Exit 62 and N.Y. 111, then north to N.Y. 25A and northeast to Stony Brook Road; from New England, take the ferry to Port Jefferson, a few miles east.
TELEPHONE: (516) 751-0555
ROOMS: 7 upstairs, 15 in motel units
RATES: EP, $25 to $35 all year; plus 7% tax, total bill.
MEALS AND ENTERTAINMENT: Breakfast 8–10, lunch 12–3, dinner 5–9 weekdays, to 10 Friday and Saturday, 12:30–9 Sunday and holidays (approx. $20 to $30 for two); no room service; jackets in dining room; piano in Sandbar dining room Friday and Saturday only.
DIVERSIONS: No sports facilities on the premises, but hiking, biking, golf, and swimming in the Sound nearby.

The Griswold Inn
Essex, Conn.

After dinner, stroll down to the boat jetty, perch on a bollard, and look across the still estuary. Sniff the night air. Listen to the clink of rigging on masts. Watch the moon shimmying

across the water. It's the perfect public ending to a day at a sea-loving spot like the Griswold Inn.

The Griswold is the same age as the United States; in the 18th century they used to build ships across the street, and during the War of 1812, the British sneaked into the harbor and burned the Essex fleet. But not, praise be, the inn, and drinks and dinner at the Gris are still a tradition with yachtsmen on this part of Long Island Sound. There's no reason why landlubbers shouldn't have some fun, too.

Essex is a lovely old Colonial seaport, its main street lined with houses that have weathered many a gale. The inn is three stories of white clapboard (with, oh dear, green plastic shutters) anchored to a two-story annex, the Hayden House. It has a small lobby-lounge with a large goblet full of jelly beans, and delightful new innkeepers. Until 1972, the Griswold had been in the same family for 140 years; now it's been taken over by a young couple, Bill and Vicky Winterer. Bill Winterer was once a Coast Guard officer, and then an investment banker, who also happens to be a gourmet cook and natural host. But he wanted to be near his 44-foot ketch, so now he has a two-hundred-year-old inn, with his ketch moored at the bottom of the street.

STEAMSHIP PRINTS, ANTIQUE PISTOLS. The dark-hued Tap Room (originally the first schoolhouse in Essex) is dominated by a girthy Franklin stove that once warmed the audience at the Goodspeed Opera House in East Haddam. Here you get your first introduction to the inn's unique collection of steamship prints and handbills, including a turn-of-the-century advertisement announcing sailings of the "*State of New York* (new and elegant steamer) leaving Hartford Wednesdays and Fridays and arriving in New York in time for early trains to the South and West."

The main collection is in the adjoining dining room, called the Covered Bridge Room, where the walls are awash in prints—some by Jacobson, others by Currier and Ives—and here and there a helpful if unheeded temperance poster (my favorite: "Large Streams from LITTLE Fountains Flow, GREAT SOTS from MODERATE Drinkers Grow"). Logs in the six-foot-wide fireplace crackle away during the winter months to cheer the landbound sailors waiting for the first glimmer of spring and a chance to unwrap their boats.

The recently restyled Library Room is a second restaurant, decorated with antique pistols, revolvers, flintlocks, carbines, and muskets; and off the main lobby there's a third dining room, the Steamboat Room. This one resembles a cabin of a posh yacht, looking aft; an illuminated painting of Old Essex, recessed into the wall, rocks gently to and fro to give you the idea you're at sea. (There's some speculation that this "motion" may be cutting down the bar sales.) That's a lot of eating and drinking space for one small inn, but in fact on summer weekends it takes all three rooms, with three sittings in each, to accommodate all the yachtsmen who come here. It's not because there's no other spot on the Sound, but because the menu is outstanding—Nantucket Bay scallops and broiled Cape bluefish from the list of local specialties; lamb pie and a brace of Canadian quail with Bulgar wheat are among the surprises. The wine list is short and to the point—enough to launch a meal if not a ship.

KNOTTY BEAMS, FOURPOSTER BEDS. The Gris's eighteen rooms, fresh as a 10-knot wind, have all been renovated in

the past few years, no mean feat when you consider that there is hardly a straight line in the place. Each one is different, each decked out with antiques or period furniture, decorated with prints chosen and framed with an artist's eye. A selection: Room 1 has knotty beams, lopsided wardrobe, twin fourposter beds; room 4 has two giant magnificent mahogany fourposter beds and views of swaying masts in the boatyard, but at times may be afflicted with rumbling sounds from an exhaust fan outside the window; the new Governor Trumbull Suite has bird-print wallpaper, exposed brick walls, exposed beams, wooden shutters, and a cabin-sized sleeping alcove. My favorite is room 3, above the lobby, with beamed ceiling, barnboard paneling, and a big old bed with a list to starboard. All the rooms have air conditioning, eleven have private bathrooms (although it should be pointed out that because these rooms were never intended to hold private johns, some of the bathrooms are tiny and separated from the room only by screens; they may offer less privacy than some couples prefer, and if you're on a first outing together you might feel more at ease with a shared bathroom down the hall).

All in all, the Gris is still one of the best values in New England.

And Essex is still one of the prettiest towns. Even if you're not a sailor there's plenty to do in these parts. Take a trip upriver on the *River Queen*. Take in a musical or play at the Goodspeed Opera House or the Ivortown Theater. Drive over to Old Saybrook at the mouth of the river. Or just sit on a bollard and dream.

NAME: The Griswold Inn

OWNER/INNKEEPER: William G. Winterer

ADDRESS: Main Street, Essex, Conn. 06426

DIRECTIONS: From the Connecticut Turnpike, either exit 64 then north 5 miles to Essex, or exit 69 to Rt. 9, then exit 3 to Essex; by rail to Old Saybrook.

TELEPHONE: (203) 767-0991

ROOMS: 18 (11 with private bath, 7 sharing baths) and 1 suite; rates include continental breakfast.

RATES 1978: EP $18.50 to $26.50 for rooms, $32.50 for the suite, all year; plus 7% tax on total bill.

MEALS AND ENTERTAINMENT: Breakfast 8:30–10:30, Hunt Breakfast on Sunday, lunch 12–2, dinner 6–9 weekdays, to 10 Friday and Saturday (approx. $14 to $18 for two); no room service; informal dress; banjo concerts Friday and Sunday evenings.

DIVERSIONS: Essex village, the Connecticut Valley, tennis (free town courts 1 mile from the Gris), golf, bikes, horseback riding, ice skating on town pond, sailing and boating nearby.

P.S. No groups ever.

Ship's Knees Inn
E. Orleans, Cape Cod, Mass.

It's not a cutesy-pie title; a ship's knee is a block of wood that connects deck beams to the frames of sailboats, and when this shingle house was built 150 years ago it was held together by ship's knees. "Now I'm having a fantastic love affair with Ship's Knees," says Jerrie Butcher, who took over the house a couple of years ago and charmed it into the most decorative hostelry on the Cape. She scoured local antique stores for ship's trunks, old whaling prints, antique maps, Windsor chairs, duck decoys, and braided rugs; then she sorted out her finds in rooms designed in one of three basic colors and fitted them out with carpets, towels, bedspreads, and sheets in coordinated colors, making simple but delightful nooks for love affairs, fantastic or otherwise. The ship's knees hold together just ten rooms, four of them with private bathrooms and color television, and one (#3) with beamed ceilings and a fireplace. There's a small lounge where you help yourself to fresh-baked popovers and doughnuts and coffee for breakfast, and out in the garden you can toss a frisbee, play volleyball, or lounge in patio furniture till the stars come home. And that's it—quiet, unassuming, impeccable, escapist. The Ship's Knees sits at the junction of a couple of residential streets, under streams of telephone company spaghetti, and across the street from an unusual little restaurant called The Quacker, where you can have simple snacks on a rustic terrace or buy the ingredients for a tasty picnic to take to the beach.

Just wait till you see the beach! Nauset Beach is part of the Cape Cod National Seashore, mile after unspoiled mile of sand and dunes, just a three-minute walk from and five-minute walk to the inn. This is paradise for off-season beach-lovers, a place to walk when the winds are churning the ocean and the seagulls are flying backwards, when the twilight comes early and eerily and turns the surfcasters into balloon-legged silhouettes; then, when your faces are all tingly, you can hurry up the hill to the color-coordinated warmth of the Ship's Knees' bedspreads and sheets.

NAME Ship's Knees Inn

INNKEEPER: Barbara and Frank Butcher

ADDRESS: Beach Road, East Orleans, Cape Cod, Mass. 02643

DIRECTIONS: Follow U.S. 6 to Orleans exit, then go east on Mass. 28 to E. Orleans and follow the signs for Nauset Beach; by air to Hyannis.

TELEPHONE: (617) 255-1312

ROOMS: 19

RATES 1978: EP, spring and fall from $14 to $25, summer from $15 to $39 (includes continental breakfast); plus 5.7% tax on room.

MEALS AND ENTERTAINMENT: Continental breakfast only (included in price, in season).

DIVERSIONS: Heated outdoor pool, indoor games (checkers, chess, etc.); golf, bicycles, hiking, horseback riding, sailing, waterskiing nearby.

Jared Coffin House
Nantucket, Mass.

Step inside the lobby and you're back in the days of the great whaling fleets of Nantucket. The public rooms are filled with Chippendale, Sheraton, Directoire, and American Federal furniture, antique oriental rugs, Chinese coffee tables, and Japanese lacquered cabinets; a sweeping stairway with a white balustrade leads you up to your guest room, which will be decorated with period furniture, authentic Colonial wallpapers, and traditional Nantucket curtains and bedspreads hand woven by local ladies. Jared Coffin, one of the wealthiest shipowners in Nantucket, built this red brick mansion on a street of mansions in 1845, and furnished it with treasures brought back from around the world by his ships. It still looks like a private home, although Coffin lived here for only one year before it was bought up by the Nantucket Steamboat Company and turned into a hotel in 1846; the Nantucket Historical Society took it over in 1961 and restored it to its original state.

The Jared Coffin House is the most famous and most popular inn on the island, which means that in summer its garden patio, Tap Room, and dining room are swarming with overnight visitors and day trippers; but it remains open throughout the year, which means you can visit Nantucket at its most Nantucketty. The islanders themselves rave about November in Nantucket, when the moors are a carpet of fall colors; but October is also a lovely month for hopping on a bike and riding along the clifftop roads, and May and June are great for tennis, golf, and playing leapfrog on the beach.

Just bring lots of sweaters to keep you warm on the moors and beach; the Nantucket embroidery will keep you warm in bed.

NAME: Jared Coffin House

INNKEEPER: Philip Whitney Read

ADDRESS: Nantucket Island, Mass. 02554

DIRECTIONS: On the corner of Broad and Centre Sts., near the top end of Main St.; to get to Nantucket Island you take the ferry from Woods Hole or Hyannis, or fly Air New England from New York, Boston, Hyannis, and other points.

TELEPHONE: (617) 228-2400

ROOMS: 41

RATES 1978: EP, from $30 to $50 all year; plus 5.7% tax on rooms, 6% on food (already included in drink prices).

MEALS AND ENTERTAINMENT: Breakfast 8–10, lunch 12–2, dinner 6:30–9:30 (approx. $15 to $25 for two), limited food service in summer (2–6); room service for continental breakfast and drinks; jackets requested in spring, fall, and winter, casual (but neat) in summer; piano with dinner, live music in the Tap Room.

DIVERSIONS: Chess, bridge, backgammon, checkers in the inn, everything else nearby (with special club rates for tennis, golf by arrangement).

P.S. Busiest July and August (like everything else in Nantucket), but also at Christmas and New Year, and getting that way in the fall; small groups off season.

The White Elephant Hotel
Nantucket, Mass.

You wake up in the morning in a flower-covered cottage to see seagulls preening themselves on the bollards and schooners riding at anchor in the harbor. If it's sunny and warm you can slip into the pool or wander over to the beach; if it's cool and misty, the way Nantucket should be, you can hop on bicycles and ride across the moors of Sargent juniper and Warminster broom. In the evening, wander down to the wharf for a moonlight view of the harbor before you return to your flower-covered saltbox cottage.

Nantucket is a nautical town, and the White Elephant is a nautical hotel, right down on the waterfront, with its lawns ending up in the harbor. It was built in 1963 by Walter Beinecke, Jr., of S&H Green Stamps, who took over most of the Nantucket waterfront and revitalized it (he's had his critics, but most people seem to feel he's done a tasteful job, remodeling the place with a feel for its shingle-saltbox heritage).

This elephant comes in six parts: the main two-story lodge with spacious, modern rooms; the Spindrift Cottages, on the lawn by the water, with roses growing up the walls, neatly furnished living rooms and bedrooms, and windows facing the harbor (which makes them the most popular rooms in the hotel); and the Captain's Court, a bunch of typical Nantucket homes the size of dollhouses, grouped around a lawn with loungers spread out beneath the locust trees. The suites in the Captain's Court cottages give you a chance to live in the style of a Nantucket seafarer—pine walls, beamed ceilings, sturdy furniture, fireplaces, and old prints and maps on the walls. The remaining components are two more sets of cottages—Driftwood and Pinegrove—and the new "The Breakers" wing, a few doors down the street, also on the edge of the harbor, with 26 deluxe rooms, which remain open all year.

NAME: The White Elephant Hotel

INNKEEPER: Ian Danielski

ADDRESS: Nantucket Island, Mass. 02554

DIRECTIONS: By ferry from Woods Hole or Hyannis; by Air New England from New York, Boston, or Hyannis.

TELEPHONE: (617) 228-2500

ROOMS: 60 rooms and 22 cottages

RATES 1978: EP, from mid-May through June 29 $40–$65 for rooms, $55–$80 for 1-bedroom cottages, from June through mid-September $55–$80 and $70–$120, from mid-September through November 1 $40–$65 and $55–$80, lower rates in winter; plus 5.7% tax on room, 6% on meals.

MEALS AND ENTERTAINMENT: Breakfast 8–10, lunch 12–2:30, dinner 6–10 (approx. $16 to $20 for two); room service 8–10 for breakfast, noon to 11 p.m. for drinks; informal dress; live music and dancing.

DIVERSIONS: Heated outdoor pool, tennis (9 courts, $10 per court per hour weekends, $8 midweek), putting green, croquet, bicycles, cardroom; golf, horseback riding, sailing, and boating nearby.

Ships Inn
Nantucket, Mass.

The Ships Inn is to the Jared Coffin House what a ship captain is to a shipowner. This clapboard house is a modest version of the Coffin house, built in 1812 by Captain Obed Starbuck as a cozy place to come home to after long voyages. It's now a cozy place where John Krebs came to after a spell as a stockbroker in Baltimore in the heavy seas of the sixties. The period furniture is sturdy, the walls are lined with prints of whaling ships and flowers, the door jambs are askew, the rooms are named for the ships Starbuck commanded, and all in all it has a salty Nantucket air about it. It's on a quiet street at the top of Main Street, away from the rabble, but still close enough to the wharf and bars and goings-on.

Downstairs, the Krebses have installed their own cocktail lounge—an unusual place where you can sit at a bar shaped like a whaling dory and have a drink while you're waiting for your place at the Captain's Table. Their restaurant has an interesting menu—beef, cheese, and seafood fondues, and baked stuffed Nantucket quahaugs. The menu is inexpensive, but the inn is a shade overpriced in the peak season; however, that's only three months of the year, and the remainder of the time it's a comfy little harbor to return to after days of exploring the island.

NAME: Ships Inn
INNKEEPERS: John and Bar Krebs
ADDRESS: Nantucket Island, Mass. 02554
DIRECTIONS: On Fair Street, which runs off to the left at the top of Main Street.
TELEPHONE: (617) 228-0040
ROOMS: 12

RATES: EP $34 (including continental breakfast) June 15 through October 15, $22 from October 16 through June 14; plus 5.7% tax on room, 6% on food and bar bills.

MEALS AND ENTERTAINMENT: Breakfast 8–10:30, no lunch, dinner 6–9:30 (approx. $14 to $20 for two); no room service; dress optional; taped jazz in the bar.

DIVERSIONS: Darts, backgammon, cribbage; hiking, biking, riding, and water sports nearby.

Seacrest Manor
Rockport, Mass.

Rockport, on Cape Ann, is something of a shorebound Nantucket—picturesque harbor just waiting to be painted, lobster pots and fish nets hanging from weathered wooden shacks. On Bearskin Neck, the stone jetty that has become the town's trademark, shingle-sided sheds and houses have been converted into artists' studios, boutiques, and restaurants. Very pretty and, in summer, very crowded. You can escape the crowds by checking into the Seacrest Manor, located on a nontourist street on the edge of town, with a view of the sea and the twin lighthouses of Thatcher Island. Walk to the end of the street and the rocky shore beckons you to take a brisk, bracing walk; on warmer days, settle into one of the shady bowers in the Manor garden, beneath the red oak and maple and linden trees, surrounded by beds of dahlias, begonias, and roses. For a view, or a tan, climb the wooden steps to the second-floor sundeck.

This turn-of-the-century manor, built for a former governor of Massachusetts, was modulated into a refined and elegant guest house in 1973: two large sitting rooms filled with antiques, paintings, and family bric-a-brac; upstairs, eight bright, cheerful and immaculate guest rooms, each with private bath. The most expensive rooms have french doors leading to their own corners of the sundeck, but you'll probably be satisfied with any of the rooms (if you have time, and a choice, look around first and take your pick). Afternoon tea is served in the living room, breakfast in a breakfast room that has more character than *dining* rooms in most hotels. But then, breakfast is kind of special too at the Seacrest Manor: Miss Lillian's spiced Irish oatmeal with chopped eggs, banana pancakes, and corn fritters. A complimentary newspaper brightens your morning (by order only on Sunday), and gentlemen may have their shoes shined simply by leaving them outside their doors at night. The governor himself could still be in residence.

NAME: Seacrest Manor

OWNERS/INNKEEPERS: Leighton T. Saville and Dwight B. McCormack, Jr.

ADDRESS: Marmion Way, Rockport, Mass. 01966

DIRECTIONS: Rockport is four miles from the end of U.S. 128, northeast of Boston; the Manor is just off Hwy. 127A (Thatcher Road), where you'll see a small sign.

TELEPHONE: (617) 546-2211

ROOMS: 8

RATES 1978: EP, from $36 to $42 May 26 through October 10, from $30 to $36 October 11 through December 30 and February 1 through May 25; plus 5.7% room tax (on special weekends, 2- or 3-day minimum stays are required).

MEALS AND ENTERTAINMENT: Breakfast 8:30–9:30, afternoon tea at 4. No liquor license, but the owners will supply mixers and ice.

DIVERSIONS: Reading, lounging, sunning, walking; tennis, golf, sailing nearby.

Wentworth-by-the-Sea
near Portsmouth, N. H.

This is a veritable *Queen Mary* of resort hotels, a leviathan with elegant salons and hallways and dining rooms, with balls and parties, dance bands, cabarets—even its own symphonietta. It rides the crest of one of the small islands at the mouth of Portsmouth Harbor, its gleaming white superstructure rising above an ocean of trees.

The Wentworth is an immense place (more than 200 rooms), rather posh, but it sails into these pages because of location—and nostalgia. It's ironic that hotels of the Colonial era seem to be thriving more successfully than hotels of the Victorian era, that hotels built to cater to the stagecoach trade are doing better than hotels built for the carriage trade. The Wentworth is an exception.

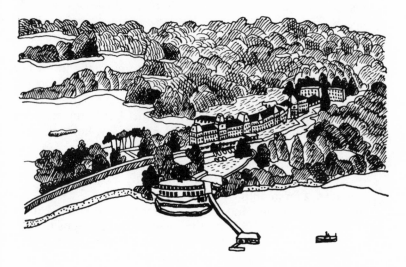

The first carriages started driving up to the Wentworth in the 1870s, and the hotel reached its pinnacle of fame in 1905, when it hosted the diplomats who signed the Russian-Japanese treaty. Ever since, it's been hosting the families of the well heeled as well as a sprinkling of celebs—Gloria Swanson, Richard Nixon, Sir John Gielgud, Ted Kennedy, Duke Ellington, Goodman Ace, Anthony Burgess, and Ogden Nash. A motley crew.

The hotel's rooms (or most of them) are big, with the gracious air of a country mansion. Each one is different but all, of course, have private baths, and the lanai suites also have enclosed porches with luxurious terrace furniture. But you don't have to stay with the crowd. The hotel has a few New England-style cottages scattered around the grounds, most of them across the street in the gardens above the sea.

PARKLIKE GROUNDS. Although the hotel is immense, you don't feel crowded because the grounds and the surroundings are so spacious. Walk across the street, through the gardens, around the pitch-and-putt course, and you come to a heated swimming pool of Olympic proportions, or the sandy beach. The hotel's private golf course, eighteen holes, skims alongside the shore half an island away, and there are first-class tennis courts out back. The cordial ever-present president-owner and his resident manager occasionally throw out a challenge to guests to a set of tennis or a round of golf; if they lose, the guest gets a free night's lodging. Don't dream—they gave away only two rooms last summer, even though the president is a shade older than, say, Bobby Riggs.

NAME: Wentworth-by-the-Sea
OWNER/INNKEEPER: James Barker Smith
ADDRESS: Portsmouth, N.H. 03801
DIRECTIONS: From Interstate 95 northbound, take exit 3 about an hour after Boston, then follow the signs to U.S. 1A, where you'll pick up the signs for Wentworth and/or Newcastle; by air to Portsmouth.

TELEPHONE: (603) 436-3100

ROOMS: 240 rooms, 20 suites, 6 cottages

RATES 1978: Complicated, but averages $80 MAP in May, June, from Labor Day through October, averages $80 MAP in July and August; plus $7.50 a couple per day in lieu of tipping, and 6% tax on total bill.

MEALS AND ENTERTAINMENT: Breakfast 8–9:30, lunch 12–1:30, coffee shop to 5 or 6, dinner 6:30–8; room service during dining hours; jacket at dinner; live music and dancing most evenings, occasional floor shows, bingo, movies.

DIVERSIONS: Outdoor heated pool, shuffleboard, table tennis; tennis (7 courts, no lights, $4 doubles per hour in July and August only); golf (18 holes $7 weekdays, $9 per day weekends); horseback riding nearby.

P.S. July and August are the social season; during the group months "there are times when the guests will encounter a banquet meal and extra ebullience . . . call Jim Smith for group month appraisal."

Stage Neck Inn
York Harbor, Me.

The name conjures up visions of sea-girt headlands and squawking seagulls and lobster pounds. And that's more or less what you find: a spit of land at the entrance to York Harbor, river on one side, beach on the other, ocean ahead, harbor astern. The inn was built (1973) to take full advantage of the site; all fifty-eight of its big, comfy rooms have a view (you pay less for the "harbor" view because it's half harbor, half parking lot), and the elegant blue-and-gilt dining room has picture windows on three sides, although here the view is partially pinched by the velvet drapes. But then if you order poached sole à la Stage Neck Inn, you won't have time for the view, so busy will you be plowing through a huge baked potato stuffed with lobster Newburg and sole filets. Follow that, if you dare, with another of the Swedish chef's specialties—deep-fried Camembert with lingonberry jam. The inn's menu is not inexpensive, but the table d'hôte dinner at $8.25 is good value: melon and prosciutto or vol au vent with creamed mushrooms, broiled swordfish, salad, dinner breads, and coffee or tea. Not a bad way to spend an evening in the fall. Afterward you can sit in a plump sofa before the big fireplace in the lobby-lounge, surrounded by paintings by local artists and Chinese vases and other antiques.

If this part of the inn looks and feels like a private home, it may be because most of the furnishings come from the Warracks' home in New Jersey, which they gave up when "Pud" Warrack quit his job as an investment banker to build an inn where he and his wife first met when they were children—among the headlands of York Harbor.

NAME: Stage Neck Inn

OWNER/INNKEEPER: Alexander Warrack

ADDRESS: York Harbor, Me. 03911

DIRECTIONS: York is just across the state line from Massachusetts, 1½ hours from Boston; exit 1 on the Maine Turnpike (I-95) puts you within a few minutes of town, via U.S. 1A.

TELEPHONE: (207) 363-3850

ROOMS: 58

RATES 1978: EP, $50 to $65 from late June to Labor Day, $38 to $53 late April to late June, post Labor Day through October; plus 15% service charge and suggested (voluntary) $2 per day for maid, 5% tax on total bill.

MEALS AND ENTERTAINMENT: Breakfast 7:30–10 (Sundays 8–11:45), lunch 12–2:30, dinner 6:30–10 (approx. $20 to $25 for two); room service for breakfast and bar; jacket required, tie requested in dining room; piano bar during week, trio on Friday and Saturday, in the lounge.

DIVERSIONS: Heated salt-water pool, beach; tennis (2 clay courts, no lights, $3.50 singles per hour); golf nearby.

Dockside Guest Quarters
York Harbor, Me.

The dock in question is opposite the neck of Stage Neck, where the York River makes a 90-degree turn and unwary skippers sometimes come to grief before the astonished eyes of the Quarters' guests rocking on the porch. It's an attractive location, although some guests may find the lobster fleet less than quaint as it putt-putts out of the harbor at six o'clock in the morning. This otherwise secluded seven-acre island complex lives up to its nautical name and location. The Maine House dates from the late eighties and retains the atmosphere of an old seadog's home, its lobby and lounge lined with model sailboats and paintings of clipper ships, cabinets filled with scrimshaw, walls lined with books on lighthouses and sailing. Guests in the five bedrooms here have a grandstand view of the river from wraparound verandas (these are also the least expensive rooms, all but one of them with private bath). The remaining rooms (the newest are only a couple of years old) are grouped in contemporary-style pine cottages along the shoreline, with rustic-nautical decor, blue-and-yellow towels like signal flags; all of them have decks with captain's chairs for lounging and thinking and watching the ducks and dories—or sailboats that run aground.

NAME: Dockside Guest Quarters
OWNERS/INNKEEPERS: David and Harriette Lusty
ADDRESS: Harris Island Road, York, Me. 03909
DIRECTIONS: York is just across the Maine border from Massachusetts; once you leave Interstate 95, follow routes 1, 1A, and 103 to York Harbor (not Village), where you'll see signs for the Quarters.
TELEPHONE: (207) 363-2868
ROOMS: 19 (5 in the Maine House, the remainder in shoreside cottages)

RATES 1978: EP from $26.50 to $44.50 from June 18 to September 17 (rates and dates subject to change), about 15% less from May 27 to June 17 and from September 18 to October 11 (except for Columbus Day weekend), closed rest of the year; plus 5% on total bill.

MEALS AND ENTERTAINMENT: Continental breakfast (in Maine House or on veranda) 8–10:30; other meals in the adjoining restaurant, operated separately (dinner 6–8, except Monday).

DIVERSIONS: Badminton, shuffleboard, parlor games, library, sailboats for rent; beach, tennis, golf nearby.

The Captain Lord Mansion
Kennebunkport, Me.

A *lord's* mansion, almost, rather than a captain's: Federalist styling with yellow clapboard walls and 160 bottle-green shutters, rising to an octagonal cupola, almost as high as the ancient elms in the yard. Inside, high-ceilinged corridors lead to elegant drawing rooms with tall windows and hand-sewn drapes, marble fireplaces and furnishings of ornatest Victoriana. Captain Lord was a shipowner who couldn't abide to see his crew sitting around on their seafaring butts while the British blockaded Kennebunkport during the War of 1812; so he set them to work building the grandest mansion on the avenue, a masterpiece with all the hallmarks of the ship carpenter's craft—including a three-story unsupported elliptical stairway and mahogany doors with chunky brass locks. A few years ago the mansion was fortunate to come into the care of Jim Throumoulos, a conservation-minded escapee from the world of corporate finance and acquisitions, who conserved, restored, and transformed the old mansion into a Ritz among guest houses. (Shirley came later as an assistant restorer, fixed up the garden, charmed the boss, and married him right here in the parlor she helped restore—there is still, apparently, justice in this world.) All the guest rooms are different, most of them larger than average, some with working fireplaces, some with fourposter beds, all spruced up in Colonial colors. Arrive early in the day, ask Jim or Shirley to show you what's available, then take your pick.

Breakfast is served family style in the *House-and-Gardenish* kitchen (two sittings, each announced by a bell), with Jim serving fresh juice, coffee, and Shirley's just-baked muffin marvels (mincemeat, peach, blueberry, or date). Between them they manage to turn a normally bleary-eyed ritual into something between a picnic and a garden party. The remainder of the day you're on your own to explore the charms and crannies of coastal Maine; but round about sunset, buy a bottle of wine, return to the mansion, climb the steps to Captain Lord's crow's-nest cupola, settle down on the bench, and watch the twilight calm settle over the harbor.

NAME: The Captain Lord Mansion
OWNERS/INNKEEPERS: Jim and Shirley Throumoulos
ADDRESS: P. O. Box 527, Kennebunkport, Me. 04046
DIRECTIONS: Follow the Maine Turnpike to the Kennebunk signs (about 20–25 miles north of the Mass. line), then follow State Highway 9A or 35 into Kennebunkport; the mansion is one block inland from the waterfront, near the yacht club.
TELEPHONE: (207) 967-3141
ROOMS: 15, most with private or semiprivate bathrooms
RATES 1978: EP $40, $44, $50, but mostly around $44 all year (or 5 nights for the price of 4); room rate includes continental breakfast, service charge, and taxes.
MEALS AND ENTERTAINMENT: Breakfast only, two sittings—8 or 9. There are plenty of dining spots in the area, and Jim or Shirley will show you a selection of menus and make reservations.
DIVERSIONS: Snoozing in the lawn chairs, boat watching from the cupola; tennis, golf, boating, theater nearby.

Seacrest Inn
Kennebunkport, Me.

This is a place to be in a gale, by the window, a roaring fire at your back, a roaring sea outside, hands clasped around a mug of mulled cider. Rocking chairs on the big veranda and picture windows in the dining room make sure you never miss a single wave.

The old seafarer's home, a green-timbered house with a steep red roof, overlooks a rocky garden, the rocky shore and the rocky sea; a skinny road runs between the garden and the shore, and there's nothing else around but private summer houses.

The inn proper has six rooms with private baths, and two bathrooms for the remaining three rooms. Try to get one of the two big rooms facing the sea, painted in soft pastel shades with turn-of-the-century Maine furniture. All the bedrooms have an ocean view—slightly angled in some cases, but an ocean view nonetheless.

If you can't get a room in the inn, settle for the small motel in the garden. These rooms are compact, but you can always pretend they're cabins on a yacht; they all have balconies facing the ocean, and such unnautical equipment as "noiseless mercury switches" and "hydronic radiant heating," and they're "scientifically constructed against sound-conduction." The attraction of the dining room, besides the view, is the price—a lobster dinner costs only about $7, depending on the day's catch. You'll find golf, tennis, riding, boating, and fishing nearby; Kennebunk Beach is within walking distance, or you can swim in the natural rock pools right in front of the inn.

Basically, a place for wave watching.

NAME: Seacrest Inn
OWNER/INNKEEPER: John M. Somers

ADDRESS: Ocean Avenue, Kennebunkport, Me. 04046

DIRECTIONS: Follow the Maine Turnpike (I-95) to the Kennebunk signs, then follow State Highway 9A to Dock Square in the center of Kennebunkport; then take Ocean Avenue, turn right at the sea, and drive along the shore road until you come to the inn.

TELEPHONE: (207) 967-2125

ROOMS: 16, and apartment

RATES 1978: EP, spring and fall from $20.50 to $23; summer, from $25 to $30; 5% tax on total bill.

MEALS AND ENTERTAINMENT: Breakfast 8–9:30, lunch 12–2, dinner 6–9 (approx. $10 to $15 for two); no room service; dress informal; recorded background music, alas.

DIVERSIONS: Bicycles, hiking trails, horseback riding, sailing/boating, waterskiing nearby.

The Squire Tarbox Inn
Westport Island, Me.

This two-hundred-year-old retired farmhouse sits contentedly between the trees and a roadway that goes nowhere. Daisies grow in the parking lot, honeysuckle berries crowd the veranda, cedar waxwings flutter from honeysuckle to oak and back again. Guests come back again too: the young couple reading and drowsing on the veranda spent a night with the Squire on their way north and returned the following day because "it's just so peaceful here." Peaceful it is: eight rooms only, a few with private bathrooms, mostly period furnishings, with the quietest nooks in the former barn, above a rustic lounge with high ceilings and serendipitous decor. It's restful, too. The most energetic activity is croquet. Or you can take a walk through the woods to Squam Lake, but be back in plenty of time for the highlight of the day—dinner in the Colonial-style dining room, its plank floors and low beamed ceiling aglow in the light of candles and the logs in the brick-and-beam fireplace. Mississippians Elsie White and Anne McInvale have been here only a year (their first inn, too), but their cuisine has already earned a high reputation around the Boothbay region. Dinner at seven consists of four courses of "modified continental" cuisine—local flounder meunière or boeuf en daube provençale, fruit salad with poppyseed dressing, chocolate mint pie, and other interesting dishes that merit a drive along a road that goes nowhere.

NAME: The Squire Tarbox Inn
OWNERS/INNKEEPERS: Elsie White and Anne McInvale
ADDRESS: Route 2, Box 318, Wiscasset, Me. 04578
DIRECTIONS: On Westport Island, between Bath and Wiscasset; from U.S. 1, follow the signs for State Highway 144, and then occasional signs for Squire Tarbox, about 15 miles from U.S. 1.
TELEPHONE: (207) 882-7693
ROOMS: 8, some with private bath
RATES 1978: EP (including continental breakfast) $30 from May 1 through October 31 (closed rest of year); plus 5% tax.
MEALS AND ENTERTAINMENT: Breakfast 8–9, no lunch, dinner 7 (one sitting, public by reservation, $21 for two for four courses); informal.

DIVERSIONS: Croquet, darts, books, games, each other; tennis, golf, and so forth back on the mainland, wherever that is.

Spruce Point Inn and Lodges
Boothbay Harbor, Me.

The view is wall-to-wall harbor and islands, rocky headlands and lighthouses, schooners and windjammers, and to make sure you can enjoy the view to the full the Druces have installed a gazebo on the embankment and wooden platforms with wooden armchairs at strategic spots along the shore. The pool is beside the sea, and you can fish off the dock, or, if you're feeling adventurous, hoist the flag and one of the ferry boats plying the harbor will stop by and take you into town. On Sundays guests board the ferry for a sunset cruise through the harbor, fortified with hot chocolate and freshly baked pastries; on Monday morning, there's a mariners' breakfast beside the sea, on Tuesday a lobster bake. With all these opportunities for enjoying the waterfront setting there's no need to insist on a room with ocean view; a room in a garden cottage fits the bill nicely (most of the rooms are a deft combination of rustic charm and modern convenience). The Spruce Point Inn has been hosting many of America's leading families for forty years, but it has a relaxed informal manner about it; it encourages families as families, but it's the sort of place where children are expected to behave like grown-ups at the appropriate times. In any case, you can always escape to the gazebo, or settle into a pair of wooden armchairs and watch the windjammers.

NAME: Spruce Point Inn and Lodges
OWNERS/INNKEEPERS: John and Charlotte Druce

ADDRESS: Boothbay Harbor, Me. 04538 (in winter, 158 Prospect Street, West Boylston, Mass. 01583)

DIRECTIONS: On a 100-acre wooded peninsula, about 5 minutes from the bustle of Boothbay proper, on Atlantic Avenue. The signs along U.S. 1 just north of Wiscasset will get you to Boothbay Harbor, about 100 miles north of the Mass. line.

TELEPHONE: (207) 633-4152; winter (617) 835-3082

ROOMS: 60, including suites and villas, and 9 in the inn itself

RATES 1978: MAP only, $74 to $84 for rooms, $84 to $90 for suites with fireplaces, from June through October (closed remainder of year); suggested 15% service charge, plus 5% tax on total bill.

MEALS AND ENTERTAINMENT: Breakfast 8–9, lunch 12:30–1:30, dinner 6:30–8, weekly lobster bakes, cookouts, etc.; no room service; jacket and tie for dinner.

DIVERSIONS: 2 pools (one fresh, one salt), putting green, croquet, 3 all-weather tennis courts (no lights); golf, boating, sailing nearby.

P.S. The social season absorbs July, August, and the first weeks of September; small groups appear in October, so your best bet here is likely to be the month of June or late September.

GREEN MOUNTAINS, WHITE MOUNTAINS

No, make me mistress to the man I love
If there be yet another name more free
More fond than mistress, make me that to thee!
POPE

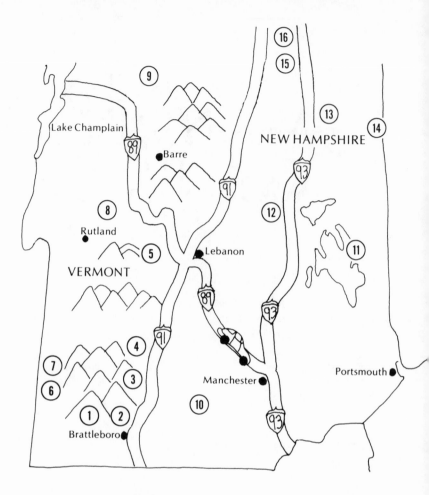

1. The Inn at Sawmill Farm
2. The Four Columns Inn
3. The Old Tavern at Grafton
4. Chester Inn
5. Woodstock Inn
6. Reluctant Panther Inn
7. Barrows House
8. Hawk Mountain

9. The Lodge at Smugglers' Notch
10. The John Hancock Inn
11. Wolfeboro Inn
12. Hillside Inn
13. Snowy Owl Inn
14. Stafford's-in-the-Field
15. Lovett's Inn
16. Franconia Inn

The Inn at Sawmill Farm
West Dover, Vt.

The old stable is now an airy lounge with a wall of window looking onto swamp maple and tamarack trees. The former stalls are bedrooms and the haymows are sleeping lofts. The cupola-crowned sugar house, where the farmer used to render the maple syrup, is now a summer card room by the edge of the swimming pool. The chess table in the bar was once a hand-cranked washing machine, and the planter on the dining room wall used to be a South Jersey cranberry rake.

Many people have converted barns; few of them have succeeded as nobly as Rodney and Ione Williams. What the Williamses have wrought is not so much a conversion as a metamorphosis. But then they started out with several advantages. Rodney Williams was, until a few years ago, an Atlantic City architect; Ione Williams was an interior decorator. The remainder of the family contributed muscle or encouragement during the transformation period, and they still play an enthusiastic part in running the inn—son Brill is the head chef, and Ione makes the fresh tomato juice served at breakfast and the black raspberry pie with sugared crust at dinnertime.

AROMATIC WELCOME. The inn gets its name from a sawmill that was erected here sometime in the late 1700s, where a branch of the Deerfield River funnels through a narrow rocky gully. You drive across this gully and up the hill a few yards to a small red building, softly floodlit by lamps artfully concealed in the stumps of trees. Step out of your car and immediately you notice the scent of apple trees and the whiff of a wood fire. Welcome to the Sawmill.

The inn's foyer is decked out like a farm shed, with yokes and harnesses, forks and hoes, and all the impedimenta of a working farm. Go upstairs, and it's nothing like a farm. Nor a hotel, for that matter. It looks more like a classy antique store—an antique store where you can lounge and eat and drink and play.

The basic structure of the 80-year-old barn is still intact. All the hand-hewn weathered beams and barnboards are original; ditto the mellowed brick and textured fieldstone. None of the original timbers were discarded; when they weren't needed in their original position, they were salvaged and used elsewhere. There's nothing phony about the Sawmill. Look up, for example, to the ceiling of the stable-lounge. Those hefty timbers are real. Note the balustrade along the library balcony—it's made from the stall dividers that once separated the cows from the bulls. There's a lot to admire in this lounge: the nonagenarian Elliot grandfather clock, the dainty Davenport desk, the copper-covered coffee table, the bronze telescope, the honest-to-goodness pans, pots, spoons, tongs, and candleholders surrounding the big brick fire. All the colors of Vermont are here—from spring's celery-tinted walls and the lime-green upholstery to the russet and copper of autumn.

FLAGSTONE FLOORS AND BARNSIDING. Beyond the lounge you have a pair of dining rooms. The first is a formal jacket-and-tie sort of place, with overhead fans, walls lined with American primitives of young girls and old ladies, and chairs that are far too slender and elegant for a public dining room. The more popular dining room is a glass-enclosed patio overlooking the apple trees and the pool, a rustic room with flagstone floors, dark-brown barnsiding, and directors' chairs to match. People drive for miles, through spring muds and winter snows, just for the pleasure of dining here: avocado stuffed with hot crabmeat, escargots bourguignonne, roast duckling with green peppercorns, rack of baby lamb persille, backfin crabmeat au gratin (the crab by special delivery direct from Crisfield, Maryland). But don't forget to leave room for one of Ione's fresh-from-the-oven pies.

OLD CIDER HOUSE. The Sawmill has only eighteen rooms, two of them "bedloft" rooms with extra twin beds (really for families or foursomes, but they make an unusual change of pace if you want to pay the higher rate). The ten rooms in the main building are different—early American, Georgian, Victorian, Vermontian—but each has its delicate little touches, like washbasins recessed in copper-topped vanity tables. Cow stalls were never intended to be soundproof, and you may still hear a hint of mooing and lowing from the adjoining rooms, but not enough to keep you awake. For more privacy (or a host of other reasons, for that matter) splurge for one of the new studio suites in the Old Cider House, with fireplaces, club chairs, sofas, dressing rooms, and king-size beds.

SEASONAL PLEASURES. West Dover is one of the oldest villages in Vermont, mostly white clapboard houses and a white church with a tall spire hidden behind a grotesquely ornate telephone pole. A quick walk along the main street and you've more or less seen West Dover, but there are plenty of activities in the neighborhood, at any season of the year. There are miles and miles of walking trails, the nearby Marlboro Music Festival in summer, the foliage in fall; but maybe the region comes into its own in winter, when you have a choice of downhill skiing at Mt. Snow, a mile and a half to the north, skating on the inn pond (bring your own skates), cross-country skiing on four-hour trails (the Williamses will make up a picnic lunch with wine), or snowshoeing through the forest. Let others shiver, however; I'll be sitting on the big sofa in the lounge with my afternoon tea, feet propped up on the copper-topped table, watching the snow fall on the tamaracks and maples—a panorama of white on white.

NAME: The Inn at Sawmill Farm

OWNER/INNKEEPER: Rodney C. Williams

ADDRESS: Route 100, Box 8, West Dover, Vt. 05356

DIRECTIONS: On Vt. 100, 6 miles north of Wilmington, halfway between Brattleboro and Bennington, and 10 miles from the Marlboro Music Festival.

TELEPHONE: (802) 464-8131

ROOMS: 13 rooms, plus 5 suites with fireplaces

RATES 1978: MAP only, $80 to $100 all year; plus 15% service charge and 5% on total bill (total bill less service charge, that is).

MEALS AND ENTERTAINMENT: Breakfast 8–9:30, no lunch, dinner 6–9:30; room service during meal hours; jackets at dinner.

DIVERSIONS: Outdoor pool and 2½-acre spring-fed pond for swimming, tennis (1 court, no charge for house guests), hiking trails, fishing; golf (18 holes, $10–$12 per round), rental bikes, horseback riding, sailing, and boating nearby; in winter, ice skating, snowshoeing, cross-country skiing, downhill skiing (1½ miles away).

P.S. Busiest in foliage and snow seasons, quietest in *summer*.

The Four Columns Inn
Newfane, Vt.

At some point on your trip, probably close to lunch or dinner, you may decide how marvelous it would be if Vermont had one of those great little inns like they have in France.

It does. *Voilà*. The Four Columns.

Poke your head into the restaurant here and you might think you're in Burgundy. Have dinner here and you may still think you're in Burgundy. The reason is, of course, that René Chardain, *le patron*, comes from France (from Champagne, rather than Burgundy), and Anne Chardain from

French Canada. What they've created is an almost-typical French auberge in Vermont.

The France-in-Vermont ambiance runs all the way through. None of the fourteen rooms are alike, and though the antique and not-so-antique furniture comes from auctions around Vermont, the print wallpapers, the curtains, and the bedspreads collectively have a look of France about them. All the rooms have private baths, and most of them have air conditioning.

The name comes from the four white columns decorating the slightly pompous facade of Kemball Hall, a house built for a Mr. Marshall Kemball back in 1830. It sits well off the main road, behind the Newfane Inn, the village green, and the county courthouse. It's in two parts—the old white house at the front, and a red barn at the rear—the two connected with a sheltered patio where you can drink and dine in summer. The restaurant, bar, and half the rooms are in the barn. At the rear, a footbridge leads across a pond, with a flock of cantankerous geese, to a trail leading up the hill (affectionately known as Mont Chardain) behind the inn.

PHEASANT AND CANDLELIGHT. This is no grab-a-snack joint. It's a place where you dawdle until the last drop of Burgundy is sipped, where you plot an entire evening that begins with a *kir* and ends with a kiss. The dining room greets you with a huge fireplace, a wall with subdued splashes of roses, a pheasant on the mantelpiece, a stag's head on the wall; the gentle lighting comes from sconces and candles; and copper pieces hanging from the dark, beamed ceiling glitter in the candles' glow. It's a mellow atmosphere. And *très intime*. No rush, no bustle. Just the quiet, unobtrusive service you get in a restaurant where the food is more important than the maitre d'.

The dishes are served up with that little extra care you associate with France, and the plate itself is carefully garnished; the waitress sweeps away the bread crumbs between courses, the plates appear and disappear without clatter.

The portions, *hélas,* are mountainous, and, doubly *hélas,* delectable to the last morsel. M. Chardain's specialties are duckling Bigarade flambée, rack of lamb, filet mignon poivre vert flambée, lobster with crab meat stuffing, trout (live from the tank or the pond), pheasant from their own farm, filet Wellington. A meal here is expensive, say $30 to $45 for two, with wine. That's the way French food is. The question is, is it worth it? That depends on who's with you.

M. Chardain's skills have been highly praised in *Life, Holiday, Vogue,* and *Esquire* (in each case when he was running the Newfane Inn across the green). Naturally, the wine list is also compiled with a little more care in such a place, and you can toast *l'amour* over a Sancerre ($9) or Gevrey Chambertin ($10)—or, if you don't let your lover see the prices, a modest Brouilly or Medoc or Pouilly Fumé.

After all that, there's nothing for it but to stumble upstairs to bed.

NAME: The Four Columns Inn
OWNER/INNKEEPER: René Chardain
ADDRESS: 230 West Street, Newfane, Vt. 05345

DIRECTIONS: On State Highway 30, 15 miles northwest of the Brattleboro exit on Interstate 91.

TELEPHONE: (802) 365-7713

ROOMS: 12 rooms, one suite

RATES 1978: EP, $30 to $40 all year; plus 5% tax on total bill.

MEALS AND ENTERTAINMENT: Breakfast 8–9:30, lunch 12–2, dinner 6–9 (approx. $20 to $25 for two); no room service; jacket requested in the dining room; piped music.

DIVERSIONS: Eating.

P.S. Closed Mondays, and for one month in spring (call ahead for dates).

The Old Tavern at Grafton
Grafton, Vt.

This may well be the ultimate New England inn.

It's historic (it opened its doors in 1801), and it had a distinguished clientele (Daniel Webster, Nathaniel Hawthorne, Ralph Waldo Emerson, Ulysses S. Grant, Teddy Roosevelt, and Rudyard Kipling, who stayed here so long one of the rooms is named after him). But historic inns often look their age, because it takes so much money just to keep them from falling down. Not the Old Tavern at Grafton, thanks to the Windham Foundation, which has restored many of the old Colonial homes in the village, and particularly this proud old inn. Now it's virtually a brand-new 270-year-old inn, with modern heating, a fire detection system, sprinklers, and an elevator. Kipling and Co. never had it so good.

When the inn first opened its doors, it was a much simpler structure than today's three-storied whitewashed

building with twin verandas overhung by the third floor, a bar in the old barn, and across the street a couple of old homes (also dating from the 1800s). The proprietors call this the "most elegant little inn in all New England." They're not kidding.

Step through the inn's main door and you're in the drawing room of a well-to-do squire—except that it's really the lobby and reception area. To the left is the Kipling Library, a blue parlor with shelves of books flanking an open fire, writing desks for dashing off *billets-doux,* and comfy sofas to settle back in with a volume of Kipling or Emerson or Hawthorne.

Upstairs in the guest rooms, you'll find the same impeccable taste. All the rooms are different, but they're all decorated with antiques and drapes and hooked rugs. Try one of the other rooms with tester beds—mini fourposters with cute embroidered canopies. The inn has thirty-five rooms spread over three buildings—fourteen in the old inn itself, the remainder in the Homestead and the Windham Cottage opposite. Normally, the words "across the street" might throw you into a tizzy. How dare they shunt you off to the annex! In this case, go. The rooms are delightful there, too. Karen's Room is all pinks and pastels, with bay windows and armchairs; Addie's Room, green and white, has a chaise longue where you can stretch out and watch the action down by the inn's swimming hole. There's another lovely old parlor in the Homestead, and a barlike lounge with TV, fireplace, and a discreet soft-drinks machine.

One of the most convivial rooms in the inn is one Kipling and his cohorts never saw. It's the Tavern Bar, an austere corner of the barn, so snug you can't avoid clinking glasses before you drink. On the other side of the bar's fireplace is the barn proper, with an even larger fireplace, puffy chairs and sofas; above it, the haymow has become a games room, with a piano, English bar billiards, and a TV set tucked away in a corner.

QUIET CORNERS, COVERED BRIDGES. The Old Tavern at Grafton is one of those places where you'll want to spend a few days. Just sampling all the quiet corners in the inn takes time: one morning writing postcards in the Kipling Library, an afternoon taking advantage of your luxurious room, cocktail hour in the Tavern Bar, an after-dinner drink in the Barn Lounge. Next day, a dip in the inn's private swimming pool in the meadow behind the Homestead. After lunch, a game of tennis. Or croquet. Or sit and rock on the porch, watching the automobiles go by every half hour or so. Or take a walk down the village street, past the antique shops, the art gallery, the general store, and the lovely old homes, across one of Grafton's kissing bridges, and wander up the leafy lane on the side of the mountain. It's so peaceful you can almost hear the butterflies flap their wings.

NAME: The Old Tavern at Grafton
INNKEEPER: Lois Copping
ADDRESS: Grafton, Vt. 05146
DIRECTIONS: On State Highway 121, about 10 miles west of Bellows Falls and Interstate 91.

TELEPHONE: (802) 843-2375

ROOMS: 37

RATES 1978: EP, from $30 to $45 all year; 5% local tax on room and food.

MEALS AND ENTERTAINMENT: Breakfast 8–9:30, lunch 12–2, dinner 6:30–8:30 (approx. $15 to $25 for two); no room service; jacket at dinner only; live music on weekends.

DIVERSIONS: Outdoor pool, tennis (2 clay courts, free), bicycles, cross-country skiing, ice skating, horse and carriage rides (in summer only), pool, Ping-Pong, skittles; hiking, horseback riding, skiing nearby.

Chester Inn
Chester, Vt.

After a while it gets to be like a movie scenario: young couple gets fed up with life in big city, moves to country, buys old inn, lives happily, but busily, ever after. In this case, the big city was Cleveland, the couple Betsy and Tom Guido, a former insurance executive, and the inn the nineteenth-century Chester Inn in southern Vermont.

It's colored pale salmon trimmed with blue, a stubby three-story building sitting well back from the main street on the village green, its facade dominated by verandas and porches where you can sit and rock and watch a day in the life of a small Vermont town. The spacious lounge has generous supplies of magazines, armchairs, and sofas grouped around a big wood-burning fireplace; the walls are lined with original paintings by friends of the Guidos, the furnishings are country primitive. Pride of place among the guest rooms goes to the Victorian Suite with authentic brocade swag draperies and a volume of Victorian poetry on the marble-topped night stand. Step through the doors of the cocktail lounge and you're insulated from the village green, on a patio with a heated pool surrounded by pink geraniums in pots; farther down the backyard there are two tennis courts and a garden growing fresh vegetables, herbs, and flowers for the inn dining room. Cleveland is lightyears away.

NAME: Chester Inn
OWNER/INNKEEPER: Tom Guido
ADDRESS: Main Street, Chester, Vt. 05143
DIRECTIONS: On Vt. 103, 15 miles northwest of exit 6 on Interstate 91.
TELEPHONE: (802) 875-2444
ROOMS: 27 rooms, including 3 suites
RATES 1978: EP, $25 to $30 all year (including breakfast); plus 10% on room rate to cover gratuities for breakfast and maid service, and 5% tax on total bill.
MEALS AND ENTERTAINMENT: Breakfast 8–9:30, lunch 12–2, dinner 6–9 (approx. $15 to $20 for two); no room service; informal dress; piano player in the lounge, Saturday only.
DIVERSIONS: Heated pool, bikes, backgammon, chess, tennis (2 courts, free to guests, ball machine); golf, hiking trails, horseback riding ($6 an hour), ice skating, sleigh rides, snowmobiles, cross-country and downhill skiing nearby; summer stock theater at Weston.

Woodstock Inn
Woodstock, Vt.

What the world needs is more Laurance Rockefellers, conservationists who have the wherewithal to put their money where their hearts are, men who'll put up beautiful inns like this one and then spend $3 million of their own money to bury telephone poles around the village green. Even before the poles went under, Woodstock was one of "the five most beautiful villages in America." It has an elliptical village green ringed with Colonial homes, four sets of Paul Revere bells in its church steeples, and a brand-new kissing bridge across the Ottauquechee River. The green, the bells, the bridge, and the river are circled by a protective bowl of hills where people ski in winter and hike in summer.

There's been an inn on this same spot on the village green since 1793, but all that remains of the earlier hostelries is the great hand-carved eagle above the portico of the 1969 inn—guardian of the inn's tradition of two hundred years of New England hospitality. Someone really cared about the details in the Woodstock Inn. Look around your room before you hop into each other's arms; note the jaunty handmade quilts, the brass hinges on the doors, the evocative photographs on the walls, the custom-designed oak furniture and the bedside table with the discreet AM/FM radio (the TV, alas, is not so discreet).

You spend your public hours in equally tasteful, restful surroundings, with ten-foot stone fireplaces, weathered Vermont timbers, a neat coffee shop, a cocktail lounge/piano bar, and an elegant blue-red-and-white dining room. In the rear, there's a broad terrace where you can dine beneath the awnings or sit in a rocker and admire the garden while readying your appetite for avocado bisque, roast leg of lamb Flamande, and Washington pie; but take your time over the decision because it's so pleasant rocking, listening to the birds twittering their evensong and the Paul Revere bells chiming the hour, as the shadows lengthen across the lawn.

ADDER'S TONGUE, DUTCHMAN'S BREECHES. Woodstock is a nice place to be any time of the year, but every lover has his favorite season. Come here in the spring and you can follow woodland trails, stepping lightly through the wildflowers—adder's tongue, Dutchman's breeches, cowslip, bloodroot, and jack-in-the-pulpit; in fall, you're sitting inside a golden bowl, and in winter you can go jingling through the streets in a one-horse open sleigh. Spring, summer, and fall you can swim in the garden pool (but no diving, it's only four feet deep); or play tennis and golf at the country club (one of the oldest courses in the country); or rent a bike ($4 a day) and go riding off down the backroads.

NAME: Woodstock Inn

INNKEEPER: C. B. Williamson

ADDRESS: Woodstock, Vt. 05091

DIRECTIONS: By car, from New York, take Interstate 91 to the White River Junction exit, then go 14 miles west on Vt. 12 (driving time 5 hours); from Boston, follow Interstates 93 and 89 to U.S. 4, then go west 10 miles (driving time 2½ hours); by air, scheduled flights to Lebanon, N.H. (an $8-per-couple cab ride from Woodstock).

TELEPHONE: (802) 457-1100

ROOMS: 110 (including a few deluxe rooms with steam baths)

RATES 1978: EP, winter and spring, $28 to $48, fall and summer, $36 to $56; plus 5% local tax on room and food.

MEALS AND ENTERTAINMENT: Breakfast 7–11, lunch 12–2, dinner 6–9 (approx. $16 to $20 for two), coffee shop open all afternoon; room service during breakfast and lunch; dress informal in winter, jacket required in dining room in summer; piano bar, live music and dancing Friday evenings.

DIVERSIONS: Heated outdoor pool, marked hiking trails (maintained by the inn), ice skating; sleigh rides, tennis (10 courts, $10 per court per 1½ hours, pro, ball machines, clinics), paddle tennis (2 lighted courts), golf (18 holes, $10 per round), bikes for rent, cross-country skiing trails; downhill skiing, horseback riding, and sailing nearby.

P.S. Small top-echelon groups most of the year, but the meeting rooms are all downstairs and you may never know there's a group in the house.

Reluctant Panther Inn
Manchester Village, Vt.

¢

Like the name, there's a touch of whimsy in the exterior (an un-Vermontlike muted mauve) and eclectic interior decor—Chinoiserie, Victoriana, an antique desk clerk's clock, hanging lanterns and planters in one of the two snug dining rooms. Most guests come here for the Panther's inventive cuisine (Greek avgolemone soup, crêpes Rangoon, breast of chicken stuffed with almond-and-apple dressing), but people who really know the place call ahead and book a room as well as a table. If it's winter, they'll specify one of the four rooms with wood-burning fireplaces. Like everything else in this 150-year-old house, the guest rooms will come as a surprise: some have carpets that continue halfway up the wall, the color schemes are unorthodox, but they all have modern bathrooms and cable TV. It all may sound rather odd, but in fact it's done with great flair, and you needn't be reluctant to spend a night or two with the Panther.

NAME: Reluctant Panther Inn
OWNERS/INNKEEPERS: Wood and Joan Cornell
ADDRESS: Box 6781, Manchester, Vt. 05254
DIRECTIONS: In Manchester *Village,* at the intersection of Route 7, West Road and Seminary Road.
TELEPHONE: (802) 362-2568
ROOMS: 6, one suite
RATES 1978: EP, $20 to $30 in spring and summer, $24 to $35 after September 15 (when rooms with working fireplaces are $30 weekdays, $35 Fridays, Saturdays, and holidays); plus 15% service charge and 5% tax on total bill.
MEALS AND ENTERTAINMENT: Breakfast 8–9, no lunch, dinner 6–9, closed for dinner on Tuesdays (approx. $20 to $25 for two); room service for breakfast; informal dress.

DIVERSIONS: Tennis, golf, bikes, hiking trails, horseback riding, winter sports all nearby.

P.S. No children or pets.

Barrows House
Dorset, Vt.

It's almost a village within a village, six houses on as many acres—Hemlock House, Truffle House, the Carriage House, the Birds' Nest, a cottage named Schubert (Charles, not Franz), and Barrows House itself, a big white mansion built back in 1784 by one of the first preachers in Vermont. The guest rooms are New England traditional (floral wallpapers, dust ruffles, patchwork comforters the maid turns down at night), except for a few rooms, in the Carriage House, which are done in dashing contemporary style. For the past five years the inn has been owned, managed, and cherished by Charles and Marilyn Schubert, an energetic and congenial couple who have laid on plenty of diversions for their guests (see below), and who'll be happy to direct you to local activities like barn sales and summer theater. But they won't be too upset if you just lounge around and enjoy the peacefulness of their garden, beside a quiet tree-lined street in the kind of Vermont village where everyone seems to be at church listening to the preacher.

NAME: Barrows House

OWNERS/INNKEEPERS: Charles and Marilyn Schubert

ADDRESS: Dorset, Vt. 05251

DIRECTIONS: Drive north or south along U.S. 7, then northeast on State Highway 30; the Schuberts are right on 30.

TELEPHONE: (802) 867-4455

ROOMS: 22, with 4 suites

RATES 1978: MAP $56 to $66 all year (discount given if you decide not to have dinner); plus 15% service charge and 5% tax on room and food.

MEALS AND ENTERTAINMENT: Breakfast 7:30–9, lunch 12–1:30, dinner 6–9 (approx. $20 to $25 for two); room service; jacket preferred at dinner.

DIVERSIONS: heated outdoor pool, sauna, 2 tennis courts (free to house guests), game room, backgammon, chess, etc., bikes for rent; golf, hiking, and horseback riding nearby; cross-country skiing (rentals available), ice skating; downhill skiing nearby.

Hawk Mountain
Pittsfield, Vt.

Turtledove Mountain would be more like it, because there's a love affair going on up here, a love affair between people and trees. "The nice thing about Vermont," as one young Vermonter once remarked, "is that the trees are close together and the people are far apart." And that's the way it is on Hawk Mountain. You have complete, unruffled seclusion (you rent homes, not rooms) among the pine, spruce, and maple trees, where kingbirds and tree swallows swoop and sing as if they're happy to be here. You'll have a terrace among the branches of the spruce and maple, and if you're here in warm weather you may find yourself spending most of your time there: brunching on the terrace, snoozing on the terrace, reading on the terrace, sunbathing on the terrace, sundowners on the terrace, dinner on the terrace, love on the terrace with the moonlight of Vermont filtering through the leaves.

Hawk Mountain is a place for two people who are happy just being with each other. There's no "action" (plenty of it, though, in Killington). You enjoy simple pleasures here—a swim in the spring-fed pond, a walk to the top of the mountain for stunning views of wave after wave of greenclad slopes (you're surrounded on three sides by the Green Mountain National Forest); walks around the common grounds in fall to pick armfuls of apples, blackberries, or raspberries.

TIMBER HOUSES, FIELDSTONE FIRES. Hawk Mountain is neither a resort nor a hotel in the usual sense, and to say it's a housing development is like calling Yehudi Menuhin a fiddler. At Hawk Mountain people buy lots, build vacation homes, and put them into a rental pool when they're not in use. You're the big winner—because for a few nights or a few weeks you have all the advantages of living in a smart vacation home in the forest without owning it. They're hardly run-of-the-mill vacation homes either: they're all screened from each other (and from the driveways) by trees, they're built of timber and finished with stain only (no paint), and even the "garbage houses" have to match the homes. A few have two bedrooms, most of them have three or four (the rates are not much different once you check into them). Decor varies from owner to owner, but most of them are summer townhouse modern; all of them have complete kitchens, terraces, fieldstone fireplaces, stacks of firewood, electric heating, picture windows filled with treescapes. The newer homes have washers, dryers, and compactors, a few have private saunas. You can request maid service or you can do without it, if you don't want to see any living creatures except the kingbirds and swallows.

When you arrive, you'll find a basket with wine, Vermont cheese, and crackers on the house; if you would like to have your refrigerator stocked, call in your order in advance. But probably the nicest way to spend your first evening is to have the front office send over a cook with all the makings of cheese fondue or a steak dinner or some other goodies, and settle down in front of your fieldstone fireplace until dinner and wine are served.

Hawk Mountain (with its cousins, Great Hawk and Timber Hawk) is the brainchild of a Harvard-graduated architect, Robert Carl Williams, and a doctor, Hugh Kopald, who grew up together in the Great Smokies of Tennessee, discovered they shared the same concern for man and nature, and found the perfect spot for turning their ideas into reality along Route 100 in Vermont.

Route 100 is known as the "Skiway," because of Killington and a dozen other ski slopes. Which brings you to two of the advantages of the three Hawks—they're year-round hideaways, and if you do decide to rejoin the world for a few hours, you'll find golf, tennis, riding, fishing, sailing, hiking, dining and dancing within a short drive of your terrace. You'll also find gas stations, junkyards, and traffic.

It's nicer up on the mountain. Stay there, and enjoy your love affair with the trees.

NAME: Hawk Mountain

INNKEEPER: Gary Gaskill (property manager)

ADDRESS: Route 100, Pittsfield, Vt. 05762

DIRECTIONS: 260 miles from New York, 155 from Boston, 18 from Rutland; from Interstate 89N take Bethel exit (#3) to Vt. 107 west to its intersection with Vt. 100, then south on 100 to Pittsfield; from Interstate 87N, take exit #20 to N.Y. 149, follow U.S. 4 east through Rutland to Vt. 100. By air, to Rutland, Lebanon, Montpelier, Burlington; by Amtrak to Whitehall or White River Junction.

TELEPHONE: (802) 746-5171; toll free (800) 451-4109

ROOMS: 60 homes

RATES 1978: EP $52 up per couple, except for Christmas/New Year's week and Washington's Birthday weekend when the rate is $102 and up; 10% discounts for stays of 5 nights or more; plus 5% tax on room.

MEALS AND ENTERTAINMENT: No meals (although a restaurant is in the plans), but you can have meals delivered from outside or a Hawk Mountain cook come cook for you, or you can go off and sample some of the dozens of restaurants in the neighborhood.

DIVERSIONS: Heated pool, spring-fed ponds, exercise rooms, hiking trails, tennis (2 courts, no lights, $5 per court per hour), squash and racquetball ($7 per court per hour); cross-country skiing (rentals), sleigh rides, ice skating, skiing nearby; golf, canoeing, trout fishing, paddle tennis nearby.

P.S. Open all year, busiest during ski weekends, during July and August, during the foliage season (but what is "busy" at a place like Hawk?).

The Lodge at Smugglers' Notch
Stowe, Vt.

You're high in the Green Mountains here: Mt. Mansfield and Smugglers' Notch are a few miles up the road, the Alpine-pretty village of Stowe is a few miles in the other direction, and no matter which way you turn the landscape is chock-a-block with forested mountains and valleys. If you want to go higher still, head for the summit of Mansfield, at 4303 feet above sea level. There's a restaurant up there: take a gondola to lunch. "Rooms $1 and up," reads a sign for the original inn, but that goes back a long way to the days when this really was a mountain lodge with bare floors and bunk beds. Now it's the sort of semiluxurious place where Kennedys and TV people stay when they go skiing on these slopes. The lodge's dining room is a proper restaurant in its own right (no place this for an après-ski bowl of onion soup), and there are games rooms, a library, and a TV lounge to fill in the gaps in your indoor hours.

But indoors is no match for the outdoors here, and even with all its comforts, the lodge is really a place to hang your bathrobes while you enjoy the seasons—the lower-decked valleys in spring, the foliage in fall, the crisp mountain air at any time.

If you're looking for a place to go in winter but don't want to be swamped by skiers, try the Lodge at Smugglers' Notch—it's just far enough from the slopes to be peaceful.

NAME: The Lodge at Smugglers' Notch
INNKEEPER: Phil Breedlove
ADDRESS: RR 1, Stowe, Vt. 05672
DIRECTIONS: 6½ miles north of Stowe village, on Vt. 108; Stowe is 10 miles from Exit 10 on Interstate 89; by air to Burlington or Montpelier.
TELEPHONE: (802) 253-7311
ROOMS: 35 rooms, 3 suites
RATES 1978: MAP only $60 to $110 from mid-June through mid-October (check with the lodge for rates beyond that date); plus 15% service charge, 5% tax on total bill.
MEALS AND ENTERTAINMENT: Breakfast 8–9:30, continental breakfast 9:30–11, lunch 12–1:30, dinner 6:30–9; room service during regular meal hours; jacket at dinner; live music during dinner.
DIVERSIONS: Heated outdoor pool, game room, hiking trails, ice skating; tennis (6 courts, $6 per court per hour, pro, ball machines, 3-day clinics), golf (18 holes, $12 per day), skiing, cross-country skiing, sleigh rides, snowmobiles; horseback riding nearby.

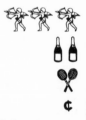

The John Hancock Inn
Hancock, N.H.

Hancock is reputed to be, quote unquote, one of the six prettiest towns in New Hampshire. That's one reason for going there. The other is the local hostelry, which has been luring travelers off the highway long before anyone ever thought of such things as prettiest villages.

The John Hancock Inn has been standing tall and stately since 1789, on a street of fine Colonial buildings, a few yards from the village green and a meetinghouse with bells forged by Paul Revere. Hancock himself never actually saw the place; apparently the Declaration of Independence wasn't the only document Hancock signed—he was also a land-speculator and put his quill to a title deed buying up several hundred acres of property in this neighborhood. Some of his local admirers voted to name the village after him (when he turned down an invitation shortly afterwards to visit the town, the snubbed villagers tried to have the name changed).

If Hancock never dined here, Daniel Webster did, and over the generations a host of notables have walked through the heavy hospitable red door of the inn—Peter, Paul, and Mary, Nelson Rockefeller, Ted Williams, and Tony Bennett among them.

Much of the inn's decor is authentic, some of it dating from the days of John Hancock, Esquire. The ten rooms (all with private bath) are decked out with braided rugs, wide floorboards, fireplaces (but no fires), wash stands, half tester beds, pencil post beds, slatback chairs with footstools, travel trunks, patchwork quilts. The most unusual room in the inn (in fact, one of the most unusual anywhere) has "primitive" murals depicting a blue-green lake-and-forest setting, painted by an itinerant artist, Rufus Porter.

The Hancock's Carriage Lounge is the snug sort of room you look forward to finding in a country inn: the seats are tufted leather benches from old buggies, the tables black-smiths' bellows, and there's a big roaring brick fireplace in one corner. Businessmen drive from miles around to have lunch here, but most diners continue through to the rear and one of three pleasant dining rooms. One is an enclosed patio overlooking the garden at the rear, another is a quiet blue-hued den with only four tables. The Hancock's cuisine is basically New England country fare, with an occasional bow to continental cuisine. The New England seafood casserole in sherry sauce is as tasty a way as any to wind up an evening.

NAME: The John Hancock Inn
INNKEEPERS: Glynn and Pat Wells
ADDRESS: Main Street, Hancock, N.H. 03449
DIRECTIONS: On N.H. 137, a few miles from U.S. 202 (between Hillsborough and Peterborough) and about 20 miles from Keene; by air to Keene.
TELEPHONE: (603) 525-3318
ROOMS: 10
RATES 1978: EP, $25.50 (including tax) year round
MEALS AND ENTERTAINMENT: Breakfast 8–9:30, lunch 12–2, dinner 6–9 (approx. $12 to $18 for two, including tax), Sundays 5–8; no room service; dress optional "but in good taste."
DIVERSIONS: Swimming in town lake, free tennis on 3 town courts, lots of hiking trails in neighborhood, ice skating on town rink; antiquing, theater, concerts, golf and skiing nearby; chess, checkers, and conversation at the inn.

Wolfeboro Inn
Wolfeboro, N.H.

There probably aren't too many Colonial inns in New England with four dented Saabs in the back yard; but then there aren't too many Colonial inns run by retired hot-rodders. That's no qualification for an innkeeper, of course, but Paul McBride also spent a long time with the Sheraton chain before coming here fifteen years ago—and that is.

The Wolfeboro Inn, which dates from 1812, has fifteen bright-and-breezy rooms, all decorated with period furniture, all with private bath or shower. Three of them have double beds, three have fireplaces.

When he wasn't denting Saabs, McBride was scouring the auctions of New Hampshire for antiques for his inn. He tracked down some beauties. The parlor has a fine set of "Praying Mantis" andirons—whirls and swirls of wrought-iron patterns crafted in Cape Cod in 1731. The huge hooked rug, on the other hand, is no antique: it was hooked a few years ago by Mary McBride. The other rooms are chock-a-block with bellows, pewter, silverware and copperware (at least they were on a recent visit, but if guests continue to pocket the pewter there may not be much left by the time you get there).

The inn's restaurant is a 130-seater, a new extension tastefully designed (by Paul McBride) to blend in with the overall decor and atmosphere, but if you don't want to eat with the crowd there's also a charming little dining room at the front of the main house.

The inn's hefty meals are welcome after a day in the fresh air on Lake Winnipesaukie. The shortest route to the lake is through the back yard, past the Saabs to the inn's private beach—only ten feet of the lake's 300 miles, but enough to introduce you to the refreshing waters. You can also borrow one of the inn's two Sunfishes and sail away across the lake.

And if you get to know Paul McBride he may take you for a hair-raising spin in his mighty racing boat. Once a hot-rodder, always a hot-rodder.

NAME: Wolfeboro Inn
INNKEEPER: Paul J. McBride
ADDRESS: 44 North Main Street, Wolfeboro, N.H. 03894
DIRECTIONS: On State Highway 28, on the eastern shore of Lake Winnipesaukie.
TELEPHONE: (603) 569-3016
ROOMS: 15
RATES 1978: $20 EP all year; plus 6% tax on room, food, and bar.
MEALS AND ENTERTAINMENT: Breakfast 8–9:30, lunch 11:30–2:30, dinner 5:30–9 (approx. $12 to $18 for two),

lounge to 1 a.m.; dress informal, "but no blue jeans, shorts, tank tops, or T-shirts please"; live music.

DIVERSIONS: Freshwater pool and sauna, 18-hole golf course ($9 per round); tennis, bicycles, hiking, horseback riding, sailing and boating, waterskiing, winter sports including skiing nearby.

Hillside Inn

East Hebron, N.H.

And hillside it is. You enter on one level (with cozy lounges and a spacious dining room), climb a few steps to traditional inn rooms, or step down to the games room, another lounge, and several modern guest rooms. Every level seems to have a veranda with rocking chairs to take full advantage of the view across the lawns and lake to the distant mountains. The Higgins family, owners of the inn, seem to be willing to spend whatever it takes to maintain an elderly inn in good condition, and innkeeper Fitzmaurice Kelley is an eager welcoming host. It's a place to go for winding down. Spend an hour browsing among the piles of magazines and books in one of the antique-filled lounges or in front of one of the four fireplaces. Or take a trip on the lake; the Indians called it Pasquany, the lake of the canoe tree, but you'll have to settle for an aluminum rowboat.

NAME: Hillside Inn
INNKEEPER: Fitzmaurice Kelley
ADDRESS: East Hebron, N.H. 03232
DIRECTIONS: On Newfound Lake, on N.H. 3A between Plymouth (exit 26 on Interstate 93) and Bristol (exit 23 on I-93).
TELEPHONE: (603) 744-2413

ROOMS: 17 in inn (plus 7 cottages, for families rather than couples)

RATES 1978: MAP from $51 to $56 all year (with rebates for meals not taken at the inn, if warned in advance); plus 6% tax on total bill.

MEALS AND ENTERTAINMENT: Breakfast 8–9, lunch 12–2, dinner 6–8:30; no room service; prefer jacket at dinner.

DIVERSIONS: Pool, lake swimming, bikes, rowboat, tennis court (free); golf and winter sports nearby.

Snowy Owl Inn
Waterville Valley, N.H.

The valley first. The Mad River shoulders its way through a gap between three mountains—Tecumseh, Snow, and Osceola—and the surrounding peaks rise above forests of spruce and pine to a height of four thousand feet or more. The scenery is, well, magnificent, and you could spend days walking and hiking here without passing the same tree twice. Even with the year-round resort that has taken root here in the past few years, this is still very much nature's own country, partly because the only way in is winding route 49 and the only way out is back along the same winding 49. Here and there among this extravaganza of trees and mountains and streams you come upon the enclaves of the Waterville Valley resort—lodges, condominiums, restaurants, and a few shops, all in tune with the setting. Of the Valley's four inns, the Snowy Owl is the wise choice.

It has been described by a leading ski magazine as "the best designed lodge in U.S. mountain resorts," which may be overstating the case, but it is certainly *one* of the most beautiful lodges in the country: weathered pine facade and a veranda lined with antique wicker chairs; a lobby rising to three stories around a massive fieldstone fireplace; rustic-modern decor highlighted with a few well-chosen antiques and owls in all forms—macramé owls, oil owls, photographic owls, carved wooden owls. One level down, there's a conversation pit in front of the big fire, then a terrace and stone steps leading down to Snow's Brook, which ripples along like something out of Schubert *lieder*. *"Bachlein, so munter rauschend zumal/Wollen hinunter silbern ins Tal."*

Right up top, up a wrought-iron spiral stairway, there's a small cupola with a bench and heater, where you can take your morning coffee (or late-night wine) and look at the treetops, the birds, the sunset, or the stars, far from the madding crowd and the Mad River.

NAME: Snowy Owl Inn

OWNERS/INNKEEPERS: Tish and Roger Hamblin

ADDRESS: Waterville Valley, N.H. 03223

DIRECTIONS: Take Interstate 93 to exit 28 and follow the signs; the valley is about one hour by car north of Concord.

TELEPHONE: (603) 236-8383

ROOMS: 37

RATES 1978: EP, $34 to $40 summer and fall, higher in winter; special tennis packages for Rod Laver clinics; plus 6% tax on total bill.

MEALS AND ENTERTAINMENT: Complimentary coffee all day, continental breakfast in winter only. The inn has no dining facilities; the Fourways Restaurant (a 2-minute walk through the trees) serves all meals including dinner from 6 to 9 (approx. $15 to $20 for two). The young ski-oriented waiters and waitresses are hearty but confused—imagine recruiting *ski* instructors in a hotel school. Dress is informal; and Fourways is also the site of the local discotheque, the Rustic Nail.

DIVERSIONS: Small pool, sauna in the inn; in the resort—tennis (18 courts, no lights, $3.50 an hour per court, Rod Laver clinics), golf (9 holes, clubs for rent), hiking trails;

in winter, ice skating, 15 miles of cross-country trails (6 full-time instructors), 32 downhill slopes.

p.s. If Snowy Owl is full, try the Hamblins' Silver Squirrel or the Valley Inn (which has an indoor-outdoor pool, platform tennis, and a few rooms with terraces).

Stafford's-in-the-Field
Chocorua, N.H.

It tops a knoll above a gravelly back road, a tall, mellowed farmhouse with a big old barn alongside, in a meadow somewhere between a village, a lake, a forest, and a mountain. If it looks like a farm outside, it feels more like a home inside. It's very much a family affair: Fred Stafford, genial and laconic, is your host, his wife Ramona is cook (usually the first words you hear about the inn are "the food is terrific"); daughter Momo, in her early twenties and pretty as spring, is the pastry chef/baker and a stickler for natural ingredients; sons Fritz and Hansel help out with the hard labor, odd jobs, and running the place. They all trekked east from San Diego a decade ago because they hankered after "something old and New England." They found the old here, in a house that dates from 1784 and took in its first paying guests in 1894, and added an extra dash of New England with a collection of milk churns, butter washers, boudoir desks, and a blacksmith's bellows that's finding its second wind as a coffee table. Charming is an overused word in describing old inns (this guide is as guilty as any), but here charming is the word. The Staffords have only seven rooms in the main house (more in the cottages at the rear, but you'll probably prefer one of these seven), and they've decorated them the way you hope a country inn will be decorated—with cheery wallpapers, braided rugs, and some tasteful family bric-a-brac. Three of the rooms have double beds, only two have private bathrooms (the others share four baths and toilets, a manageable ratio). The dainty rooms on the top floor have corner windows looking straight into the leafy limbs of maples—you feel like you're waking up in a tree house.

A HAPPENING EVERY NIGHT. The focal point of the inn is the antique-filled dining room, and the highlight of the day is dinner. It's served at a rural 6:30, which may seem early, but most guests actually start congregating long before. (The inn has no liquor license, but Fred provides setups and ice and you just help yourselves.) This is the time to sit in a rocker on the porch to watch evening settle over the gentle countryside; it's a time, too, to greet your fellow guests, and you may find yourselves rocking beside a musician or writer, corporate lawyer, or museum curator. Bringing people together is what Fred Stafford enjoys most about innkeeping, and since the evening meal is served dinner-party style, with Fred at the head of the table, "every evening becomes a happening . . . people react beautifully." Good food helps, of course, as much as good conversation—four courses of wholesome home cooking, with vegetables and berries fresh from the garden, bread warm from the oven, and entrées that range from New England to India to France to California/Mexico, depending on how Ramona sizes up that day's guests. By the time you've sipped your coffee you appreciate the wisdom of the 6:30 start, because even after four courses of "terrific food" you have time for a nightcap on the porch (or, as the bugs sometimes insist, indoors among the serendipitous antiques in the parlor) and *still* get to bed ahead of your usual schedule.

NAME: Stafford's-in the-Field
INNKEEPERS: Fred and Ramona Stafford
ADDRESS: Chocorua, N.H. 03817
DIRECTIONS: Chocorua is on N.H. 16, between Lake Winnipesaukie and the White Mountain National Forest,

about ten miles from Conway; the inn itself is a few miles from the village, on N.H. 113.

TELEPHONE: (603) 323-7766

ROOMS: 23, including 7 in the inn itself

RATES 1978: MAP only, $58 to $64 all year; plus 12% service charge, and 6% on the total bill (before the service charge is added).

MEALS AND ENTERTAINMENT: Breakfast 8:30–9:30, no lunch, dinner 6:30, served family style; no room service; informal dress; occasional musical events in the big barn, without intruding on the peacefulness of the inn; no liquor, bring your own (set-ups provided).

DIVERSIONS: Walking, swimming in the lake, canoeing, climbing Mount Chocorua; tennis, golf, summer theater nearby; cross-country skiing on the grounds (skis for rent), downhill skiing nearby.

P.S. Open all year, except for the period between late October and December 26; busiest in summer and foliage seasons.

Lovett's Inn
Franconia, N.H.

Down a steep, winding country road you go, between cliffs of spruce and pine and birch, until the scenery opens out into a meadow and you cross a brook and into Lovett's. Guests in the cottages often spot deer and foxes and bears padding across the meadow, but even if you don't spot any wildlife the surrounding White Mountain scenery is exhilarating.

The main house here goes back 170 years, and it's been run continuously by two generations of Lovetts. They've filled it with appropriate antiques and collectibles to preserve its stone-wall beamed-ceiling personality, yet they've managed to add a few contemporary cottages (each with picture windows and terrace, some with fireplace) in the garden at the rear without spoiling the setting. Most important for some guests, though, the family has managed to tack on a kitchen that wouldn't look out of place in an inn twice the size. Lovett's is famed for miles around for home cooking, which, even with all the fresh herbs and vegetables from the garden, is more cosmopolitan than country: a typical dinner here might consist of black bean soup with Demerara rum, pan-broiled chicken in brandy or curried young lamb with Franconia chutney, topped off with fudge rum pie or macaroon crumble.

Obviously, the Lovetts expect their guests to turn up in the dining room with farmers' appetites primed by fresh air and exercise, and there's certainly plenty of both in these parts: walking, hiking, trips up mountains on aerial tramways or cog railways, to say nothing of horse shows, auctions, flower shows, and country fairs. Or just sitting in the fresh air in the garden, waiting for a fox or deer to appear.

NAME: Lovett's Inn

OWNER/INNKEEPER: Charles J. Lovett, Jr.

ADDRESS: Profile Road, Franconia, N.H. 03580

DIRECTIONS: Near exit 38 of Interstate 93, just after it leaves the White Mountain National Forest.

TELEPHONE: (603) 823-7761

ROOMS: 22 (8 in the inn sharing 5 bathrooms, the remainder, with private baths, in cottages; some with fireplaces)

RATES 1978: MAP $44 to $64 all year (EP available on request), including 6% tax.

MEALS AND ENTERTAINMENT: Breakfast 8–9, no lunch, dinner 6:30–7:45; no room service; jacket and tie at dinner.

DIVERSIONS: Heated outdoor pool, hiking trails, lawn games, table tennis, pool; tennis, golf, horseback riding, winter sports nearby (cross-country rentals at the inn).

Franconia Inn
Franconia, N.H.

Old Zebedee Applebee, they say, was the first innkeeper in these parts, building his Colonial-era tavern on the same spot where the Franconia stands today; and although this particular inn was built in the thirties, as a farmhouse, it exudes something of the atmosphere of a Colonial tavern. In any case, how often do you find a country inn with indoor tennis courts?

The Franconia has been through some up-and-down years recently, and gone through several twentieth-century Zebedees, but for the past few seasons it has been owned by Wade and Rachel Perry of Lincoln, Mass., who've plowed more than $100,000 into refurbishing the rooms. The most interesting nooks, on the second floor, have knotty pine walls throughout, even in the shower stalls and closets, which gives them the look of cabins on a nice old-fashioned yacht. The inn's dining room serves up staple fare in a relaxed, softly lit atmosphere, decorated with antiques and hanging planters. When there's a chill in the New Hampshire air, guests can gather around the big old fireplace dating from 1862, a reminder at least of the inn's heritage.

NAME: Franconia Inn
INNKEEPER: Dwight W. Blakeslee
ADDRESS: Route 116, Franconia, N.H. 03580
DIRECTIONS: Take exit 38 from Interstate 93, then go 2 miles west on Route 116.
TELEPHONE: (603) 823-5542; toll-free outside of New Hampshire (800) 258-8985
ROOMS: 29

RATES 1978: MAP only, $56 to $76 in spring, $60 to $80 remainder of year; plus 6% local tax on total bill.

MEALS AND ENTERTAINMENT: Breakfast 8–9:30, continental to 10, no lunch, dinner 7–9; no room service; informal dress.

DIVERSIONS: Heated outdoor pool, cross-country skiing (rentals), bikes, tennis (6 clay courts, 2 indoor, pro, ball machines, clinics, "special rates for guests"); golf, horseback riding, other winter sports, trips up the mountains.

IN AND AROUND THE BOSKY BERKSHIRES

O, my Luve is like a red, red rose
That's newly sprung in June;
O, my Luve is like the melodie
That's sweetly play'd in tune . . .
BURNS

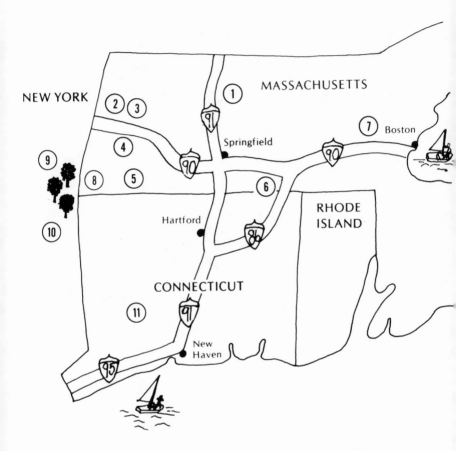

1. Deerfield Inn
2. Wheatleigh
3. The Gateways Inn and Restaurant
4. The Red Lion Inn
5. The Flying Cloud Inn
6. The Publick House
7. Longfellow's Wayside Inn
8. Stagecoach Hill Inn
9. Swiss Hutte Inn
10. Oliver House
11. Harrison Inn
    and Conference Center

Deerfield Inn
Old Deerfield, Mass.

When they buried the telephone cables here a few years ago the villagers had a party, and when they finally had to chop down the 300-year-old elm tree in front of the Asa Stebbins House some of the old-timers wept. Old Deerfield is that kind of village.

And Deerfield Inn is that kind of inn. Where else can you dine off polished mahogany tables with silver candelabras and English antique cutlery? Or sleep in guest rooms with reproductions of eighteenth-century wallpapers? The inn was built in 1884, and although it's been titivated in recent years, it still has the feel of a coaching house. All twelve rooms have private baths and electric blankets, and all except one have twin beds. Room #3, at the rear, has a lovely plush love seat in a corner by the windows, surrounded by lacy curtains.

BYE, BYE, TWENTIETH CENTURY. The sunny veranda lounge looks out on a view consisting almost exclusively of a gigantic catalpa tree, whose branches seem as eager to grow down as up, fringed in spring with orchidlike blossoms. Through the blossoms you get a glimpse of the white clapboard walls of the Joseph Stebbins House, built in 1774, and a foretaste of what's in store if you can coax yourself out of your Hitchcock chair to go for a stroll.

The Street (that's what they call it—simply The Street) is lined with elms and maples and more than fifty fine old houses from the eighteenth and nineteenth centuries. Most of them have been restored, but instead of being mere museums (more than a hundred period rooms are open to visitors), they're actually people's *homes*. Some people call this the prettiest street in all America and they may be right—just elms, maples, houses, gardens, and Deerfield prep school on the common. No neon, no telephone poles.

The Street wasn't always so peaceful. At dawn on February 29, 1704, a band of Indians crept into town, burned homes, killed forty-nine settlers, and then marched the remaining 109 through the snow to Canada, 200 miles away. One of the local museums still exhibits a door axed by a tomahawk.

Deerfield Academy was founded in 1799 with the motto "Be Worthy of Your Heritage," and since then the entire village seems to have adopted the sentiment. And back in 1952 a well-to-do couple by the name of Flynt fell in love with the place and set up the Heritage Foundation to preserve the village in its unspoiled state. Hence the spic-and-span Deerfield Inn, where you can nod off in early New England surroundings and not have to worry about the Indians sneaking in.

NAME: Deerfield Inn

INNKEEPER: Philip Di Benedetto

ADDRESS: Deerfield, Mass. 01342

DIRECTIONS: *Old* Deerfield is just off U.S. 5, three miles south of Greenfield, which in turn is at the intersection of U.S. 2 (the Mohawk Trail) and Interstate 91.

TELEPHONE: (413) 774-3147

ROOMS: 12

RATES 1978: EP, $24 to $28 all year; plus 8% tax on food and beverages, 5.7% on room.

MEALS AND ENTERTAINMENT: Breakfast 7:30–9:30, lunch 12–2, Monday through Saturday, dinner 6–9, Monday through Saturday, Sunday 12–3 and 5–8 (approx. $12 to $18); snack shop open 10 a.m.–4 p.m.; no room service; informal dress.

DIVERSIONS: The museums of historic Deerfield are the main attraction; hiking and skiing nearby.

Wheatleigh
Lenox, Mass.

There must be a St. Lenox up there somewhere watching over this charmed village. First there's all that beautiful Berkshire hill-dale-and-forest scenery; then the Tanglewood Music Festival with its magical evenings of lawns, stars, and the Boston Symphony; and now when you go there you can stay in a Florentine villa, once the home of a contessa.

Wheatleigh was built in 1893 or thereabouts, a wedding gift from an American tycoon to his daughter and her Spanish count. It's very Italianate, a piccolo palazzo: circular courtyard with large fountain, glass-and-iron marquee above the main door, great hall with chandeliers and polished oak floors, grand stairway illumined by Tiffany stained-glass windows. The twenty-two acres of gardens are decorated with terraces and statuary, an old-time swimming pool, and what looks like a campanile but is really a water tower. A couple of years ago Wheatleigh was acquired and restored by David Weisgal, a youngish New York philanthropist and fund raiser, and now he and his fiancée run the inn on the lines of house parties in a gracious country home. Weisgal himself rustles up pancakes and bacon-and-eggs for his guests; and either he or Ms. Brooks-Dunay are on hand to greet new arrivals and show them to their rooms, with a casual request to remember to sign the register at some point.

This being a private home, the bedrooms are all different: half of them are deluxe (almost mini-suites, some with terraces and fireplaces), a few are quite cramped (but they're several dollars less expensive, so don't scoff at them). Furnishings are mostly antiques and period pieces, including some beds with white frilly half-canopies. The most romantic of the lot is the Aviary Suite, in a separate wing connected to the main house by an ivy-covered galleria; it's on two levels, sitting room downstairs, with iron steps spiraling up to a second-floor nest with fluffy carpets and twin beds. It really was an aviary at one time; and it's now popular with musicians (Leonard Bernstein and my favorite pianist, Claudio Arrau, among them) because they can just squeeze a piano into the sitting room. If privacy is a consideration, the Aviary also has a private entrance from the courtyard. Cocktails are served on the terrace, by the pool, or in the library, dinner in the cozy candlelit dining room or in the enclosed porch at the rear. The menu is restricted to three entrées each evening, one of them Italian, in keeping with the villa's heritage. The house wine, too, is from Verona, a gentle reminder that you're here to play Romeo and Giulietta (or even Marcello and Sophia). So order a carafe of Ristoro and a couple of glasses, and enjoy the stars. *"E lucevan le stelle . . . e olezzava la terra."*

NAME: Wheatleigh

OWNER/INNKEEPERS: A. David Weisgal and Florence Brooks-Dunay

ADDRESS: P. O. Box 824, Lenox, Mass. 01240

DIRECTIONS: For Lenox, take the Mass. Pike to the Lee exit, then follow the signs for Lenox; in town, go left at the Curtis Hotel onto Stockbridge Road, turn right at the bottom of the hill, and continue for about 1½ miles to the Wheatleigh driveway.

TELEPHONE: (413) 637-0610

ROOMS: 18 rooms, including 10 deluxe and 2 suites (11 rooms and suites in winter)

RATES 1978: EP (including full breakfast) $30 to $45 in spring; in July and August $40 to $55 weekdays, $65 to $80 weekends (discount for stays of 7 days); lower rest of year; plus 5.7% tax on room.

MEALS AND ENTERTAINMENT: Breakfast 8–10, lunch 12–2:30, dinner 6–9 (daily except Tuesday in July and August, approx. $22 to $25 for two); no room service; informal dress (but stylish); pianist in lounge on weekends.

DIVERSIONS: Pool, walking, tennis (one court, free), sailboat
and rowboat (free) on Stockbridge Lake; golf, horseback
riding, winter sports nearby.

The Gateways Inn and Restaurant
Lenox, Mass.

The Bicentennial was supposed to be *America's* big year but
Czech-born Gerhard Schmid also came out of it smelling of
roses. First he won a slew of gold medals in the International
Culinary Olympics in Frankfurt. Then he was invited to prepare a civic banquet for Queen Elizabeth in Boston's town
hall—no mean feat when you consider the rudimentary
kitchen facilities there, but it turned out to be a triumph, the
queen polished off her dessert, and Prince Philip said his
thank-yous in fluent German. To cap the year, the Schmids
bought this country inn (with kitchens that are far from rudimentary) and now they are working happily ever after.

Their mansion (square, white, and flat-roofed, more London than Lenox) was built around the turn of the century for
Harvey Procter of Procter & Gamble fame. A huge ma-
hogany-paneled hallway leads to a pair of elegant dining
rooms and a large bar named, inexplicably, The Thistle; a
flight of handsome mahogany stairs leads up to the dozen
guest rooms on the second floor. Half of them, more or less,
have private bathrooms, four have fireplaces (working, but
only when lit by a member of the household). The two most
in demand are the large corner chambers above the main
portico, but Gateways regulars will settle for any room, just to
be within reach of the dining tables. Cuisine, as you can
imagine, is everything here, even to the point where the
menu admonishes concertgoers to select from the list of
special items ready to be served rather than rush the kitchen

and try to gobble down a gourmet meal before dashing off to Tanglewood. During the festival, the tireless Schmids also serve supper (including such uncommon but musical-sounding dishes as Viennese Pariserschnitzel), or you can have postconcert pastries and coffee (seven types of cappuccino alone), served in the bar.

Devote at least one full evening to a leisurely meal, even if that means arriving a day early or leaving a day late. The menu features rack of lamb and beef Wellington for two-somes, pheasant in season, and some house specialties like veal Wisconsin (with mushroom duxelles and Wisconsin cheese, rolled in egg and sautéed) and sole Washington (with lobster and lobster sauce)—presumably in honor of that memorable Bicentennial year.

NAME: The Gateways Inn and Restaurant
OWNERS/INNKEEPERS: Gerhard and Lilliane Schmid
ADDRESS: 71 Walker Street, Lenox, Mass. 01240
DIRECTIONS: On Routes 7A and 183, in the center of town.
TELEPHONE: (413) 637-2532
ROOMS: 11 doubles, 4 with fireplaces
RATES 1978: EP, $24 without private bath, $28 with private bath, May 1 to July 1 and Labor Day to October 31; $38 and $28 and $34 July 1 to Labor Day; *in both cases, higher on weekends;* lower rates in winter; plus 5.7% tax.
MEALS AND ENTERTAINMENT: Breakfast 8–10:30, no lunch, champagne brunch on Sundays 11–3, dinner 5:30–9 most of the year, 5:30–10 in summer, served indoors or on the terrace (approx. $25 to $30 for two); late supper during Tanglewood Festival, or coffee and pastry in the bar; no room service; informal dress.
DIVERSIONS: Eating.
P.S. May be closed for a week or two in spring or fall—call ahead for reservations.

The Red Lion Inn
Stockbridge, Mass.

Stockbridge has one of the prettiest main streets in America, ending at one of the country's most famous inns. The original Red Lion was built in 1773 to serve the stagecoaches between Boston and Albany, and rebuilt more or less in its present form in 1897, with its classic long veranda dotted with a dozen wicker rocking chairs. Through the years it has hosted "everyone from Hawthorne and Longfellow and Roosevelts to Aaron Copland, Bob Dylan, and Gene Shalit."

When it was bought ten years ago by Jack and Jane Fitzpatrick, a Stockbridge couple who run Country Curtains (a mail order company that ships all over the world), the inn was renovated from top to bottom, spruced up with period wallpapers specially produced by an old mill in northern Massachusetts, and, of course, with curtains. Curtains in all their variety—muslin, gingham, organdy, with ruffles, tiebacks, and knotted fringes. No two rooms are identical, but they all have air conditioning and room phones, two-thirds of them have private baths, and one-third of them (the thirty-odd rooms that stay open in winter) have television. Rooms #212 and #112 are big, bright corner chambers—one with rose-patterned wallpaper and matching upholstery, wicker headboards, marble-topped coffee table; the other with pink paper, floral carpets, twin beds, rockers, and wing chairs. More recently the big house round the corner was bought up by the inn and converted into four fairly luxurious suites; a new manager has taken over the reins; and fifteen thousand flowering plants have been installed in the courtyard. If you can't get here when they're in bloom, come in winter to admire the Christmas-card setting (like something from an old *Saturday Evening Post* cover, which it was, since Norman Rockwell has lived around the corner for years and painted this venerable centenarian many times). Go walking in the frost or snow, wrap your arms around each other to keep warm, then hurry back to the Red Lion for a drink in the wood-paneled warmth of Widow Bingham's Tavern.

NAME: The Red Lion Inn
INNKEEPER: William C. Manger
ADDRESS: Stockbridge, Mass. 01262
DIRECTIONS: Five miles southwest of exit 2 on the Mass. Pike, at the junction of U.S. 7 and Mass. 102.
TELEPHONE: (413) 298-5545
ROOMS: 96 rooms, 4 suites, some rooms sharing bath
RATES 1978: EP all year, May, June, September, October from $20 to $32, suites $38 to $48; July and August from $26 to $48, suites from $56 to $84; lower rates in winter; plus 5% tax on total bill.
MEALS AND ENTERTAINMENT: Breakfast 7:30–10:30, lunch 12–2:30, dinner 6–9:30 (approx. $15 to $20 for two), sandwiches to 1 a.m.; informal dress in courtyard and tavern, jacket and tie in main dining room; live music in Lion's Den Bar downstairs.
DIVERSIONS: Small heated outdoor pool; tennis, golf, bicycles, hiking, horseback riding, white water and lake canoeing, winter sports nearby.
P.S. Crowded on weekends in summer (especially Tanglewood weekends) and during the fall foliage season (when reservations are essential for the inn *and* dining room).

The Flying Cloud Inn
New Marlboro, Mass.

Most of the old inns in New England are smack dab on the village green or main street, but here's a Colonial-style retreat far out in the country, at the end of back roads leading to byways, surrounded by a couple of hundred acres of birch, beech, tamarack, and a dozen kinds of apple trees. You wake with the lark, go to bed with the chickadees, and the big bad world never intrudes on your peace. No phones, no TV, no crowds. You spend your days simply: swimming in a spring-fed unpolluted pond; wandering through maple and hemlock trees in search of beavers and otters and muskrats; picnicking at "Uncle's Cabin" atop the hayfield, looking across the hills into Connecticut. There are tennis courts (one clay, one all-weather) a few dozen paces from the back door, table tennis in the barn and badminton on the lawn, rowboat and kayak on the pond. If you ever wanted to sample cross-country skiing, this is the place to learn because you can borrow, not rent, the equipment; and if you're an accomplished skier you can go exploring six miles of trails on the property, miles more through the state forest next door. Or you can simply sit in front of the big fire and roast chestnuts. At the Flying Cloud, you're part of a world detached in time and place, but if you want to sample civilization, culture awaits only a few miles away along quiet country roads at Tanglewood, Jacob's Pillow, and Red Fox Music Barn. Only Mozart or Bach could lure you away from a spot like this.

The Flying Cloud was originally a farmhouse, built in 1771 by New England shipwrights and named for one of the great American clipper ships, a white clapboard cottage with plank floors and hand-wrought oak and chestnut beams. All ten rooms are different and each is furnished with antiques; take a stroll through the house and pick out your bed—with muslin canopy, with pencil posts, with pineapple or acorn knobs. All are charming places to spend loving nights, and if you're reluctant to leave them in the morning, you'll find opaque window shades installed specially for late sleepers.

The Flying Cloud can be a convivial place, and guests usually gather for pre- and postdinner drinks on the screened porch or around the fire in the lounge; but the Shaker-style dining room has candlelight and tables for twosomes who want to be just twosomes. Dinners, served family style, feature good, wholesome fare, with broccoli, squash, lettuce, or beans fresh from the garden, soups made from stock, bar-becued lamb or roast beef, occasional continental dishes like veal parmigiana or beef bourguignonne, followed by musk-melons or strawberries from the inn garden. But what may surprise you in such a small inn is the quality of the wine list, which David Schwarz has selected with the kind of care you expect in a much larger establishment—Chassagne Mon-trachet Bourée 1970, Château Pichon Lalande 1967, Meur-sault Cuvé Maurice Chevalier 1973. Top that with a vintage port (Taylor Fladgate 1960) or cognac Briand VSOP, on the porch, surrounded by birch and beech and tamarack.

NAME: The Flying Cloud Inn

INNKEEPERS: David R. Schwarz (owner), Martin and Beverly Langeveld

ADDRESS: Star Route 70, Box 143, New Marlboro, Mass. 01230

DIRECTIONS: By car from New York, take Interstates 684 and 84 to Conn. 8 North, then go west on U.S. 44 to Conn. 183 (just outside Winsted), where you make a right turn and go north another 14½ miles to the inn. From Bos-ton, take the Mass. Pike to exit 2 (Lee), then go south on Mass. 102 and U.S. 7 to Mass. 23 and Mass. 57, where you fork right (about ¼ mile beyond the New Marlboro village green) and follow a tiny sign to The Flying Cloud. By private or charter plane to Great Barrington.

TELEPHONE: (413) 229-2113

ROOMS: 14

RATES 1978: MAP only, $64 to $90 all year (including, in ad-dition to breakfast and dinner, all gratuities and the use of all facilities—among them tennis in summer, cross-country skiing in winter); plus 5% tax on room, 6% tax on food.

MEALS AND ENTERTAINMENT: Breakfast 8:30–10, lunch 1 (but only if requested at breakfast time), dinner 7 (one sitting, served family style) or, in summer during the fes-tival season, at 6:30 weekdays, 6 Friday and Saturday; no room service; informal dress; "entertainment consists of good conversation on the porch in summer, by the fire in winter."

DIVERSIONS: Spring-fed pool for swimming, bicycles, walking trails, fishing, croquet, parlor games, tennis (2 courts, no charge, pro in summer, ball machines, clinics), cross-country skiing (6 miles of trails, equipment for *loan*, not rent), sledding, ice skating, rowboat and kayak on pond; golf, horseback riding, downhill skiing nearby (and positively *no* snowmobiles).

P.S. Open all year except April and November; busiest in July, August, and October; some small business groups, but the innkeepers welcome groups of *friends*—who can arrange to have special wine-tasting parties or take over the entire inn for a few days. Think about it.

The Publick House
Sturbridge, Mass.

Lafayette once warmed his *derrière* before the huge open fireplace in the taproom. The taproom is now the dining room and you can feast yourself before the same fire—on onion popovers, baked lobster pie or prime ribs, cranberry bread or pumpkin muffins.

The Publick House was first established as a coaching tavern in 1771, by Colonel Ebenezer Crafts, a legendary innkeeper who could lift a barrel of cider and drink from the bunghole. He also equipped and drilled a company of cavalry on the common opposite the inn, and marched them off to help Lafayette in some of his skirmishes. The tavern did a hefty business because of its location at one of the busiest crossroads in the Colonies. "The old fordway at Tantiusque" was the route taken by the Indians when they carried corn to the Pilgrims in Plymouth; in turn, the first white settlers

traipsed over the same route on their first ventures westward. Later, the Old Colonial Post Road ran through Sturbridge. Ben Franklin traveled along it when he was deputy postmaster of the thirteen Colonies and made a field trip to most of his post offices.

This is the era you still breathe when you step beneath the lantern and through the door of the Publick House.

APPLES BY THE BEDSIDE. If Lafayette had stayed the night he would have slept in a room that hasn't changed much to this day. He might not recognize the wallpaper on the landing but it's so jolly and patriotic it would probably have sent him off to bed with his heart as warm as his *derrière*. The period furniture and lurching floors have been joined by discreet concessions to the twentieth century—like tiled bathrooms, cuddly towels, telephones, air conditioning, and a sprinkler system. The twenty-one rooms in the old inn, plus another six rooms, not quite so "period," in a newer wing, all welcome you with a bowl of apples on the bedside table. But don't spoil your appetite. Your innkeeper has some tasty dishes waiting downstairs.

The Taproom, with its big fire and curtained windows, is a pleasant enough spot, but lovers will probably prefer the inn's Barn Restaurant, where the hand-hewn beams and timber stalls make quiet nooks for diners who want to look into each other's eyes while dipping into their lobster pies.

You can round out your dinner with a cognac in the cocktail lounge downstairs, another cozy low-ceilinged spot. But be warned—the combo may be playing, amplified, and you can bet your bottom dollar they're not playing "Let tyrants shake their iron rod."

SUGARING-OFF PARTIES. If you're here on a Yankee Winter Weekend (January through March) the inn will also entertain you with hot buttered rum, roast chestnuts, roast venison, and mincemeat pie, square dancing, sleigh rides through Old Sturbridge Village, and sugaring-off parties; then wake you next morning with the aromas of an open-hearth breakfast—hickory-smoked bacon, porridge with maple syrup, and hot apple pan dowdy.

In spring, the county's orchards are fluffy with apple blossom; in the fall, you can visit the orchards, pick your own McIntoshes, and then wander off, hand-in-hand, away from the village and the highways, and find yourselves a leafy glade for an afternoon of munching, drowsing, and day-dreaming.

Or you can visit Old Sturbridge Village. It's a corny, touristy sort of thing to do, but do it anyway if there aren't too many people around. Old Sturbridge Village is a 200-acre re-creation of a New England country town of the late eighteenth and early nineteenth centuries—forty fully furnished homes, shops, a meetinghouse, and costumed hosts and hostesses to show you around and demonstrate how your ancestors used to spin, weave, make pottery and brooms, and grow herbs. Hop on the horse-drawn carry-all wagon for a jaunt around the village, and buy your sweetheart old-fashioned penny candies at the General Store.

NAME: The Publick House
INNKEEPER: Buddy Adler
ADDRESS: On the Common, Sturbridge, Mass. 01566

DIRECTIONS: Take exit 3 from Interstate 86, exit 9 from the Mass. Pike, and follow the signs.

TELEPHONE: (617) 347-3313

ROOMS: 27, with 3 suites

RATES 1978: EP, from $28 to $32 all year; plus 5/7% tax on room, 6% on food and beverages.

MEALS AND ENTERTAINMENT: Breakfast 7:30–11, lunch 12–4, dinner 4–8:30 Sunday through Thursday, 5–9 Friday and Saturday (approx. $14 to $18 for two), supper till 11:30; room service 8 a.m. to 8:30 p.m.; informal dress; live music and dancing in the cocktail lounge (downstairs).

DIVERSIONS: None at the inn, but plenty of sightseeing, tennis, golf, horseback riding, skiing, and sleigh rides nearby.

Longfellow's Wayside Inn
South Sudbury, Mass.

"As Ancient is this Hostelry/As any in the Land may be . . ." So rhymed, precariously, Henry Wadsworth Longfellow.

He wrote and set his *Tales of a Wayside Inn* in this very hostelry. Alas, this makes it superhistoric, and a place that many Americans feel they ought to see, even if they've never managed to get beyond "Listen, my children, and you shall hear/Of the midnight ride of Paul Revere." They come out from Boston by the coachload. This puts you, the guests, almost in the category of exhibits in a museum, not much fun for most lovers unless they're the kind that fancies an audience.

Still, the Wayside Inn is such a delightful old place it's worth bucking the busloads; in any case, during the off-season (October through June) there's only a scattering of day trippers. Then you have the place practically to yourself because there are only ten guest rooms to begin with (it must have been a tight squeeze when King Ibn Saud and his retinue dropped in). They're not the most elegant in Massachusetts, but they're charmingly furnished with period pieces, and they all have phones, air conditioning, and private baths. Most of them were tacked on a long time after Longfellow rhymed, but two of them are authentically ancient: room #9, with its plank floors, pine walls, low beamed ceiling, sconces, sideboards, and armchairs; and room#10, which is smaller, with tiny windows, red curtains, and antique tables (but no phone).

PATRIOTS, POETASTERS, AND TEAMSTERS. This inn is so old it goes back to the days *before* stagecoaches. The original two rooms were built in 1686—the date that led Longfellow to rhyme his lines claiming it as the oldest inn in the country. In those days guests came galloping up on horseback or lumbering up by oxcart; they warmed themselves in the taproom and then retired upstairs to a sort of dormitory, now known as the Drovers' Room, where there were five beds for the teamsters. The inn was built by a David Howe and called the Howe Tavern, but by the time of the Revolution it had become the Red Horse. It was still owned by a Howe, Colonel Ezekiel, who gathered a group of Sudbury farmers in his taproom before marching them off to the field at Concord. When the fracas got properly under way, the colonel dined here with George Washington, who was on his way to Boston to take command of the army. The inn got its present name, of course, from Longfellow, who actually spent only two weekends here.

The inn stayed in the Howe family until the turn of the century, when it started to decay. Henry Ford bought it in 1920 and fixed it up (some say *over*fixed). He stayed there many times, and often invited his friends over for a few days—Edison, Firestone, the Prince of Wales. In 1953, the inn caught fire, but fortunately on a freezing morning; when the firemen poured on water it turned to ice and froze the fire. Otherwise, the entire inn might have been destroyed. It was restored in 1958 with a grant from the Ford Foundation, and the inn is now run by its own foundation dedicated to preserving it as an historical and literary shrine. It's non-profit; any money you spend there goes to keeping the place in tiptop condition.

You can tell the money isn't wasted the minute you set eyes on its neat, russet-colored clapboard exterior, rather like the shape of a haystack, and the trim lawn guarded by two tall oaks. It's set back a hundred yards from the main road on a twisting country lane, or as Longfellow put it, "A region of repose it seems/A place of slumber and of dreams/Remote among wooded hills."

On your right when you go through the door is the Old Bar Room—an austere, timbered room with the original settle, pewter sconces, hutch tables, and chairs. Across the hall is the Longfellow Parlor, one of the rooms where Long-fellow supposedly wrote and recited some of his tales. It's still furnished with authentic period items, including "the first spinet in Sudbury," and other items mentioned in the poem. The Longfellow Bedroom upstairs is preserved as an example of the sort of room people used to stay in back in the eigh-teenth century, with pencil post bed, Spanish-foot chairs, and a 1710 highboy.

Most of the trippers who visit the inn stop off for lunch or dinner in the big Colonial-style dining room at the rear, but the Red Horse Room is cozier, a publike sort of place with hovering beams, slat-backed chairs, and wooden tables. The menu is basically New England, but with something for everyone—Yankee beef broth with barley, roast Mas-sachusetts duckling, baked fresh scrod, ribs of beef, filet mig-non. You've read of many inns that bake their own bread, but the Wayside Inn goes one better—its rolls and muffins are made from flour and meal stone-ground at the inn's own grist mill, down the road.

NAME: Longfellow's Wayside Inn
INNKEEPER: Francis J. Koppeis
ADDRESS: Sudbury, Mass. 01776

DIRECTIONS: On U.S. 20, the old stagecoach route, midway between Boston and Worcester, and an easy drive to places like Concord, Lexington, and Sturbridge.

TELEPHONE: (617) 443-8846

ROOMS: 10

RATES: EP $23.78 (including tax) all year; 6% tax on food and drinks.

MEALS AND ENTERTAINMENT: Breakfast 7–9:30, lunch 11:30–3, dinner 5:30–9 weekdays, 12–8 Sundays (approx. $20 to $25 for two, reservations essential); no room service, except breakfast if you make arrangements with the front desk the night before; jackets requested in the evening.

DIVERSIONS: No pool, no sports, just lovely countryside; the first Saturday in October is Minute Man Day, to be seen or avoided depending on your tastes.

P.S. Given the kind of monument this is, the inn's trustees and so on are concerned about the image, so please act like a properly married couple here.

Stagecoach Hill Inn
Sheffield, Mass.

For candlelight dinner in the Colonial dining room, you can choose blackbird pie or Alderman's Carpetbag, polished down with a tankard of Watney's Red Barrel; when you've sated yourself, wander through to the timbery Tap Room, settle down before the fire, and sample a rarity from the inn's Locked Scotch Cabinet or Locked Brandy Cabinet—say, a twenty-year-old Royal Reserve by Arthur Bell, or a Biscuit Debouche Extra Cognac. From the Tap Room it's only a few steps through the pine-scented garden to your room.

The Stagecoach Hill Inn is something of a curiosity—an old coaching house that was also the village poorhouse, and now billing itself as "the English Inn in the Berkshires," a red-brick building hidden by a clump of maple trees. Behind the inn is a two-story red shingle cottage, the former poorhouse, with the four best rooms in the inn; beyond that are the lawns, and two three-room chalets furnished with antiques and period pieces. The best rooms are #10 and #11 in the Poorhouse, under the eaves, with chintz curtains and pretty but uninspired decor. But chances are you won't be in a mood to analyze the decor after you've feasted in the dining room, which is what you come here for in the first place. Scottie Burns and Wilbur Wheeler have made a gallant attempt to get away from the standard steak and lobster fare; in addition to the blackbird pie and Alderman's Carpetbag (it's a sirloin with a "secret pocket" stuffed with half a dozen oysters) their menu lists steak and mushroom pie, veal a l'estragon, and chicken livers Rumaki. Prices are in the $8 range, except for the Carpetbag, which carries a $10.95 tag.

This is a place to come and gorge yourself (if you can overlook the background music) and stop over between trips to Tanglewood, Jacob's Pillow, Music Mountain, the Music Barn and all the other summer lures of the Berkshires. When there's racing at Lime Rock, sports car buffs come here and paint the inn red.

NAME: Stagecoach Hill Inn
INNKEEPERS: Scottie Burns and Wilbur Wheeler
ADDRESS: Route 41, Sheffield, Mass. 01257
DIRECTIONS: On Mass. 41, a scenic winding highway that doesn't really go anywhere and seems to be in no particular hurry to get there, 10 miles south of Great Barrington.
TELEPHONE: (413) 229-8585
ROOMS: 6 rooms, 2 suites
RATES 1978: EP (including taxes) $23.25 and $26.45 for rooms, $31.70 for suites, all year (except March).
MEALS AND ENTERTAINMENT: Dinner only, 6–10 weekdays, 5–9 in winter, 2–9 Sundays (approx. $20 to $25 for two); no room service; informal dress; live music weekends.
DIVERSIONS: Walking, skiing, cross-country skiing, golf, tennis, horseback riding nearby.

Swiss Hutte Inn
Hillsdale, N.Y.

Behind the lodge, a steep hill struggles up to the highway; facing the lodge, across the meadow, is Catamount. The view is everything: you see it from the balcony of your room, when you're dining on the patio or outdoor terrace, when you're relaxing in the two wooden armchairs on the jetty by the pond. Even the Rode Gluckel Bar has its windows angled to take in the mountain view.

The Swiss Hutte lodge was a farm before the Breens converted it into a lodge and tacked on a motel wing. There's nothing grand about the Hutte; it's rustic in a yodelly sort of way, a pleasant, friendly place in a sheltered setting. You can swim in the spring-fed pond by the edge of the meadow, or in the heated pool (by the side of the lodge but actually in Massachusetts); walking trails wind up into the forest and lead you miles away from everyone. In winter you can skate on the pond, ski cross-country along the trails you hiked in winter, or ski the slopes of Catamount.

The rooms are so-so (all with TV, private bath/shower, individually controlled heating or air conditioning, balcony but no phone), but the lodge itself has a piney, flowery atmosphere that puts you in the mood for a hearty meal—the inn's specialty: scampi Dijonnaise, roulade de porc Cordon Bleu, that sort of thing, with a few items such as schnitzels, sauerbraten, and steaks in the $8 to $12 bracket. Any of the Swiss Hutte's dishes tastes more scrumptious on the terrace surrounded by pine, crabapple, and honey locust trees, with the stars over Catamount and the brook trickling by beyond the pond.

NAME: Swiss Hutte Inn
INNKEEPER: Thomas M. Breen
ADDRESS: Route 23, Hillsdale, N.Y. 12529

DIRECTIONS: On N.Y. 23, 3 miles east of Hillsdale, 7 miles east of the Taconic Parkway, and 30 minutes from Tanglewood and Jacob's Pillow festivals.

TELEPHONE: (518) 325-3333

ROOMS: 20, 1 suite

RATES 1978: MAP $70 from May 28 through October 16, EP $35 from October 16 through November 1 (closed during November); plus 15% service charge on MAP, and 6% tax on total bill.

MEALS AND ENTERTAINMENT: Breakfast 8–11, lunch 12:30–2:30, dinner 5:30–9:30 (approx. $18 to $22 for two); no room service; informal dress; background music during dinner.

DIVERSIONS: Heated pool, 2 freshwater ponds, tennis (2 courts, $6 per hour per court), putting green with sand traps; hiking, horseback riding nearby; skiing, cross-country skiing (with rentals), ice skating, across the meadow on Catamount.

Oliver House
Ancram, N.Y.

Lovers' hotels have a way of popping up in the most unexpected places. If you draw a line on your map seven miles due west from the border between Massachusetts and Connecticut, you'll find the as-yet-unsung hamlet of Ancram, New York. Or, if you wander off the Taconic Parkway some lovely weekend, you suddenly may find yourself in a little country crossroads town where two energetic young men have restored and are running a diminutive eighteenth-century opera house, a fanciful Victorian emporium, and a snug turn-of-the-century inn called Oliver House.

Stop for high tea and stay the night. There may be a Viennese operetta or Gay Nineties musicale to delight your evening hours (or a showing of Jeanette MacDonald and Nelson Eddy in *Rose Marie,* or something fun with Fred and Ginger). And even if you don't need to augment your Tiffany tea service or stock up on silk flowers, it's always fun to browse in Simon's General Store. Ancram is a living restoration of the Victorian era; just park the car and forget the last ninety years. Mind you, there are only five rooms in old Doc Oliver's place, and everyone shares the "Necessary Room" with its gloriously big old tub, but if U.N. diplomats don't mind, why should you? You'll have an antique chest to tuck your undies into, a family Bible to read, and (in all but one of the rooms) a double bed with carved headboard to snuggle in. Oliver House was a home and a home it still is, where lovely meals are served to polite and interesting people.

L.E.B.

NAME: Oliver House

OWNERS/INNKEEPERS: John-Peter Hayden and Donald Richard Chapin

ADDRESS: Ancram, N.Y. 12502

DIRECTIONS: From the Taconic Parkway, take the Jackson Corners exit, follow county road 7 and signs for Ancram: from Route 22, go west to Copake, county route 7A/7 and Ancram signs.

TELEPHONE: (518) 329-1166

ROOMS: 5

RATES 1978: EP (with continental breakfast) $20 all year; plus 6% tax, *no* tipping permitted.

MEALS AND ENTERTAINMENT: Continental breakfast only, lunch 12–4, high tea 4–5:30, dinner 6:30–8 (approx. $25 to $30 for two, again no tipping); no liquor license, bring your own wine and/or booze; no room service; informal dress; occasionally a piano in the dining room.

DIVERSIONS: Walking, exploring, antiquing, and other nice country pastimes.

P.S. One of the nicest times to visit Ancram is during the Christmas season, when Messrs. Hayden and Chapin deck the entire town in twinkling lights and flood the side yard of Oliver House for ice skating. Their annual Victorian Christmas is Currier and Ives incarnate.

Harrison Inn and Conference Center
Southbury, Conn.

Put this down as a possibility for a windy, wintry weekend. You can curl up in snug rooms that look like pages from a California homes-and-gardens magazine: cedar walls, rattan chairs, handwoven wall hangings and blowups of photographs, custom-designed wood-block closets, a bath-and-a-half, and stereo and TV. Without ever venturing beyond the inn's cedar-sided walls you can soak in a sauna, work out in an exercise room, play pool, listen to Dixieland, watch old movies, shop in one of the most unusual bazaars this side of Ghirardelli Square, and dine in a pubby restaurant.

If you come on a mellow day you can swim in the heated pool, or sit in the gazebo and look at the gardens and listen to the stream. There are a pair of all-weather tennis courts, a golf course on the other side of the stream, and bikes and horses to take you through the countryside.

All this sounds like a pleasant country inn, and that's how Harrison Inn promotes itself, but it's really nothing like a traditional New England country inn. It's located in a residential community, and it's part of the Harrison Conference Center, geared to seminars and groups of executives from all those corporations proliferating around Hartford and in Westchester. That doesn't sound too romantic, but the truth is that the elderly inhabitants seem to keep to themselves and the executives all go home on weekends, when the inn is taken over by a youngish, moderately swinging clientele. And it is an interesting inn, warm, snug, and comfortable in winter.

NAME: Harrison Inn and Conference Center
INNKEEPER: Robert J. Anderson
ADDRESS: Heritage Village, Southbury, Conn. 06488
DIRECTIONS: Take Interstate 84 to exit 15, then drive to Conn. 67 and follow the Harrison signs.
TELEPHONE: (203) 264-8255
ROOMS: 121 rooms, 9 suites
RATES: EP $47 to $57 for rooms, $80 to $114 for suites in spring (rates not available for remainder of year); plus 7% tax on total bill.
MEALS AND ENTERTAINMENT: Breakfast 7–9 (continental only 9–10), lunch 12–2, Sunday brunch 11–2:30, dinner 6–9 (approx. $12 to $25 for two); no room service; jacket and tie Friday and Saturday; live music and dancing.
DIVERSIONS: Outdoor pool sauna, therapy pool, exercise room, hiking trails, game room, tennis (2 courts, lights until midnight) all free of charge; golf (9 holes, $8 per round), bikes for rent; horseback riding nearby.

FROM THE SHAWANGUNKS TO THE ALLEGHENIES

How silver-sweet sound lovers' tongues by night,
Like softest music to attending ears! . . .
SHAKESPEARE

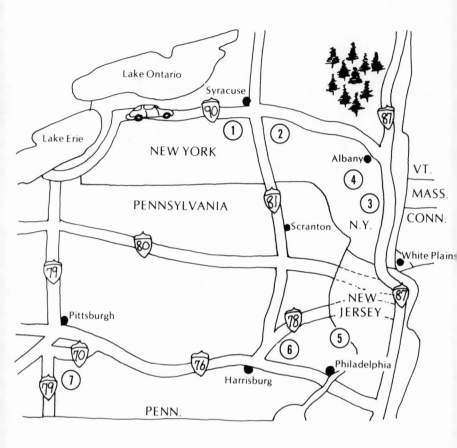

1. Sherwood Inn
2. Alexander Hamilton Inn
3. Mohonk Mountain House
4. Auberge des Quatre Saisons
5. 1740 House
6. Tulpehocken Manor Plantation and Inn
7. Century Inn

Sherwood Inn
Skaneateles, N.Y.

¢

The Sherwood Inn is a find. First for Joy and Bill Eberhardt, who bought it four years ago and now are busily—and faithfully—restoring the 170-year-old rooms. Next for a travel writer in search of hotels that *haven't* answered the clarion call of the Howard Johnsons. Finally, for the two of you in search of a room with a view in a pleasant little town in the Finger Lakes.

Skaneateles is the kind of town you can relax in and enjoy. No sights that *must* be seen or dressy events to attend, but great old houses to walk or ride a bike past, tidy shops to poke around in, and fun things to do, like dinner on the mailboat while it makes its rounds, or a polo match on Sunday afternoon, or a sailing regatta on the lake. Which neatly brings us to the subject of how nicely the Sherwood Inn is situated. Skaneateles caps the north end of long-and-skinny Skaneateles Lake. Now, guess what hotel sits right at the tip of the lake with the best view in town. And if it's that view you're after, ask for "B" (as in Bridal Suite); it's big and bright and papered in blue flowers that confirm the Eberhardts' good taste and their intention to blot out a World War II era "refurbishing" by reinstating furnishings in keeping with the hotel's beginnings, in 1807, as a stagecoach stop.

But before taking "B", have a look at the suite at the end of the hall. The Garden Suite (Room #18) is nice, isn't it? All those windows and the array of hanging plants shading you from view. You could lie in bed tonight, bathed in the freshness of this greenery, with the lake sparkling outside your

window and moonlit shadows flickering across the garden
room floor, listening to the chirping of the crickets.

L. E. B.

NAME: Sherwood Inn

OWNERS/INNKEEPERS: Joy and Bill Eberhardt

ADDRESS: 2700 West Genesee Street, Skaneateles, N.Y.
13152

DIRECTIONS: Skaneateles is on U.S. 20 (the old stagecoach
road), 17 miles southwest of Syracuse (or exit 40 on the
New York Thruway), and the inn is just west of the
town square.

TELEPHONE: (315) 685-3405

ROOMS: 12 (with expansion "in the old style" planned for
1978)

RATES 1978: EP, from $15 to $25 with continental breakfast
included, all year; plus 7% tax on total bill.

MEALS AND ENTERTAINMENT: Breakfast anytime, lunch
11–2:30 (to 4 in the lounge), Sunday brunch 11–2 in
summer, dinner 5–10 weekdays, 2–8 Sunday, 5–11 Friday and Saturday (approx. $9 to $15 for two); no room
service; informal dress; piano in the bar Friday and
Saturday, classical piano nightly in the dining room.

DIVERSIONS: None at the inn, but the village has lighted public tennis courts which are flooded for ice skating in winter; golf, tennis, hiking, and winter sports nearby.

Alexander Hamilton Inn
Clinton, N.Y.

¢

Clinton is a college town; in fact, it's a two-college town. One
is Kirkland for Women, named for a man who sought government money to provide higher education for the Indians; the
other is all-male Hamilton College, named for the U.S. Trea-

sury Secretary who granted the necessary funds. Nice as it would be to think that Alexander Hamilton once had sheltered in the house, it's doubtful he ever visited Clinton; the naming of the Inn simply perpetuates local gratitude.

The place has a lively history nevertheless. It was built in 1820 by a Yale lawyer named Othneil Williams, well known in the area for his skillful defense of one G.W. (as in George Washington) Loomis, horse-thief and plunderer, never indicted. But Othneil died before the house was completed, whereupon Othneil, Jr. and his vivacious wife Delia finished the project, fancifully installing silver faucets when indoor plumbing became the thing to do. Delia made sure the house was the social hub of Clinton and achieved her zenith of one-upmanship when they hosted President Grover Cleveland for the town's Centennial.

Although principally a restaurant now, the Alexander Hamilton has five homey guest rooms on the second floor, all with private bath and each individually decorated and lovingly wallpapered in Williamsburg florals. The spacious Washington Room on the front of the house has an appealing view of the wide front lawn and the village green. All done in blue and lilac, it has an inviting chaise longue, high four-poster beds, and a black marble fireplace; its only disadvantage is the bathroom, which—although private—requires a quick dash past the house's main staircase. Fortunately this is the only room requiring such "adjustment" and its spaciousness makes up for the inconvenience.

The cozy brown-and-gold Hamilton Room across the hall has the only double bed in the house; the brown-and-blue (and rather masculine) Franklin Room at the back, the only refrigerator; the blue-and-white Clinton Room, the only other fireplace. But probably the most totally pleasing room in the house, all things considered, is the cheerful blue-and-beige Madison Room, a biggish room made bigger and brighter by a floor-to-ceiling bay of windows, with a biggish bath made bigger and brighter with a floor-to-ceiling mirror. Too bad the double bed was wasted on the Hamilton Room.

L.E.B.

NAME: Alexander Hamilton Inn
INNKEEPER: Gino Russo
ADDRESS: Clinton, N.Y. 13323
DIRECTIONS: Take the New York Thruway to exit 32; from there Clinton is 6 miles south via routes 233 and 412 East, and the inn is tucked into the northwest corner of the village green.
TELEPHONE: (315) 853-5555
ROOMS: 5
RATES 1978: EP $25 all year; plus 4% tax.
MEALS AND ENTERTAINMENT: Breakfast 8–10:30, lunch 12–2:30, Sunday brunch during the academic year, dinner 5:30–8 weekdays, 1–8 Sunday, 5–10 Friday and Saturday (approx. $12 to $15 for two), restaurant closed on Monday; room service by request; informal dress; soft recorded music.
DIVERSIONS: Tennis, golf, antique-hunting nearby.

Mohonk Mountain House
Mohonk Lake, N.Y.

It's eye-boggling. A rambling, gabled, turreted, eighth-of-a-mile-long Victorian château, 1250 feet up in the mountains, with a lake at its doorstep and miles of wilderness all around. From a distance it looks like medieval Nuremberg, from close up like a Disney fantasy elongated for Cinemascope. Inside it's even more stunning: walls and balustrades of intricately carved birch, square columns with carved capitals, leaded and textured glass, pierced-wood screens, "Sultan's Corners" with plush banquettes, bentwood settees, velvet-covered love seats, a pair of five-foot Japanese cloisonné vases flanking a parlor organ and a Steinway concert grand.

"FOREVER WILD." The whole massive anachronism is the
cherished preserve of a family called Smiley. The first Smi-
leys started it all back in 1869, when they built a summer
house for their friends; hence the word "house" rather than
"hotel," because the fourth generation of Smileys still like to
think of it as a private country house (some country house,
with 305 rooms and 150 fireplaces), and love to show guests
around the gardens or entertain them with a recital on the
Steinway. They're Quakers, and you have to put up with a
few eccentricities: no smoking in the dining room or main
parlor; no drinking in public places except during dinner
(you can tipple in your room if you like, and the hotel will
supply you with set-ups); you may not play the piano in the
lounge between two and five in the afternoons; you won't
find TV or room phones in the uncompromisingly Victorian,
somewhat stodgy rooms; but you can forgive these trivia
when you see what else the family has done for you. A few
years ago they turned over 60 percent of their land (a tidy
$10 to $15 million worth of real estate) to the Mohonk Trust
to ensure that the mountain wilderness will be "forever wild."

Forever wild, and forever enjoyed, because the Smileys have set things up so that you can fill your days with un-polluted pleasures. Sun yourself on the sandy beaches (that's right, sand even at 1250 feet). Paddle a canoe across the lake. Put a dime in a dispenser for a handful of fish food to feed the trout. Ride horses along forty-five miles of woodland trail lined by spruce, birch, and beech. Wander hand-in-hand through the gardens of red salvia, snapdragons, asters, and zinnias; sniff the mignonette, heliotrope, and shrub roses. All over the gardens and up the side of the mountain, the Smi-leys have built tiny gazebos (about 150 of them) of weathered hemlock with thatched roofs where you can rest, kiss, and admire the view across the Shawangunk Mountains and Rondout Valley to six states. You can go sightseeing by horse-drawn carriage, play golf or tennis, or sit on a veranda and rock the hours away to dinnertime; in winter you can go cross-country skiing, snowshoeing, sleigh riding, or skating.

Outdoors, there's something for almost everyone, but the hotel itself may not be everyone's cup of afternoon tea. The rooms, for example, are not as large, stylish, or comfortable as the rates might lead you to expect (be sure to pack slip-pers, because some well-trodden carpeting has still to be re-placed); but for those who enjoy something unique, a keep-sake of bygone gracious days, Mohonk offers magnificent surroundings and crystal-clear air—and hour after hour, mile after mile of Quaker quiet.

NAME: Mohonk Mountain House
OWNERS/INNKEEPERS: Vice president, Ben H. Matteson; resi-dent manager, Frank A. Hamilton; owners, Smiley fam-ily.
ADDRESS: New Paltz, N.Y. 12561
DIRECTIONS: The hotel is 6 miles west of New Paltz, about 90 from New York City; by car, take the N.Y. Thruway to exit 18, then follow New Paltz's Main Street until you come to the bridge over the Wallkill River, then turn right and follow the signs for Mohonk; by rail to Pough-keepsie, where you can arrange to have a Mohonk car

meet you; by air, to Stanton Airport, 10 minutes from the hotel.

TELEPHONE: (914) 255-1000; NYC tie line, (212) 233-2244

ROOMS: 305, with 21 tower rooms and 8 cottages (which can accommodate 2–6 people, available from mid-May to mid-October); almost half the rooms have fireplaces; a few have running water but no bathrooms.

RATES 1978: AP $76 to $118 from mid-May through mid-October, slightly less (say, 12½%) in winter; plus 7% tax on total bill. (*Note:* the top price includes a fireplace, a luxury which is in fact costing you about $20 a night, including one large bundle of wood.)

MEALS AND ENTERTAINMENT: Breakfast 8–9:30, lunch 12:30–2, dinner 6:30–8; room service during meal hours; jacket and tie in dining room; dancing, Saturday nights May to October.

DIVERSIONS: Spring-fed lake half-mile long with bathing area and beach; tennis (6 courts, $4 per court per hour, pro facilities), golf ($5 per round Friday–Sunday only, *free* golf Monday–Thursday); hiking trails, horseback riding ($10 per hour), cross-country skiing (rentals), boating, winter sports, trout fishing, shuffleboard, croquet, lawn bowling, sleigh rides, carriage rides—all on premises. Also bridge, chess, Ping-Pong, TV rooms.

P.S. Busiest in summer, small groups remainder of year; if you want to go on a sleigh ride, reserve the ride when you reserve your room.

Auberge des Quatre Saisons
Shandaken, N. Y.

Lie on the lawn, with the birds singing and the brook chuckling, and let the cooking smells that wisp past your noses lull you to Burgundy. Walk into the dining room and everything confirms that you're in a small French provincial inn—the pine walls, the checkered tablecloths with white napkins, the French accents, the way the wine appears on the table before the food. Even the new chalet wing wouldn't look out of place in the Haute Savoie. Your map tells you you're in the Catskills, but a long way from the Catskills in spirit. This is France, from the aperitif on the porch to the first sip of Beaujolais, from the *soupe à l'oignon* to the deliciously gooey *profiterolles*. You come here to eat, and between meals you can frolic in the pool, sun yourselves on the lawn, play volleyball, Ping-Pong, or tennis—all within sniffing distance of the kitchen. You can take long lonely walks through sixty-five acres of woods behind the hotel, or just sit on the porch and watch the big white cat chase a chipmunk.

The auberge is a mile or so from busy Route 28 on unbusy Route 42, a dark-shingled lodge on a tiny hill surrounded by a hillside of trees. Its rooms, too, are more Burgundian than Catskill—piney walls, lino floors with skimpy rugs, and so small you have to embrace every time you turn around. Most of the rooms in the lodge don't have private baths; if you want that kind of extravagance, and room to move around without getting into a clinch, take a room in the chalet. Twice the space, but half the charm.

As if it weren't enough to have the birds, the trees, the brook, the tennis, the Frenchness, and the *profiterolles,* the Auberge keeps its most endearing quality when it presents your bill—what you'd normally pay for just a room in most inns buys you room *and* breakfast *and* dinner at the auberge.

NAME: Auberge des Quatre Saisons

OWNERS/INNKEEPERS: Annie and Dadou Labeille

ADDRESS: Route 42, Shandaken, N.Y. 12480

DIRECTIONS: About 120 miles or 2 hours and 15 minutes from New York by N.Y. Thruway to exit 19 (at Kingston), then by U.S. 28 to N.Y. 42; or by Palisades Parkway to Thruway entrance 9, then to exit 19.

TELEPHONE: (914) 688-2223

ROOMS: 37, including one suite

RATES 1978: MAP from $42 to $54 all year; plus 7% tax on total bill.

MEALS AND ENTERTAINMENT: Breakfast 8–9:30, no lunch, dinner 6:30–9:30; no room service; informal dress.

DIVERSIONS: Pool, tennis court (free), hiking trails, fishing, hunting; golf and horseback riding nearby.

1740 House
Lumberville, Pa.

Lumberville slumberville—this small village drowses alongside the Delaware River and the Pennsylvania Canal, about three miles upstream from the Stockton Bridge. This is the place where Harry and Janet Nessler decided to build their dream inn when they gave up the real estate business in New York a few years back.

The 1740 House is a warm, friendly place, right on the edge of the canal and surrounded by sycamores, pines, oaks, and boxwood, and banks of asters, roses, and rhododendron. River Road runs by on the other side, almost as silently as the canal. This is what peace is all about. "The folks who feel insecure without color TV in the room and a piano bar in the cocktail lounge should stay away," says Harry Nessler. "They'll hate it here." In fact, not only is there no TV or piano, there's no bar either. The 1740 part of the 1740 House is an old stable, but most of the inn is a modern cedar-sided structure, blissfully at one with the surrounding trees. You wake to nature, you dine with nature, you play in nature. The inn has acres of windows; each of its twenty-four rooms overlooks a panorama of river and woods and canal, and if that's not enough step out onto your own patio and take in the whole depth of the scene—the greenery, the scent of the forest, the chirping of birds, the swish of a canoe along the canal.

Breakfast is served in a small dining room filled with ivy, a lemon tree, gardenias, and begonias, overlooking the river. It's buffet style—great pitchers of orange juice, pots of coffee, a pewter pot filled with boiled eggs, heaps of freshly baked croissants, rolls, and cold cereals.

After breakfast, tiptoe down the rickety steps with English ivy growing all over them that look as though they've been there since 1740, untie one of the two canoes or the rowboat, and go for an expedition along the canal. You won't have to worry about rapids and white water here—the most ruffled the water gets is when a mosquito flits down for a drink. The inn has its own small pool, and there are golf, tennis, and fishing in the neighborhood. In winter, someone lowers the level of the water in the canal so that you can go ice skating or ice boating. The rooms, in fact the entire inn, are handsomely highlighted with antiques. (Bucks County is a region of fine old family homes and when someone dies the antiques often go up for auction; a lot of them have ended up here.) The reading table that holds the register, for example, is a copy of one found in the governor's palace in Williamsburg. Two of the rooms are in the old part of the structure—Room #2, with thick stone walls and beamed ceilings, was once this stable; and Room #23, with a cathedral ceiling and wide oak beams, was once the hayloft, both adjoining the pool. Otherwise, all the rooms are new, with wall-to-wall carpeting, individually controlled central heating and air conditioning, and sparkling bathrooms with tubs and showers. The original house, which was formerly an antique store, is now the sitting room. Here you'll find lurching floors and old ceiling boards, with comfortable antiques and a big wing chair, as well as Mariah, a Labrador retriever, and Molly, a longhaired dachshund, in front of the log fire. The Nesslers' motto is, "If you can't be a house guest in Bucks County, be ours." Be theirs.

NAME: 1740 House
INNKEEPER: Harry Nessler
ADDRESS: River Road, Lumberville, Pa. 18933

DIRECTIONS: On State Highway 32, about 10 minutes north
of New Hope and the exit from U.S. 202, or about 30
miles from Philadelphia.

TELEPHONE: (215) 297-5661

ROOMS: 24

RATES 1978: EP (including buffet breakfast) $33 weekdays,
$38 weekends and holidays; plus 6% tax.

MEALS AND ENTERTAINMENT: Buffet breakfast 8–10:30, no
lunch, dinner 6–8 (approx. $20 for two); no room ser-
vice, no liquor license, but the inn will provide ice and
setups if you want to bring your own; jackets suggested
for dinner.

DIVERSIONS: Small pool, rowboats (free), walking; tennis and
golf nearby.

Tulpehocken Manor Plantation and Inn
Myerstown, Pa.

Go easy as you drive around the big barn because the ducks
may be sitting in the middle of the road. And if no one an-
swers the doorbell, it's probably because Jim Henry is out
mending the east fence; he'll be back soon, so just pull up
one of the fourteen chairs on the veranda and enjoy the
shade of the two tall maple trees.

Tulpehocken is a working farm that also takes in a few
tourists and sightseers because it's old, unique, and historic
(it's now listed in the National Register of Historic Sites); it
was built about the same time as the Republic, by a German
settler who quarried his own limestone and cut the timber
from the family's own groves of walnut trees. The original
two-story building has had several additions, including a
mansard roof, a third story, and an ornate two-story veranda.

The other buildings on the property are unique for this part
of the world—they're built Swiss-style over a groundfloor
walk-through archway.

The farm was bought up about ten years ago by the Nissly family and Jim Henry, who've restored it and filled the
bedrooms with furnishings of the period. Filled? Stuffed.
Clogged. Like the creation of a benign Charles Addams. You
squeeze your way to bed past a jumble of Victoriana, Belgian
glass doors, handcarved walnut banisters, painted slate man-
tels, handcarved yellow pine doors, brass table lamps, Hitchcock chairs, Windsor chairs. One of the rooms has a fourposter bed and matching chest of drawers, another a bed
with a headboard over eight feet tall and weighing between
500 and 600 pounds (the man who designed that must have
been quite a performer—or a braggart). The farm has twenty-
seven rooms in all; nine of them are in the adjoining cottages
(with kitchenettes and private baths, but with nothing like
the personality of the manor rooms). The eighteen rooms in
the manor house share three bathrooms (a fact that didn't

faze some multimillionaires who stayed there a few months ago), and they all have ugly little plastic TV sets—except one.

THE ROOM. The exception is the room sightseers pay to see. The Room George Washington Slept In. I've tried to avoid that chestnut all the way through this guide, but in the case of Tulpehocken it's justified, because Washington slept here not once but three times. You should know this, because if you happen to rent the room he slept in (first floor, front, left) you'd better be prepared to rise early or be caught *in flagrante delicto* by a family of sightseers from Ponca City.

Get up, then, and take a look around the farm. Count the cattle (fifty-nine registered Angus), or take a walk along quiet paths that follow streams and a stretch of the old Union Canal. Tulpehocken is a lazy place, a place to lie on the grass, chew a blade of grass, and dream dreams, or in winter a cozy place to curl up with a good book or something. It would be the ideal hideaway if you didn't have to leave the place every time you want a coffee, Coke, or chocolate chip cookie; if only Ms. Nissly could be persuaded to leave a jug of juice or a pot of coffee on the sideboard for breakfast. If the ducks don't get out of the way and let you drive to the local diner you may not get breakfast at all.

NAME: Tulpehocken Manor Plantation and Inn
OWNERS/INNKEEPERS: Ms. Esther E. Nissly and James W. Henry
ADDRESS: R.D. 2, Myerstown, Pa. 17067
DIRECTIONS: In Pennsylvania Dutch Country, 5 miles east of Lebanon, on U.S. 422; to get there from the Pennsylvania Pike take the Lebanon/U.S. 72 exit, and from Interstate 78 take the exit for Pa. 501, which you take to U.S. 422, then go west 12 miles.
TELEPHONE: (717) 866-4926
ROOMS: 6, including cottage units with kitchens
RATES 1978: EP $20 and $30 all year.
MEALS: No meals.
DIVERSIONS: exploring the countryside; golf nearby.

Century Inn
Scenery Hill, Pa.

Route 40 used to be the National Pike, which was the main east-west route in the early days of the Union. Century Inn opened for travelers and stagecoaches a few months after Washington began his second term, and by the time his old buddy Lafayette passed this way on his Grand Tour of 1825, the massive stone walls already had a covering of ivy. Other guests in the coaching days included Andrew Jackson, the James K. Polks, General Zachary Taylor, and Chief Black Hawk, on his way to Washington as a prisoner of war. An historic little spot, it hasn't changed character much since those days. Its rooms are almost like antique shops: walls are draped with odd bits and pieces—giant corkscrews, copper utensils, prints, duck decoys; a five-by-seven-and-a-half-foot fireplace in the small dining room is festooned with pots, pans, skillets and ovens; the main lounge has not one but two brick fireplaces, an eighteenth-century cherry highboy with scroll top, and a collection of rare glass from the once-famous Albert Gallatin glass works down the pike. The inn has only six guest rooms, all with private tub-showers. No TV (there's one in the lounge).

The inn's two-and-one-half-story facade has a big, white veranda for rocking on, and there's a garden at the rear for lounging in. Otherwise, there's nothing to keep you here by day. The village of Scenery Hill belies its name in a shamelessly nondescript manner, but the countryside to the south is Pennsylvania at its pastoral best. Spend a couple of nights here; breakfast early, and then drive off to a quiet glade or stream for a picnic, and don't come back until the setting sun has cast a facelifting glow on Scenery Hill; then dine on baked stuffed pork chops or breaded shrimps or the inn's famous roast turkey in the main dining room, a bright, cheerful place with fresh flowers on the table.

NAME: Century Inn

INNKEEPERS: Nancy and Bob Scheirer

ADDRESS: Route 40, Scenery Hill, Pa. 15360

DIRECTIONS: From Interstate 70W take Bentleyville exit to Rte. 917 south, continue to Rte. 40, then go 1 mile east to the inn; from Interstate 79, take the exit to Rte. 40, then go east 9 miles to the inn.

TELEPHONE: (412) 945-6600 or 945-5180

ROOMS: 5 rooms, one suite

RATES 1978: EP $20 and $22 all year; plus 6% state tax.

MEALS AND ENTERTAINMENT: Breakfast 7–10, lunch 12–4:30, Sunday dinner 12–7, otherwise dinner 4:30–8 (approx. $12 to $15 for two); no room service; informal dress.

DIVERSIONS: The countryside.

IN AND AROUND THE CHESAPEAKE BAY

Omnia vincit Amor: et nos cedamus Amori . . .

VIRGIL

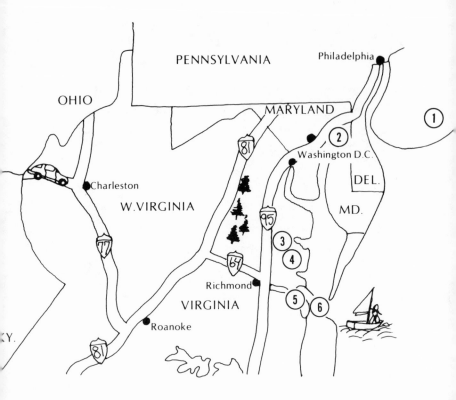

1. The Mainstay Inn
2. Robert Morris Inn
3. The Tides Inn
4. The Tides Lodge
5. Colonial Houses
6. Williamsburg Inn

The Mainstay Inn
Cape May, N.J.

"Innkeeping is a lot easier than teaching English to a bunch of high-school kids," according to ex-schoolma'am Sue Carroll; which doesn't speak very highly of school kids since innkeeping for the Carrolls has involved two solid winters of scraping and painting fifteen-foot-high ceilings, making lace curtains for twenty-four very tall windows, and tacking lace trim to sheets and pillowcases for every room of their pride and joy. But this stalwart pillared mansion has probably never looked better since it was built in the Victorian heyday of Cape May, a gambling club for southern gentlemen who quit their Mississippi plantations to spend their summers by northern shores. Now Tom and Sue Carroll have refurbished its ten rooms with Victoriana—massive beds and wardrobes to match the proportions of the main rooms, smaller pieces for the half-dozen nooks in the former maids' quarters. Except for two of the smaller rooms, which somehow manage to incorporate private facilities, guests share two bathrooms, one of them with its original copper bathtub encased in walnut paneling. There are touches of a comfortable home everywhere—patchwork quilts, braided rugs, potted plants (even in the cupola)—and staying here would be like visiting a favorite aunt if it weren't for the youthful, affable Carrolls. Despite all the work that has to go into keeping the mansion shipshape, they still seem to consider their Mainstay as a means of entertaining—friends, guests, neighbors, everyone. It's a relaxed, informal place ("we seem to use a lot of first names in introductions around here"), and a blessing if you have an urge to visit Cape May. The town is noted for its Victorian buildings (more than six hundred of them, some of them restored, some of them tottering), a couple of streets with gaslight, an Atlantic beach, and the wildness of Cape May National Seashore. But if I were going back to Cape May the attraction would be to spend a couple of relaxing days at The Mainstay: breakfast on the porch, idle chitchat with fellow guests, a ride on one of the veteran bicycles; a game or two of croquet on the unpredictable lawn, until it's time for afternoon tea in the ornately Victorian parlor, beside the big fireplace, the ten-foot gilt mirror, and the shelves of Thackeray. Then I'd climb the steps to the daintily decorated cupola to watch the sun go down on Cape May's gingerbread.

NAME: The Mainstay Inn

OWNERS/INNKEEPERS: Tom and Sue Carroll

ADDRESS: 635 Columbia Avenue, Cape May, N.J. 08204

DIRECTIONS: By car, to the south end of the Garden State Parkway or via the Lewes-Cape May ferry.

TELEPHONE: (609) 884-8690

ROOMS: 10

RATES 1978: EP (including breakfast and afternoon tea) from $25 to $32, March to December (closed remainder of year); plus 5% tax.

MEALS AND ENTERTAINMENT: Breakfast 8–9:30, afternoon tea 4; no room service.

DIVERSIONS: Croquet, monopoly, a few bikes; beach three blocks away, National Seashore a few miles away; tennis (indoor and outdoor), golf, horseback riding a few miles away.

Robert Morris Inn
Oxford, Md.

Robert Morris was a prominent English merchant who met a curiously unheroic end in the Colonies when he was fatally

wounded by the wadding from a gun firing a salute in his honor. The Robert Morris *you* might have heard of was his son—a close friend of George Washington and fund-raiser for the Continental Army.

The inn was built as a private home in the earliest days of the eighteenth century by ship's carpenters using the techniques of shipbuilding—wooden pegged paneling, fourteen-inch square beams and pilasters fastened with hand-hewn oak pegs, that sort of thing. The house was purchased for Robert Morris Senior in 1730 and first became an inn at the time of the Civil War. It sits by the edge of the Tred Avon River, just by the boarding point for a ferry that's been in operation continuously for two hundred years and hauls half-a-dozen cars at a time across the estuary. It's still very much a Colonial-style inn. Four of the rooms have the original handmade wall paneling; the fireplaces were built of brick made in England and used as ballast in sailing ships; the mural panels in the dining room were made from wallpaper samples printed 125 years ago on a screw-type press using woodcuts carved from orangewood.

The inn has thirty rooms, all with air conditioning, but otherwise they're very basic—no phones, no TV, and only five of them have private bathrooms. Your best bets are room #1, which has both a bath and a view, and #15, which has a pencil post bed so high you need a set of steps to get up to it.

There are seven more rooms (and three bathrooms) in the Lodge—a big Victorian house a few yards along the bank of the river, with spacious lawns and verandas overlooking the Tred Avon traffic.

The public rooms at the inn are plusher—the delightful Riverview Lounge with the original wood-pegged wall panels, one of the old brick fireplaces, and an antique grandfather clock. The dining room is decked out with silk drapes, chandeliers, and Hitchcock chairs; and the beamy Tap Room, where you can sip a hot toddy or buttered rum before a big brick fire, is all wooden and nautical. The menu's *pièce de résistance* is a glutton's Special Seafood Platter—chilled gulf shrimp and lump crabmeat, deep-fried crab cake, shrimp, clams, stuffed shrimp, and broiled crab imperial and filet of rockfish. Too much? Then try the crab and shrimp Norfolk, another local dish. Ask Maître d' John Miller (from Oxford, England, to Oxford, Maryland, by way of Claridge's in London and Luchow's in New York) to recommend a wine from his well-stocked cellar.

MUNGING AND JOUSTING. The Robert Morris Inn sets the atmosphere nicely for Colonial Oxford and its surroundings, and it's a perfect base for discovering the oddities of Chesapeake Bay—Baymen "munging" for terrapin; "gunkholes," or creeks, with names like Canoe Neck or Ape Hole or Antipoison; the skipjacks and bugeyes—the last working fleet of sailing vessels in the entire country; the jousting tournaments over in Talbot County. In summer there are several regattas. When you hear a starting gun go off—duck. The wadding can be dangerous, remember?

NAME: Robert Morris Inn
OWNERS/INNKEEPERS: Wendy and Ken Gibson
ADDRESS: P. O. Box 26, Oxford, Md. 21654
DIRECTIONS: From the Delaware Memorial Bridge, take Md. 13 south to Md. 301 and Md. 50 to Easton, then go west on Md. 333; from the Chesapeake Bay Bridge, follow highways 50, 301, and 50 to Easton; from the Chesa-

peake Bay Bridge Tunnel, take U.S. 13 north to Md. 50, go west to Easton, then take Md. 333 to Oxford. By boat, follow the Choptank River to the Tred Avon River and tie up at the protected anchorage at Town Creek.

TELEPHONE: (301) 226-5111

ROOMS: 30 (with 3 sets of connecting rooms); 1 cottage; 1 apartment

RATES 1978: EP, year round (open all year except Christmas), from $21 to $42; plus 5% tax on total bill.

MEALS AND ENTERTAINMENT: Breakfast (served daily, times vary), lunch 11:30–4, dinner 5–9, Sunday 1–8 (approx. $18 to $25 for two); no room service; jacket required in dining room, dress informal in taproom and tavern.

DIVERSIONS: Swimming in the river (from early spring); tennis, golf, bicycles, sailing/boating, goose and duck hunting (November–January) nearby.

The Tides Inn
Irvington, Va.

Some inns treat you to hayrides or sleigh rides, but the Tides Inn welcomes you with cruises aboard its yachts—the "whiskey run" at sunset, or a dinner cruise by moonlight, from Carter's Creek into the Rappahannock River and then out to the Chesapeake Bay, on the Stephens family's private yachts—which range from forty-six feet to the stately hundred-footer *Miss Ann*.

Everywhere you turn here, you see water. The creek surrounds the inn on three sides; lounges, terraces, dining rooms, and most of the guest rooms look out over water; lunch is served in a gazebo above the water; there's a seaside heated pool, and a tiny beach with swivel-and-tilt wicker sunchairs; the inn's second "parking lot" is a marina where waterborne guests tie up for the summer.

The Tides Inn sits on a low hill overlooking the creek, surrounded by twenty-five acres of lawns, Virginia pine, and crepe myrtle, with the Virginia scents of magnolia and azalea competing with the salty tang of the water. (They also have piped music humming from the trees, which may be therapeutic for the trees but doesn't do much to enhance the quiet atmosphere.)

The setting, in other words, is superb; and the hotel itself is not far behind. A bit stuffy maybe (you can't set foot in the lobby after six without a tie), but its other blessings more than make up for that: the ninety rooms range from elegant and simple (in the four-story lodge) to elegant and luxurious (the semisuites in Lancaster House and Windsor House); and there's plenty of pleasant activity to keep you going until it's time for the whiskey run.

BY FERRY TO THE GOLF COURSE. You can rent pedalos and sailboats, play tennis for free; and if you want to play golf, you walk down to the water, board the *Gondola,* and cross the creek to The Tides Lodge (see next listing). Evenings you can dance in the Chesapeake Club (a bottle club open to guests, because the inn doesn't have, and doesn't want, a liquor license). Most of the staff, like Curtis Sampson, has been with the inn since it opened twenty-five years ago, and they all perform with the friendly, dignified service you expect in Virginia. Even in the Northern Neck of Virginia. Irvington is on that patch between the Rappahannock and the Potomac, a relatively uncrowded but historic corner of the state: Route 3, which takes you to the inn, is known in these parts as Historyland Highway because George Washington, Robert E. Lee, and President Monroe were born nearby, just in case you get bored swiveling and tilting on the beach.

NAME: The Tides Inn
INNKEEPER: Robert L. Stephens
ADDRESS: Irvington, Va. 22480

DIRECTIONS: By car from the north, take U.S. 301 south from Baltimore to Va. 3 (a few miles after you cross the Potomac) and follow it east for about an hour to Irvington; from Richmond, take Interstate 64 and Va. 33 to West Point and Saluda, then turn right to the Rappahannock River Bridge and The Tides Inn.

TELEPHONE: (804) 438-5000

ROOMS: 100, with 4 suites

RATES 1978: AP only, from $90 to $106 in spring and summer, from $94 to $110 in fall (the inn may be closed for a few weeks in winter); plus 4% tax on total bill.

MEALS AND ENTERTAINMENT: Breakfast 8–9:30, lunch 12–4, dinner 7–9; room service during meal hours; jacket and tie at dinner; live music and dancing.

DIVERSIONS: Outdoor pool, 4 tennis courts ($1 per person per hour), two 18-hole golf courses, one 9-hole course ($9 per day), bicycles, sailing/boating, waterskiing.

The Tides Lodge
Irvington, Va.

Toss the word "golf" into the creek and you're left with a secluded location, up a creek, miles from anywhere, on a peninsula surrounded on three sides with water and on the fourth with a golf course; a modern two-story lodge with edge-grained fir siding hemmed in by mountain laurel and wildflowers, where you can breakfast on a private balcony and watch the morning mists rise and the early birds swooping for the early fish. Even if you never set foot on the first tee, you can fill your days with sailing and outboard boating, tennis, putting, swimming in a heated pool, fishing, lounging in hammocks strung out among the trees, or cruising in the lodge's sixty-five-foot yacht.

The Tides Lodge is kid brother (it was opened in 1969) to The Tides Inn, above; it's owned by the same family and shares most of the other's facilities, but it's operated as a separate entity and has a personality all its own—amiable, relaxed, and less formal than the inn. The lodge's forty rooms all have balconies with views of the water, color TV, room phones, and so much tartan decor that going to bed here is almost like cuddling under a kilt.

The tartan is in honor of Sir Guy Campbell, the revered golf course architect from St. Andrews, who helped design the lodge's links; he also has a tartan-splashed lounge named in his honor, where you can drink a toast to his memory before dinner. The pubby dining room features local delicacies—Rappahannock soft shell crabs, Chesapeake Bay shad roe, or roast Urbanna duckling. If you're ever up the creek, this is as nice a way as any to go.

NAME: The Tides Lodge

INNKEEPER: E. A. Stephens, Jr.

ADDRESS: Irvington, Va. 22480

DIRECTIONS: Same as for The Tides Inn, but branch off a few miles farther west from Va. 3.

TELEPHONE: (804) 438-6000

ROOMS: 48 rooms, 1 villa

RATES: MAP $76 to $80 all year (EP available in summer); plus 4% tax on total bill.

MEALS AND ENTERTAINMENT: Breakfast 8–10, lunch 12–3, dinner 4–11 in Binnacle II, 7–9 in dining room (approx. $12 to $20 for two); room service 8–10; jacket at dinner; live music and dancing.

DIVERSIONS: Pool, sauna, shuffleboard; tennis (3 courts, 1 lighted, $4 per hour per court), golf (two 18-hole courses, $9 per day), bicycles, canoes, sailboats, paddleboats for rent.

P.S. Spring is the busiest season; occasional small groups at other periods.

Colonial Houses
Colonial Williamsburg, Va.

Wake up in a canopy bed. Throw open the shutters, push aside the honeysuckle and dahlias, listen to the birds singing in the mulberry trees. Beyond the trim white picket fence and holly hedge is Virginia's Colonial capital. In the evening, you can sip salmagundi and juleps in taverns where Washington and Patrick Henry dined, and Jefferson wooed his fair Belinda; afterward, stroll arm in arm along cobbled streets uncluttered by cars or crowds. There you have the magic of these Colonial cottages: when the crowds have gone trudging off to pseudo-Colonial cells in nearby motels, you can give your chunky latch key a twist and step into the real thing.

This is a world of brass andirons and rag rugs, wing chairs and pewter sconces; some have fireplaces, most have kitchens. The majority of these dozen-odd Colonial Houses were actually the homes of eighteenth-century Virginians, and the remainder were Colonial-style kitchens and laundries, now converted into some of the most captivating lodgings in the country. They've been restored and furnished to the last detail in the style of their periods; but without detracting from their ambiance they somehow manage to incorporate air conditioning, private bathrooms with adjustable spray showers, and other contrivances even Franklin and Jefferson never imagined. (From the outside, incidentally, they're so authentic looking many tourists think they're exhibits and try to come in. Or in some cases peep through the windows. Be prepared.) The Colonial Houses are operated by the Williamsburg Inn (see next listing), and their guests enjoy all the services of the inn, including room service; but the Houses get a category all to themselves here because they are *so* special. Where else can you have dinner for two served on a mahogany dining table lighted by silver candelabras, in

a private heavy-beamed dining room? Then settle back in
a Chippendale sofa before a log-burning fire, there to sip a
glass of port before climbing the stairs to a dormer bedroom
and your canopy bed?

For details, see Williamsburg Inn.

Williamsburg Inn
Colonial Williamsburg, Va.

"Resort" is hardly the word that springs to mind when someone mentions Williamsburg, but that's just what you'll find
here—one of the most attractive resorts between Maine and
Florida. Step through the inn's french doors into the garden
and see what you find: two golf courses disappearing into the
loblolly pine and magnolia trees, half a dozen tennis courts,
two lawn bowling courts (and a lawn bowling *pro*), croquet,
putting green, driving range, and a pair of outdoor pools
screened from the rubbernecking hordes. All of them right
on the doorstep of an inn fit for a queen, an emperor, several
presidents, sheiks, and other grand panjandrums on state
visits to the USA, who arrive every few months at the inn's
imposing facade of arches and columns, framed by trees and
set off by a curving driveway lined with an honor guard of
flowers. Indoors, it looks like a mini-White House—Regency
lounge with twin fireplaces, chandeliers, fresh-cut flowers,
Kittering reproduction furniture, and velvet drapes that are
changed with the seasons. All very gracious, very *Virginia*.
Likewise the spacious guest rooms (with the exception of a
contemporary garden wing called Providence Hall).

Likewise the dining room, a spacious candles-and-
chandeliers salon that transforms the dinner hour into an
event. (Even children have to dress up in their best bibs-and-
tuckers to dine here.) This is an inn that takes its clarets and
cuisine seriously: an authentic sommelier will guide you
through an extensive wine list, the *chef de cuisine* (from

Belgium, via Washington's swank Jockey Club) beckons you to the realm of the epicure with dishes like braised quail with tournedos Rossini. You're only one block from all the wonders of Colonial Williamsburg, yet dining here, staying here, playing here you're insulated from the masses of day trippers.

NAME: Colonial Houses and Williamsburg Inn

INNKEEPER: James C. Miles

ADDRESS: Colonial Williamsburg, Va. 23185

DIRECTIONS: By car, take Interstate 64 to route 60, follow 60 to York Street, Francis Street, and the inn; by air to Newport News, then 20 miles by limousine or taxi to the inn; by Amtrak to Williamsburg.

TELEPHONE: (804) 229-1000

ROOMS: 145 rooms in inn, 79 in Colonial Houses, including 22 suites

RATES 1978: EP, $35 to $65 for rooms all year (suites higher); plus 4% sales tax on total bill.

MEALS AND ENTERTAINMENT: Breakfast 7:30–10, lunch 12–2 (indoors or outdoors), dinner 6:30–11 (approx. $25 to $30 for two); room service 7:30 a.m. to 11 p.m. (including Colonial Houses); jacket and tie in Regency Dining

Room at dinner, no shorts at any time; dancing to a live orchestra Friday and Saturday in Regency Dining Room, piano or harp nightly in Regency Lounge, recitals Sundays in East Lounge.

DIVERSIONS: Two heated outdoor pools, croquet, putting green, shuffleboard, chess, checkers, etc., lawn bowling and lawn bowling pro; bicycles for rent, tennis (6 courts, no lights, $2.25 per person per hour, pro shop, ball machines, clinics), golf (2 18-hole courses, $10 per day); horseback riding nearby ($5 an hour).

P.S. Open all year, crowded in July and August and on holiday weekends, best times spring and fall, and a pleasant hideaway in winter (especially in a Colonial House); some conventions, but they tend to be confined to the adjacent Providence Wing.

THE SHENANDOAH VALLEY— UP HILL AND DOWN DALE

We'll gently walk, and sweetly talk,
Till the silent moon shine clearly . . .
BURNS

1. Wayside Inn
2. Skyland Lodge
3. Big Meadows Lodge
4. The Homestead
5. Peaks of Otter Lodge
6. Boar's Head Inn
7. The Greenbrier
8. Pipestem State Park Resort

Wayside Inn
Middletown, Va.

The Wayside Inn has known the sighs of lovers for 175 years but it still greets you with the charm and low-ceiling, lop-sided elegance of those early days when Virginia dandies rode up in their coaches with sweet southern belles. The inn has just been through a ten-year refurbishing, courtesy of Leo Bernstein, a D.C. banker and avid collector of Americana, who drove past the inn one day, liked what he saw, and bought it within an hour. (If that isn't avid collecting, what is?) Since then he has decked it out with close to a million dollars' worth of Americana and, here and there, Britannica; the two lounges alone are almost museums—with George Washington looking down from above the fireplace on a Beau Brummel commode, an early Blickensdorfer portable type-writer, an English coin sorter, a petit-point chair and leather scroll footrest. Leo Bernstein's great hero is George Washington, and you can't go anywhere in the Wayside without G.W.'s beady eyes looking down on you from an engraving, painting or statuette—sometimes alone, sometimes with Martha.

You'll find them upstairs in the guest rooms, too. Espe-cially in room #16, a big green room with a pair of canopied double beds, a tallboy, chest of drawers, and half a dozen prints of G.W. Room #1 has a canopied double bed, fireplace, braided rug, circular commode, and a few steps leading down to a real bathroom (all of the inn's rooms have private bathrooms and air conditioning, but no TV); room #10 is a flamboyant nest with red velvet bedspreads and drapes, twin mahogany beds with gilt embellishments, and a hefty curli-

cued dresser—since the room is at the rear, it's quieter than its decor. All twenty-one rooms are different, and your preference will probably depend on your taste in antiques.

So many people want to dine here that the Wayside has had to expand to six dining rooms (the most romantic being the candlelit Slave Kitchen). Don't get caught up in the bustle. Grab a couple of the seven white rockers out on the veranda and listen to the birds in the bushes until the throngs have gobbled their ham and trotted off to the theater.

A few yards down Main Street you come to the 259-seat, air-conditioned Wayside Theater (another Bernstein project) where you can see professional productions of plays, musicals, and revues in summer; in winter, the theater hosts festivals of historic and unusual movies. Beyond Main Street, all the pastoral prettiness of the Shenandoah Valley is at your pleasure. Try some of the quiet back roads that wind up into the Shenandoah Mountains—they haven't changed much since the days of Virginian dandies and southern belles.

NAME: Wayside Inn
INNKEEPER: Cathy J. Castro

ADDRESS: 7783 Main Street, Middletown, Va. 22645

DIRECTIONS: Take Interstate 81 to exit 77, drive west a mile to U.S. 11, then go left into Middletown's Main Street.

TELEPHONE: (703) 869-1797

ROOMS: 21, with 7 suites

RATES 1978: EP, spring and summer from $14 to $32; slightly lower in the winter and fall; 4% local tax on room, food, and bar.

MEALS AND ENTERTAINMENT: Breakfast 7:30–11:30, lunch 11:30–3 Monday–Saturday, dinner 5–9 Monday–Friday, 5–10 Saturday, 12–9 Sunday (approx. $12 to $16 for two); no room service; informal dress; live music.

DIVERSIONS: Horseshoes, volleyball, badminton, softball, chess and checkers; hiking, horseback riding, skiing, sailing/boating nearby.

Skyland Lodge
Shenandoah National Park, Va.

Chase a white-tailed deer through the hickory and pignut. Take a deep breath and sing, "O Shenandoah, I long to hear you" into the wind. Scramble over the rocks for a picnic beside a waterfall. Lie on the grass and tickle each other's ears with columbine, while you read Spenser: "Bring hither the Pink and purple Columbine/With Gillyflowers/Bring Coronation and Sops in wine/Worn of Paramours./Strew me the ground with Daffadowndillies . . ." All around you are 300 square miles of wildlife preserve, rustling with deer, black bear, woodchuck, and gray fox; meadowlarks and indigo buntings skim through the staghorn sumac and chokecherry; and in spring, lousewort, bebb's zizzia, and columbine paint the meadows.

The location is close to beatific—the highest point on the Skyline Drive, that marvelous ambling highway that snakes along the spine of the Blue Ridge Mountains. Skyland's 160 rooms are spread out among lodges and cottages with names like Bushytop, Raven's Nest, Hemlock, and Wildwood, scattered among the pines and hemlocks, and all on different levels so that every room seems to have a view across the shimmying Shenandoah. The rooms are so-so, but at least they're piney and rustic; they all have private bathrooms, but no room phones. And no TV, so you'll just have to look at the stars.

Big Meadows Lodge
Shenandoah National Park, Va.

A ninety-two-room, stone-and-timber brother of Skyland Lodge, also operated by the Virginia Sky-Line Company. Like Skyland, its main attraction is its peaceful, nature-loving location on top of the Blue Ridge Mountains, screened from the traffic by pine and hemlock and lawns. Big Meadows is nine miles south of Skyland; all the information below applies to both, except where indicated.

NAME: Skyland Lodge
INNKEEPER: David F. Emswiler
NAME: Big Meadows Lodge
INNKEEPER: Bruce Fears
ADDRESS FOR BOTH: P. O. Box 727, Luray, Va. 22835
DIRECTIONS: Both are on the Skyline Drive—Skyland, 9 miles
    south of the intersection with U.S. 211; Big Meadows,
    19 miles south of U.S. 211
TELEPHONES: (703) 999-2211 for Skyland, (703) 999-2221
    for Big Meadows
ROOMS: 158 and 6 suites in Skyland, 92 and 6 suites in Big
    Meadows.

RATES 1978: EP from $18 to $27 spring through fall, from early November through late March $18 at Big Meadows (Skyland closed); plus 4% tax on total bill.

MEALS AND ENTERTAINMENT: Breakfast 7:30–10, lunch 12–3, dinner 5:30–9 (approx. $6 and up for two), winter hours at Big Meadows 7 a.m. to 6 (7 on Friday and Saturday); no room service; informal dress; live music.

DIVERSIONS: Horseback riding ($4 an hour, not available in winter), rental bikes at Big Meadows, hiking trails, game room at Skyland.

P.S. Try to avoid weekends and holidays, and especially weekends at fall foliage time; make a reservation well in advance, and *always* before you go up onto the Highway, because with a 35 m.p.h. speed limit it takes a long time to get back down.

The Homestead
Hot Springs, Va.

Back in the unhurried, unruffled days before the Civil War, Virginian high society whiled away its summers on a grand tour of the mineral springs in the Allegheny Mountains— from Warm in the north, southward to Hot to Sweet to White. A week here, a week there. Nowadays they head straight for Hot Springs and the magnificent Homestead.

The Homestead sweeps you up into a mountain world where sixteen thousand acres of forests and streams and meadows blot out the humdrum and the mediocre. You can go riding here day after day, mile after mile, and never trample the same soil twice; you can take leisurely strolls through the gardens, or rugged hikes that will leave you massaging thighs for therapeutic rather than aphrodisiac reasons; you can relax in mineral baths or saunas, take buckboard rides, play a set or two of tennis on a dozen courts, or a round of golf on three beautiful pine-lined courses; you can float in an outdoor or an indoor pool—and how many mountain resorts treat you to a sandy beach for sunning yourselves?

CHAMBER MUSIC, AFTERNOON TEA. The Homestead is one of America's great classic resorts, built on a scale you don't see too often these days—a towering château of 615 rooms that looms over the forest and rooftops of Hot Springs. When you enter The Homestead, you find yourselves in the Great Hall—a nave of sixteen pillars and fourteen chandeliers, great log-burning fireplaces, a solarium, and a string orchestra playing chamber music during afternoon tea. That's just the Great Hall—you've still to visit the lobbies and lounges and shopping arcade. Everything at The Homestead is on the grand scale, and if you start to wonder how a hotel like this manages to survive in this day and age, wander down to the lower level of the new $8 million South Wing, where you'll see suites of meeting rooms to house the conventions that keep those 615 rooms busy throughout the year. The Homestead is now one of the nation's classic convention hotels—a description which should instantly eliminate it from this guide; but the truth is that even with half a dozen conventions and seminars in the house, there's no overcrowding, and no hint of strained service.

The Homestead was geared to mollycoddle the mollycoddled, and the emphasis is still on service that takes everything in its well-ordered stride even if they no longer have waiters who dance with stacked trays on their heads. In return, it expects a little class from its guests, and the hotel's brochure reminds you that "gentlemen must always wear coats when dining"; and even with "young ladies can wear contemporary bathing suits" this is clearly no place for people who like to spend their vacations lounging around in stained jeans. You come to The Homestead to show off a beautiful woman in beautiful gowns, to make an entrance in the dining room, to command attentive service from maitre d', head waiter, waiter, wine steward, and busboy.

On the other hand, if you don't want to go through the fuss of dressing up every night, slip into a robe and order up room service. The Homestead has the right kind of rooms for casual, bathrobe evenings, with soothing pastel colors and comfortable furniture. The most coveted rooms have parlors and big screened porches high above the gardens; the quietest rooms are in the eleven white clapboard cottages in the garden; and the plushest rooms are the penthouse duplexes in the new South Wing, with spiral stairs leading to bedroom balconies. Up in that cozy love nest you're light miles from the conventions and the fol-de-rol.

NAME: The Homestead

INNKEEPERS: Thomas J. Lennon (president), W. Dan Reichartz (vice-president)

ADDRESS: Hot Springs, Va. 24445

DIRECTIONS: On U.S. 220, 80 miles north of Roanoke, 15 miles north of Interstate 64; by air, to Ingalls Field 17 miles away (daily scheduled air taxi flights); or by Chessie System to Covington, where you'll be met by limousine.

TELEPHONE: (703) 839-5500

ROOMS: 590, plus 78 parlor suites

RATES 1978: Not available at press time, but probably about 5% higher than 1977 rates—from $120 to $132 AP spring through fall, a few dollars less in winter; plus 15% service charge, plus 6% tax on room and food.

MEALS AND ENTERTAINMENT: Breakfast 7:30–10, lunch 12:30–2, afternoon tea 4, dinner 7–8:30 (approx. $30 and up for two); room service during meal hours; jacket and tie at dinner; live music, dancing nightly, movies.

DIVERSIONS: Outdoor heated pool, therapy pool, sauna, exercise rooms, health spa, hiking trails, lawn bowling, carriage rides, skeet and trap shooting, tennis (15 courts, no lights, $3 per person per hour, pro shop), horseback riding ($8 first hour, $6 thereafter), golf (3 18-hole courses, one of them rated among the nation's top 30 by *Golf Digest,* $12 per day); skiing, sleigh rides, and ice skating in winter.

P.S. If you'd like to enjoy all these facilities but stay in more modest surroundings, make a reservation at the nearby Cascades Inn (703-839-5355), in the hamlet of Healing Springs.

Peaks of Otter Lodge
near Bedford, Va.

Here's another dreamy location—by the edge of Otter Lake, across from Sharp Top, Flat Top, and Harkening Hill, in the Shenandoah National Park. In spring the meadows are jubilant with merrybells, trillium, and columbine; in fall with joepyeweed, goldenrod, and bottled gentian. You can follow mile after mile of hug-and-cuddle trails through sweet birch, black cherry, pignut, pine, and oak; or find a quiet spot to watch for a meadowlark, chickadee, or white-breasted nuthatch. In the evening, elk and white-tailed deer sometimes wander down to the lake for a sundowner. This is strictly a place for basking in nature and love. There's no swimming pool, no tennis court. Just unspoiled, unhurried nature.

And the Virginia Peaks of Otter Company has taken the trouble to erect a rustic lodge that harmonizes with the surroundings—rough-hewn pine walls, slate-topped dressers and tables, cane-backed chairs, acres of glass for admiring the views, acres of lawn for lounging by the lake, and all rooms with balconies or patios facing the lake. The main lodge has an open veranda and a glass-enclosed lounge facing the lake, a downstairs bar, and a raftered dining room with tables for twosomes by the window. You can dawdle over Allegheny Mountain trout or Virginia country ham, while you watch the sun set over Flat Top and the moon slip past Sharp Top. (Meals here are a bargain, by the way—two people can dine for around $10.)

Get to bed early, but leave the balcony door open and you can be awakened by the meadowlarks and chickadees.

NAME: Peaks of Otter Lodge
INNKEEPER: Roger H. Henderson
ADDRESS: P. O. Box 489, Bedford, Va. 24523
DIRECTIONS: On the Blue Ridge Parkway at the junction with Va. 43 (or Mile 86, if you begin at the beginning), 10 miles northwest of Bedford, about 20 miles north of Roanoke.
TELEPHONE: (703) 586-1081
ROOMS: 58
RATES: EP $27 all year (with dinner *included* in the rate between December 1 and March 31); plus 4% tax on total bill.
MEALS AND ENTERTAINMENT: Breakfast 7:30–10:30, lunch 11:30–2:30, dinner 5–8:30 (approx. $10 to $20 for two); no room service; dress optional.
DIVERSIONS: Hiking trails, sleigh rides in winter.
P.S. Busy with families in summer, book far ahead for the fall foliage weeks.

Boar's Head Inn
Charlottesville, Va.

This part of Virginia is America's Sussex—rolling meadow-lands, forests and streams, spic-and-span farms, a peaceful land where the landed gentry of yesterday (Thomas Jefferson and James Madison among them) built country estates, and where the landed and unlanded gentry of our day still ride to hounds. Appropriately, the best inn for miles around gets its name from Shakespeare.

The Boar's Head is a complex of well-proportioned buildings in Colonial style tacked onto an old grist mill. It's part of a new housing estate with landscaped grounds, a pair of lakes with ducks and trout, gardens of magnolia and box-wood, a nine-hole golf course, and eighteenth-century calm.

The grist mill is over a hundred years old, but it had to be taken to pieces beam by beam and moved to this site; its great forty-three-foot beams now house the Old Mill Room restaurant on the ground floor with some of the inn's hundred-odd guest rooms upstairs. The original fifty-four guest rooms are the most interesting, some with dormer windows and log-burning fireplaces, some with pine-paneled walls and set-in beds. (The new rooms are first-rate—but motley.)

The lobby is decorated with oak paneling and authentic dark oak antique furniture. The whole place is very decorative, but somehow contrived, somehow closer in spirit to Norman Rockwell than William Shakespeare. Or Thomas Jefferson, for that matter.

Besides the nine-hole golf course, tennis courts, swimming pool, and sauna, there's a Boar's Head Sports Club with more tennis courts (including indoor), platform tennis courts, and a squash court. Inn guests can join the club for $6 a day.

On the whole, the Boar's Head is a pleasant enough, relaxing inn, but it is less a resort than a base for exploring the attractions of this part of Virginia—Jefferson's exquisite and fascinating Monticello, his elegant campus for the University of Virginia.

These are places to savor, so avoid weekends and holidays. And that advice applies equally to the Old Mill Room at the Boar's Head. It gets crowded on weekends, and you have to make a reservation for dinner even if you're a guest. The restaurant's menu lists items like "escargots à la Provincial," whatever that is, but when the chef sticks to tavernlike dishes such as roast beef, he does well. But remember to make a reservation.

NAME: Boar's Head Inn

INNKEEPER: Charles E. Holliday

ADDRESS: Ednam Forest, Route 250, West Charlottesville, Va. 22901

DIRECTIONS: Follow the U.S. 50 bypass, 2 miles beyond the intersection with U.S. 29; or by air, scheduled service, to Charlottesville.

TELEPHONE: (804) 296-2181

ROOMS: 90, with 7 suites

RATES 1978: EP, $36 double, suites $52, all year; 6% local tax on room and food.

MEALS AND ENTERTAINMENT: Breakfast 7–10:30, lunch 12–2, dinner 6–9:30 (approx. $18 to $24 for two); room service 7 a.m. to 9 p.m.; jacket and tie in dining room; live music and dancing.

DIVERSIONS: Outdoor pool, sauna, tennis (sports club, daily membership fee $6, 14 outdoor courts with lights, 3 indoor courts, pro and clinics), bicycles; hiking, horseback riding, skiing, ice skating nearby.

The Greenbrier
White Sulphur Springs, W. Va.

There's a touch of *Last Year at Marienbad* about The Greenbrier: a string trio plays for afternoon tea, chandeliered corridors lead you to more chandeliered corridors, couples stroll arm in arm across acres of lawns. Occasionally, someone sips a glass of the mineral water from the sulphur spring, and some of the old-timers may be reminiscing about the day the Prince of Wales sat in with the orchestra during a gala ball.

More likely the guests are trying to recall names and faces not from last year's spa, but from last year at the insurance executives' conference, or the convention of ad biggies; because The Greenbrier is another classic resort, like The Homestead, that now keeps its aristocratic head above water by filling most of its rooms with conventioneers. They haven't taken over completely, because fortunately a lot of people still recognize that The Greenbrier is a great spot to vacation.

CHAMPAGNE AND WATERMELON. The Greenbrier owes its fame and fortune to a spring with water that tastes and smells something like a hard-boiled egg that's been lying in the bottom of a rucksack for a week. The Indians knew of its curative powers; then a Mrs. John Anderson came along in 1778 and from that point on White Sulphur Springs became one of America's great spas. Robert E. Lee spent a lot of time here, riding Traveler around the estate and admiring the gaggles of south'n belles and the budding beaux who regaled them with champagne and watermelon. They've been followed through the years and social upheavals by tycoons, dukes, lords, princes, shahs, sheiks—and now conventioneers. The Greenbrier is one of the largest resort hotels in the world, and there are a lot of well-heeled and well-traveled types who'll tell you it's one of the best. Marienbad would

probably have to look a long way back in its memory book to match the present opulence of The Greenbrier.

Its palatial facade gleams in the clear mountain air, white and massive against the dense green of the pine-clad mountains all around. Across the parklike garden, the hilltop Presidents' Cottage reminds you that no fewer than nineteen U.S. presidents have visited White Sulphur Springs, and the rows of piazza-fronted cottages running from either side take you back to the days of Robert E. Lee. (One of the rows actually houses an artists' colony, where you can buy handwoven tweeds or handmade pottery.)

The Chesapeake & Ohio Railroad, which built it, didn't stint on The Greenbrier: the hotel has 650 rooms, and no two are alike; the ashtrays at the entrance are antique Chinese rice bowls (and every time they're cleaned out the porter imprints the sand with The Greenbrier's special script-type logo); it has its own fire department, and every room is linked directly with a warning control panel in the firehouse; forty-nine gardeners and groundsmen tend the lawns and the fifty-four fairways; thirty-three chefs whip up everything from scrambled eggs to tête de veau tortue; and the swimming coach has more gold medals than Mark Spitz.

LOVER'S LEAP. Don't let all this abundance turn you off. The Greenbrier is *so* big you can easily escape to quiet corners. Take a walk, for example: you have a choice of thirteen trails, from a quarter mile to ten miles (one of them ominously named Lover's Leap). You're not going to find too many conventioneers up there; in fact, you're not going to find too many anythings up there except shagbark hickory, big tooth aspen, Virginia pine, and staghorn sumac. If you decide to go riding on some of the hotel's 200 miles of private trails, you don't even have to go to the stables to pick up your mounts; the groom will deliver them "at the appointed hour" in the riding circle by the north entrance.

When you get back from your ride, stop off in the clubhouse terrace overlooking the golf courses and sample the sumptuous buffet lunch. You have something like ninety dishes to nibble from.

You can pamper yourself silly in a place like this, and you can leave feeling like a million. Of course, it helps if you *arrive* with a million. Elegance doesn't come cheaply these days.

NAME: The Greenbrier

INNKEEPER: John S. Lanahan (president and managing director)

ADDRESS: White Sulphur Springs, W. Va. 24986

DIRECTIONS: By car, take Interstate 64 to the White Sulphur Springs exits, then U.S. 60 one-half mile west of town; by train, daily Amtrak service practically to the doorstep; by air, daily scheduled flights by Piedmont to Greenbrier Airport.

TELEPHONE: 650 rooms, 68 suites, 28 villas

RATES 1978: MAP only, from $120 to $140 all year; plus $10 per couple per day service charge, and 3% tax.

MEALS AND ENTERTAINMENT: Breakfast 7:30–10, no lunch, dinner 6:30–8:45; room service 7 a.m. to midnight; jacket and tie at dinner; live music and dancing.

DIVERSIONS: Heated outdoor and indoor pools, sauna, exercise room, hiking trails, bikes for rent, platform tennis, trap and skeet shooting, indoor bowling, billiards, backgammon, tennis (20 courts, 5 lighted, $6 per court per hour outdoors, $12 per court per hour indoors, pro shop, ball machines), golf (3 18-hole courses, $10 per round), horseback riding ($8.50 per hour); winter sports nearby.

P.S. Busiest seasons are summer and fall, with some conventions all year, but think of winter—indoor pool, indoor tennis, sumptuous dining, long walks in untrampled snow.

Pipestem State Park Resort
Hinton, W. Va.

This is the poor man's Greenbrier. However, if you're looking for a room with a view, you'll see more trees and more mountains from the lodge at Pipestem than you could see if you climbed the flagpole at Greenbrier. Pipestem is a state park high in the Appalachians. It gets its name from *spiraea alba,* a hollow-stemmed plant that the Indians used for making peace pipes. The hills around here are covered with this *spiraea alba,* as well as forsythia and dogwood and blooming redbud, and pines and firs.

The main lodge is an overpowering seven-story timber-and-stone lodge perched on the edge of the hill. Its rooms are motelly, but who cares with that magnificent view out there beyond your balcony. All 129 rooms in the lodge have private bathrooms, room telephones, television, and individually controlled heating. There are also cottages snuggled among the trees, but even with fireplaces and porches they're more suitable for families than lovers.

CANYON-BOTTOM LODGE. The most unusual feature of Pipestem is Mountain Creek Lodge. This is a two-story complex of thirty guest rooms 1000 feet down in Bluestone Canyon, at the edge of a winding mountain stream. The only way you can get down to the pleasant, comfortable motel-type rooms is by a 3600-foot aerial tramway (it's free, and runs more or less at your convenience). There's also a café/restaurant down there, so you have no reason to surface.

All the facilities of the lodge take advantage of the superb view—even the indoor swimming pool has windows two floors high, so you can frolic around in the pool even in winter and enjoy the layers of mountains covered with snow-like mounds of whipped cream. As a guest of the resort you have access to the state park's sporting facilities—miles of walking and riding trails, a nine-hole and an eighteen-hole golf course, tennis courts, archery ranges, and an outdoor theater. But nothing they perform there can be as dramatic as that view.

NAME: Pipestem State Park Resort

INNKEEPER: Arch Knighton

ADDRESS: Pipestem, W. Va. 25979

DIRECTIONS: Complicated. It's on W.Va. 20, about 16 miles from Hinton or Princeton (the southern end of the West Virginia Turnpike); or about 50 miles southwest of White Sulphur Springs and Interstate 64. By air to Bluefield.

TELEPHONE: (304) 466-1800

ROOMS: 129 rooms, 14 suites, 25 cottages

RATES 1978: EP $20 to $26 from April 1 through October 31, lower remainder of the year; plus 3% sales tax.

MEALS AND ENTERTAINMENT: Breakfast 7–2, lunch 12–2, dinner 5:30–9:30 (approx. $10 to $20 for two); no room service; dress optional; theater and musical shows in the amphitheater.

DIVERSIONS: Outdoor pool (unheated), indoor pool (heated), sauna, game room, archery, hiking trails, tennis (7 courts)—all free; golf (one 18-hole, one 9-hole, $7 for 18), horseback riding ($5 the first hour), bikes for rent.

FROM THE CAROLINAS TO THE KEYS

What men call gallantry, and gods adultery,
Is much more common where the climate's sultry . . .
                                                    BYRON

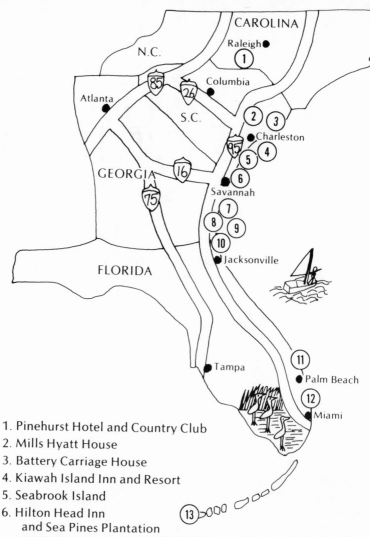

1. Pinehurst Hotel and Country Club
2. Mills Hyatt House
3. Battery Carriage House
4. Kiawah Island Inn and Resort
5. Seabrook Island
6. Hilton Head Inn
   and Sea Pines Plantation
7. The Cloister
8. The King and Prince Hotel
9. Greyfield Inn
10. Amelia Island Plantation
11. The Breakers
12. Boca Raton Hotel
13. Pier House

Pinehurst Hotel and Country Club
Pinehurst, N.C.

Smack in the middle of the Tar Heel State there's this little New England village, where azaleas, dogwoods, and camellias bloom amid holly and long-needle pines, where well-heeled young sports enthusiasts bound out of bed in the crisp clear morning air to play golf, swim, sail, play more golf, shoot skeet, fish, then play more golf. Or tennis.

Pinehurst is a hotel, cuddled into a town, surrounded by a country club, in the middle of a forest, on top of a hill, in the heart of North Carolina farm country. It's an enclave first developed more than eighty years ago by a Boston soda-fountain manufacturer named Tufts, as a place for the idle rich to while away their time when it was too late for New Hampshire, too early for Palm Beach. Tuft's frail health responded well to the balmy climate of the Carolina Sandhills, particularly when he found he could buy 5000 acres for $5000. He called in Frederick Law Olmsted (the same Olmsted who laid out New York's Central Park and Washington's Mall) and together they laid out the land and planted their trees exactly where they wanted them to be; then Tufts called in a Scot named Donald Ross to design a golf course or two, and he laid out *five*—all teeing off from and chipping back to the same sprawling clubhouse. If you've heard of Pinehurst, chances are it was a golf nut who told you about it.

Now Diamondhead Corporation of New Orleans (which bought Pinehurst in 1971) plans to go one, maybe two, stages further, and make the name Pinehurst known from coast to coast as an all-round resort. They're chipping millions of dollars into the project, building condominiums and villas along those hundred-plus fairways. They've refurbished the spacious, stately old hotel (it was formerly the Carolina), dredged a two-hundred-acre lake for recreation, laid out a score of tennis courts around a new tennis clubhouse, installed a complete health club with a masseur-masseuse team to run it, and now they're finishing off their *sixth* golf course. The result is one of the liveliest, friendliest, snappiest resorts on the East Coast, doing a booming business in golf packages and videotape tennis clinics with Aussie pros.

But is it romantic? Not exactly, but it is peaceful, stylish, *invigorating;* and even with all the activity, Pinehurst has lots of quiet spots hidden away on its thirteen thousand acres of pine and sycamore, where you can escape, hand in hand or bike by bike, among the azaleas and dogwoods and camellias.

L.E.B.

NAME: Pinehurst Hotel and Country Club
INNKEEPER: A. M. Stratta
ADDRESS: P. O. Box 4000, Pinehurst, N.C. 28374
DIRECTIONS: By car, from U.S. 1 west on State Highway 211 at Southern Pines; by air, Piedmont can fly you to Fayetteville (the closest major airport), Charlotte, or Raleigh/Durham, with connecting flights (Resort Commuter Airlines) to Pinehurst/Southern Pines Airport, 4 miles from the hotel, or by limousine, a drive of approximately one hour. By Amtrak, to Hamlet.
TELEPHONE: (919) 295-6811; toll-free (800) 334-9560
ROOMS: 260, including 10 suites and 10 villas
RATES 1978: EP, $37 to $52 from May 26 through September 10, $62 to $72 from May 16 through May 25 and September 11 through November 13; plus 15% service charge and 4% tax.
MEALS AND ENTERTAINMENT: Breakfast 7–9:30, lunch 12–2, dinner 7–9 (approx. $18 to $24 for two); room service, more or less dining-room hours; jacket and tie for dinner; live music and dinner dancing nightly.

DIVERSIONS: Outdoor and indoor pools, therapy pool, sauna, exercise rooms, archery, hiking; tennis (20 courts, 4 lighted, $4 per hour, pro shop, clinics), golf (*six* 18-hole courses, $10–$12 per round), horseback riding ($7 per hour), sailing and canoeing ($5 per hour), trap and skeet shooting, bicycling.

Mills Hyatt House
Charleston, S.C.

"Bathing rooms for gentlemen are fitted up in good style, convenient to the barber's pole . . ." wrote a local newspaper on the opening of Mills House in 1853; and it was probably such style and convenience that persuaded Robert E. Lee to estabish his quarters there when he commanded the Charleston garrison. Now, 125 years and a $6-million facelift later, there are private bathing rooms for gentlemen *and* their ladies, fitted up in tiled and gleaming style, and hop-and-skip convenient to the canopied beds. What you have at the Mills Hyatt House, in fact, is something unique—one of the oldest hotels in the country looking as if it were built yesterday. Which is more or less what happened.

A group of Charlestonians who were proud of their heritage (and few people are prouder of their heritage than Charlestonians) got together to buy the venerable but rather dilapidated Mills House. They planned to spend half a million dollars repainting it and installing private bathrooms. But the local fire department, proud of *its* heritage, said nix, it's a fire hazard. So the gallant group then decided to raze the innards and rebuild virtually from the ground up. The bill came to something like $6 million. But it was worth it—at least from the point of view of guests who only have to put up $30 or so for all this luxury.

GASLIGHT AND GARDEN PATIO. If Robert E. Lee came clattering down Meeting Street today he'd recognize the old place—wrought-iron balconies, gas lamps, the elegant tripartite doors, a mansionlike lobby with a sweeping double staircase, a garden patio with a three-tiered fountain. He'd feel at home in the interior but he might not recognize the individual decorations. One of the prime movers behind the renovation was a successful Wall Street bachelor, Dick Jenrette, who fell in love with Charleston, bought one of the stately townhouses down by the waterfront, and got involved with his neighbors in preserving the aristocratic feel of the city. He's a lover of antiques, and you'll now find an impressive collection in the Mills Hyatt House—a Regency-styled zebrawood table, Chinese Ming portraits, French clocks, Empire candleholders, a black lacquered Dutch bombe chest, and a pair of mirrors from a Viennese hunting lodge, all from the early nineteenth century. You even sign in on a marble-and-brass inkstand on a marble registration desk.

The room you check into is furnished in a style that suggests rather than re-creates the 1800s—canopied (but squeaky) beds in fabrics that match the drapes, leather Queen Anne wing chairs, footstools, silver and copper table lamps, and such modern touches as princess telephones, individual temperature controls, and color TV. All 240 rooms are attractive, but the eight poolside rooms ($48) have French doors leading to little wrought-iron porches next to the pool. If you want the best in the house, ask for the Mary Boykin Chestnut Suite (if you can't remember that mouthful, it's the one on the seventh floor).

MIRRORED ALCOVES, CHÂTEAU LAFITE-ROTHSCHILD. There are many beautiful things in the Mills Hyatt House and one of the most beautiful is the Barbados Room, a forty-table dining room with small alcoves in mirrored arches just big enough for two, fresh flowers on the table, candles in brass candlesticks, pewter plates, ceiling fans, rattan chairs, and an overall atmosphere redolent of the Caribbean island that gives the room its name (another touch of heritage—

many of the first settlers in Charleston came up from the islands). Even breakfast can be something special here: papaya lightly flavored with fresh lime juice, shrimp *pâté* and grits, waffles with creamed chicken, beaten biscuits, honey and muscadine jelly. The menu will introduce you to some of the dishes that distinguish Carolina cooking: conch stew, conch salad, oyster pie, Myrtlebank lump she-crabmeat cocktail, Charleston she-crab soup, langouste Calhoun (lobster, mushrooms, in cream and sherry sauce, served in the shell), roast duckling Carolina (with peaches and baked apple), Huguenot torte and strawberries Mills House (marinated in Grand Marnier and served with ice cream, cognac, and crème chantilly).

They've really created one of the country's prettiest restaurants here, which is hard luck on the staff because in a less beguiling setting the service probably wouldn't remind you of Joe's Corner Café. There is, for example, a surprisingly good wine list, from Beaujolais Village at $3 for the half bottle to a Château Lafite-Rothschild at $42; but if you have any respect for good wine you'll order the Beaujolais rather than watch a superb burgundy being whirled and twirled and juggled like a drum major's baton. Fortunately, the Beaujolais happens to be rather good for the price.

CANDLELIGHT, WINE, MUSIC. Don't let the few failings in service put you off coming here. The Mills Hyatt House would be worth visiting even in Gary, Indiana. As it is, it happens to be in one of the loveliest cities in the South—one of those places that people always want to call "a grand old lady." There's still enough of the aristocratic Charleston left to let you savor the atmosphere of the antebellum South. The promenade down by the waterfront, lined by more stately townhouses than you could raise a top hat to, is one of the most handsome cityscapes in America—particularly when the mist comes rolling in from Fort Sumter like candy floss. The Mills Hyatt House will rent you a map and cassette recorder (for $5.20) if you want to take a walking tour past the homes, Catfish Row (the one that inspired *Porgy and Bess*), and the old Slave Market (farmers' market on weekdays, flea market on weekends). Around Easter you can take a tour through the interiors of half a dozen of these historic homes and gardens; some evenings also feature galas in the houses, with candlelight, wine, chamber music, or concerts of spirituals. Dinner in the Barbados Room, chamber music in the Nathaniel Russell House, love in the Mary Boykin Chestnut Suite—that's not such a bad way to spend an evening anywhere.

NAME: Mills Hyatt House

INNKEEPER: Eric Brooks

ADDRESS: Meeting and Queen Streets, Charleston, S.C. 29401

DIRECTIONS: By car, take the Meeting Street/Downtown exit from Interstate 26, then follow Meeting to Queen; also, by scheduled air and Amtrak services to Charleston.

TELEPHONE: (803) 577-2400

ROOMS: 230 rooms, 7 suites

RATES 1978: EP, from $43 to $49 all year; plus 4% tax on total bill.

MEALS AND ENTERTAINMENT: Breakfast 7–11, lunch 12–3, sandwiches 3–5, dinner 6–11 (approx. $25 to $30 for two); room service 7 a.m. to 11 p.m.; jacket and tie at dinner; piano or combo in lounge, harp in dining room on selected evenings each week.

DIVERSIONS: Outdoor pool; sightseeing, harbor trips, bikes, horseback riding, boating nearby.

P.S. Busiest months are March through May (that is, around Easter and when the gardens bloom and homes are open for tours), and now also during the Spoleto Festival (May 27 to June 10 in 1978).

Battery Carriage House
Charleston, S.C.

You're welcomed with a glass of sherry from a cut-glass decanter; you cuddle up in a canopy bed; breakfast is served, on a silver tray, in the wisteria arbor. Here's your chance to savor something of the gracious life-style of Old Charleston.

One of the glories of this city, hinted at in the paragraphs on the Mills Hyatt House, is the parade of imposing mansions and walled gardens facing the waterfront, and there can be few visitors without a secret longing to stay in one of them. Now you can. Well, almost. Frank Gay and his family live in hundred-year-old Battery Mansion, four floors of verandas, columns, and shutters rising to a mansard roof; the two-story Carriage House, in the quiet walled garden at the rear, has now been converted into an elegant guest house. Each of the ten rooms is decorated with historic Charleston wallpapers and draperies; furnished with Madison dressers, gilt mirrors, canopy beds, and other period pieces; then inducted into the twentieth century with dial-a-massage showerheads, FM radios, color TV, alarm clocks, room phones, air conditioning, concealed pullman kitchenettes, and refrigerators with complimentary soft drinks and wine. These are very elegant snuggeries—maybe too snug for some people, but then the intention is not to spend all your time indoors. Explore Charleston. Grab a pair of the "beaten-up old bikes" and go riding off through narrow alleys and streets to the historic sights. Frank Gay or one of his colleagues is always on hand with advice on what to see and where to dine.

On the other hand, after breakfast in the wisteria arbor, with the birds chirruping in the trees, the farthest you'll

travel may be across the garden to the hammock slung between a pair of palm trees. That's gracious living, too.

NAME: Battery Carriage House
OWNER/INNKEEPER: Frank Gay
ADDRESS: 20 South Battery, Charleston, S.C. 29401
DIRECTIONS: By car, take the Meeting Street/Downtown exit
   from Interstate 26, then follow Meeting to the wa-
   terfront.
TELEPHONE: (803) 723-9881
ROOMS: 10
RATES 1978: $48 (including continental breakfast, bicycles,
   bottle of wine, and soft drinks), all year; plus 4% tax on
   total bill.
MEALS AND ENTERTAINMENT: Breakfast only, from 7:30
   "until anytime," served in your room or in the wisteria
   arbor.
DIVERSIONS: Bicycles, tiny pool, walking, sightseeing.
P.S. Busiest March through May and during Spoleto Festival
   (May 27 to June 10 in 1978).

Kiawah Island Inn and Resort
Kiawah Island, S.C.

In a place with so many delights, where do you begin? With
the Sandbar, maybe. It's a wall-less bar on top of the dunes,
but it's been given a separate observation deck by the edge of
the beach, and (a small point, but somehow typical of the
care that has gone into Kiawah) an unusual countertop
crafted ingeniously from driftwood, its crevasses filled with
hundreds of tiny seashells and then covered with peekaboo
plastic, at once practical and appropriate to the setting.

And what a setting! Kiawah Island is ten miles of virtually private beach, low sand dunes on the Atlantic side and low-lying marshland on the creek side, secluded, unspoiled, subtropical, the habitat of wild ponies and white-tailed deer, alligators and river otters. Since 1976, the alligators and otters have shared their swamps with eagles and birdies—on eighteen fairways of championship caliber, designed by Gary Player; its lagoons and dunes are now dotted with villas and townhouses, all in contemporary cedar-and-cypress styling, set among live oaks and palmettos.

The people who designed Kiawah (a company called Wallace, McHarg, Roberts & Todd) had a chance to polish and refine their concepts at Sea Pines and Amelia, a pair of plantations farther south, with the result that their third try, Kiawah, is one of the most beautiful resorts in the country. Its felicities of design seem to have been created not so much in harmony as in a spirit of camaraderie with its surroundings. The inn itself has deep porches front and rear, each with its quota of wicker rockers, and even the second-floor Topside Lounge has an open deck for guests who want to observe the dunes and ocean as they sip their juleps. The two dining rooms compete with each other in the charm of their decor: in the Jasmine Porch, bamboo shades, wood-bladed fans, hanging plants, and cane-back chairs with leaf-patterned cushions; the Charleston Gallery is an intimate candlelit salon, half a dozen tables for seven-course dinners. Service and cuisine match the surroundings (the minted noisette of lamb was superb).

The guest rooms, in two three-story cedar-and-cypress wings, are spacious, restful, carefully color coordinated, and decorated with framed charts of Charleston harbor and pen-and-ink drawings of Charleston landmarks or something equally appropriate. One flaw, though. You really have no alternative to the air conditioning—no louvers, no screens, no ventilators (I have the same reservation about the Jasmine Porch, a Caribbean-style room just crying out for a trade wind, and already equipped with fans and louvered screens). The solution may be to stay in one of the handsome villas or townhouses with screened porches (the Beach Townhouses are particularly attractive, but pricey); or come to Kiawah in fall or winter when you probably won't need air conditioning. But come anyway. Here's a place worth visiting.

Kiawah is Kuwaiti-owned, but the only hint of its ownership is a volume on Islamic culture, tucked away on a library shelf in the Topside Lounge, between Evelyn Waugh and Charles C. Colson; if this is what petrodollars can do, the average resort developer should be made to pump gasoline.

NAME: Kiawah Island Inn and Resort

INNKEEPER: R. Scott Morrison

ADDRESS: Kiawah Island, S.C. 29455

DIRECTIONS: Kiawah is 24 miles southeast of Charleston. By car, take Interstate 26 to U.S. 17S (about 7 miles), go left on State Highway 20, and follow the signs for 17 miles to Kiawah Island. By air, scheduled services to Charleston Airport (50 miles by limousine, $10 per couple each way); by Amtrak to Charleston.

TELEPHONE: (803) 559-5571

ROOMS: 300, including 150 in the inn, the remainder in town-houses and villas.

RATES 1978: EP, from $42 to $57, March through October (special sports and vacation plans available); plus 15% service charge on meals, and 4% tax on everything.

MEALS AND ENTERTAINMENT: Complimentary coffee in your room on request, breakfast 7–10, lunch 11:30–2, Sunday brunch 12–3, poolside lunches and snacks, dinner 6–10 (approx. $20 to $25 for two in the Jasmine Porch, $37 per couple for the 7-course dinner in the Charleston Gallery); no room service, except for continental breakfast; informal dress, except for jacket and tie in the Charleston Gallery; piano (quiet) in the dining room, combo (noisy) and dancing in the lounge upstairs; no liquor on Sundays.

DIVERSIONS: Freshwater pool, therapy pool, sauna, bridge and backgammon; tennis (9 courts, 2 lighted, 2 all-weather, $8 per court per hour, pro shop, clinics), golf (18 holes designed by Gary Player, $10 a round, driving range, putting green), bikes ($1.50 per hour), Hobie cats, jeep safaris through maritime forests ($5–$10); horseback riding nearby.

P.S. Golf and tennis year round, with the best months late September to November (still warm enough to swim in October) and early March through April; some conventions.

Seabrook Island
Seabrook Island, S.C.

You could almost jump across the creek that separates Kiawah from Seabrook (the islands), but the resorts are isolated from each other, hints of rooftops on a distant beach. At Seabrook, you register at the sales office, beside the paddock, before you check in with the guard and drive through the main gates; there's no inn here, only a variety of condominiums and private homes, ensconced in lush semi-tropical foliage. It's quiet, secluded, very private. The best values for couples are the High Hammock Villas, clusters of two-story townhouses adjoining the golf course, where luxurious one-bedroom suites (equipped down to the very ironing board) cost $60 a night. Since they sleep four people, you could enjoy even better value if you took along a compatible couple. Villas H, I, L, O, and P of this group are close to boardwalk decks on top of the dunes—perfect spot for sunset watching. For $110 a day you get a dreamhouse—a Beach Club Villa, handsomely designed, handsomely furnished, handsomely located on the quietest part of Seabrook's 3½-mile beach, facing the North Edisto River and the shrimp boats. These Beach Club Villas have *three* bedrooms; if you wanted a bargain in this case you'd have to round up *two* compatible couples, but make sure *you* get the upstairs bedroom with the private sundeck.

Seabrook is strictly a place for enjoying the open air—crabbing, searching for sand dollars, bird watching, swimming, and turtle watching (Seabrook is the nesting ground of the great loggerhead turtle). The hub for socializing is the Beach Club—pool, snack bar, cocktail lounge, and an air-conditioned dining room ruled over by a chef who's a stickler for freshness, so you can never be quite sure what's on the menu; but chances are you'll be able to sample the local seafood hauled ashore on the boats you see going up and down the North Edisto River.

NAME: Seabrook Island

INNKEEPER: Richard L. Erb

ADDRESS: P.O. Box 436, John's Island, S.C. 29455

DIRECTIONS: 25 miles southeast of Charleston; by car, Interstate 26 to U.S. 17, then follow the signs along State Highway 20; by Amtrak or air to Charleston ($20 per couple one-way by limousine).

TELEPHONE: (803) 559-5521; out-of-state toll-free (800) 845-5531

ROOMS: 200 in various formats in villas and townhouses

RATES 1978: EP, $60 for 1-bedroom villas to $110 for villas sleeping 6; plus 15% service charge on food and bar bills, $1 per day for maids, 4% tax on total bill.

MEALS AND ENTERTAINMENT: Breakfast 7:30 a.m. to 8 *p.m.*, lunch 12–2, dinner 7, 8, 9 (approx. $20 to $25 for two); no room service; jackets in the evening; piped music in the dining room, occasional live music.

DIVERSIONS: Freshwater pool, walking trails, crabbing (gear available); tennis (6 fast-dry courts, $2.50 per person per hour, pro shop, ball machines, practice areas, clinics), golf (18 holes, $10 per round), bikes ($1 per hour, $5 per day), Hobie monocats for rent, horseback riding (trail rides $7, sunset rides, sunrise rides, jump trails available but only with proper garb).

P.S. Dick Erb, one of America's most experienced resort managers, took over the running of Seabrook just as this guide was going to press, so you can expect a few changes and improvements by the time you get there.

Hilton Head Inn and Sea Pines Plantation
Hilton Head Island, S.C.

Not Conrad—William. William Hilton was the English sea captain who discovered the island back in the 1600s. At one time it was all plantations, forty-five square miles of rice and cotton and loblolly pines; now Hilton Head is pine-to-pine resort, with golf courses by the dozen and tennis courts by the score.

The Sea Pines Plantation company started the fashion a decade ago, and the most popular corner of the island is still this 5200-acre resort community, the entire southern tip of Hilton Head, surrounded by four miles of white beach, criss-crossed by marshes and lagoons, looking and feeling appropriately semitropical under palmetto and bamboo and live oaks with mossy whiskers. There are hammocks under the trees, boardwalks across the marshes, environmental beach walks and a 572-acre forest preserve that's home to a galli-maufry of winged creatures—hawks, eagles, quail, dove, and ibis.

SPORTS GALORE. Jack Nicklaus designed one of the plantation's three courses, Arnold Palmer designed another, and the Harbour Town links has been called "one of the ten greatest tests of golfing skill in the world" by a leading golf magazine. There are more than four dozen tennis courts within the plantation alone and a local resident, Stan Smith, is the head pro. You can go riding, hiking, swimming, crabbing, shrimping, or sailing, and there are no fewer than four hundred bikes available for rent. Not many resorts can offer you such an abundance of facilities, but probably even fewer dangle so many types of accommodations before your eyes.

First, the inn. The Hilton Head Inn was the first hotel on the island (in the early sixties), but it's been enlarged and remodeled in recent years; some of the two-story brick-and-cypress wings have sprouted an extra story, and the main lodge has a new Crow's Nest Lounge with crow's-nest views of the beach and ocean. The inn's 204 guest rooms (new and original) have been decked out with beachy colors and contemporary paintings and prints, but they also have several *practical* attractions. For a start, they're more spacious than normal, with separate dressing areas and bathrooms, a balcony or patio with chairs and occasional table for breakfast alfresco; other features include coffee makers, wet bars, and in most cases refrigerators. Add a sitting room to these standard features and you have a Cottage Suite, most of them secluded among the foliage, a shade more private than the regular rooms. The inn is right at the entrance to the plantation proper, a short ride by bike or free shuttle bus from the main plantation activities.

If you prefer to be closer to these activities, rent a room, suite, townhouse, or villa inside the plantation. There are a thousand or more options, all built within the past decade, finished in cedar and cypress to blend with their surroundings, most of them equipped with kitchens, wet bars, refrigerators, television, the larger suites and villas with dishwashers, dryers, and other frills. Probably the most romantic of the plantation accommodations are the circular "tree houses" among the pine trees. Tennis players seem to prefer the Heritage Villas, adjoining the Racquet Club (the courts where, apparently, everyone wants to play, although they are the most expensive on the resort). If you're looking for a lively pseudo-Portofino atmosphere, check into an apartment at Harbour Town, a circular harbor inspired by Mediterranean fishing villages, with half a dozen restaurants, outdoor cafés, and boutiques in chic colors—ivory, taupe, and salmon, to name a few.

I think my preference would be the section known as South Beach, a secluded self-contained nouveau hamlet at the very tip of the island, Calibogue Sound and beaches on one side, a placid cove on the other with marina, dockside Italian restaurant and a tavern in Nantucket style. All rather confusing, isn't it? Then just check into the inn (you have access to all the other facilities, and you can charge bills to your room), or write to Sea Pines Plantation for the brochure describing all the types of accommodations—sixteen categories in the plantation, five in the inn alone. Even Hilton can't beat that—Conrad, not William.

NAME: Hilton Head Inn and Sea Pines Plantation
INNKEEPER: Austin L. Mott III
ADDRESS: Sea Pines Plantation, Hilton Head Island, S.C. 29948
DIRECTIONS: The inn is 31 miles from Savannah, 95 from Charleston. By car, take U.S. 17 to the intersections of Ga. 170 or U.S. 278, then go east and follow the Hilton Head signs (once you cross the toll bridge you still have another 10 miles to go); continue to Sea Pines Circle, go left to Coligny Circle, then go right. By air, scheduled service to Savannah, then by limousine or air taxi service to the Island airport; by Amtrak, to Savannah.
TELEPHONE: (803) 785-5111
ROOMS: 204, including 28 Cottage Suites (plus the thousand-odd rooms, studios, and villas at Sea Pines Plantation)
RATES 1978: EP from $36 to $54 in spring, $36 to $56 in summer, $30 to $46 in fall; plus 5% tax on total bill.
MEALS AND ENTERTAINMENT: Breakfast 7–11, lunch 12–2, dinner 6:30–11 (approx. $15 to $20 for two), sandwiches during the day in the Crow's Nest Lounge, various other restaurants in Sea Pines Plantation; room service 7 a.m. to 10 p.m.; jacket in the dining room (reservations required); combo and dancing in two lounges. No liquor on Sundays.
DIVERSIONS: Three outdoor and indoor freshwater pools, putting green at inn; in the plantation, tennis (53 courts at several locations, 5 lighted, $6–$10 per court per hour depending on location, plus pros, ball machines, videotape, clinics), golf (3 18-hole courses, $12 to $18 per round), horseback riding, hiking trails, sauna and exercise rooms, sailing school (spring through fall), 400 bikes for rent.

P.S. Open all year, busiest Easter, July, and August, but you can play golf, tennis, and other sports at any time of the year; check for conventions.

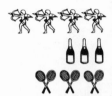

The Cloister
Sea Island, Ga.

You should really arrive at The Cloister in a shiny surrey topped by a tasseled fringe and pulled by a pair of frisky white horses. This is the quintessential plantation South, a dreamy other-worldly Eden where the Spanish moss dangling from the live oaks sets the pace for the whole island. The relaxed atmosphere begins at the main lodge, with its patios and plashing fountains, and wafts across manicured lawns to the five miles of superb private beach and 12,000 acres of unspoiled dunes, forests, and marshes. If you're on your first visit you'll be welcomed as someone they'd like to see back again; and the thousands who do come back year after year are welcomed with an enthusiasm that goes beyond fine old southern hospitality. There's a very special ambiance about The Cloister, closer to a country club than a hotel, closer to a country home than a club; credit the old-fashioned ideas of the owners.

KEEPING BEHIND WITH THE JONESES. A remarkable family with an unremarkable name, Jones, has owned The Cloister since 1928. They're a bit behind the times: they plow all their profits back into the hotel; they've expanded slowly because they never build an additional room until they have the cash in the kitty, and until they've had a chance to train extra staff and inculcate them with the special Cloister brand of service; and while other resorts point merrily to their new rooms and condominiums, the Joneses haven't cluttered their plantation with subdivisions. It may sound like a funny way

to run a hotel these days, but what the Joneses and their staff have created is one of the three or four finest resorts along the Atlantic Coast. Maybe *the* finest.

In many ways The Cloister is a perfect resort: it's detached from the everyday world, yet it's accessible; it basks in a delightful climate the year round; it's immaculate (the staff takes tremendous pride in the place—like old family retainers rather than employees); it's well-groomed outside (the hotel employs fifteen gardeners and a hundred groundsmen, and even the lamps that light the trees at night are disguised as lily pads); because of its unspoiled acres you have a marvelous sense of freedom, of quiet spaces where you can wander off and do your own thing; it's restrained and soft-spoken, but far from stuffy (when New Year's Eve in 1972 fell on a Sunday, a day on which Georgia law forbids the sale of liquor, The Cloister celebrated the Hong Kong New Year, twenty-four hours early, and then topped off the shindig with a pantry raid in the wee dry hours of Sunday morning).

DINING IN, OUT, ON THE BEACH. The Cloister mollycoddles you when it comes to dining. Where would you like to have breakfast? On your patio (with linen tablecloth), in the dining room, at the beach club—or a late breakfast in the Solarium with its two huge cages of parakeets and finches. Lunch? Dining room, beach club, golf club—or a picnic in a quiet grove screened by Spanish moss. Afternoon tea? In the Solarium. For dinner you can choose the dining room and the serenading of a string orchestra (it's a huge Y-shaped dining room so the music won't overwhelm the meal), or you can join an oyster roast on the beach. Best of all, call room service and have the waiter bring your dinner over by bicycle; then, if you're staying in a beachfront villa, you can finish your bottle of Pouilly-Fuisse on the balcony, the air soft and balmy, the palms riffling in the breeze and a full moon shimmering on the surf.

The beachfront villas are the first rooms to be filled (the other seventy-two rooms are in cottages or the main building), but spend a few days at The Cloister even if you have to take a chauffeur's room. And even if you have to arrive in a newfangled horseless carriage.

NAME: The Cloister

INNKEEPER: Ted Wright

ADDRESS: Sea Island, Ga. 31561

DIRECTIONS: By car, via Interstate 95 and U.S. 17 from the north, via U.S. 25/84/341 from the west, then join the causeway at Brunswick (about 10 miles from Sea Island). By air, scheduled services to Brunswick or Jacksonville (75 miles); by Amtrak to Thalmann (30 miles); limousine service from airports or station.

TELEPHONE: (912) 638-3611; out of state toll-free (800) 841-3223

ROOMS: 234 rooms, 100 suites (plus luxurious private homes available for rent by the week)

RATES 1978: AP only, from $84 to $148 through May 31, from $74 to $140 June 1 through November 30, from $76 to $112 December 1 through February 28; plus 10% of room rate (minimum $9) per day service charge, plus 3% tax on total bill.

MEALS AND ENTERTAINMENT: Breakfast 8–9:30 (to 10 Sunday), lunch 12–2 (to 4 at golf club), dinner 7–8:30; room service during meal hours; jacket for lunch, jacket and tie for dinner (in the dining room); combo and dancing in the dining room, harp concerts and other recitals.

DIVERSIONS: Two outdoor pools, beach club, hiking trails, miniature golf, lawn bowling, bikes for rent, tennis (18 courts, no lights, $6 per court per hour, pro shop, clinics), golf (two 18-hole, four 9-hole courses, $11 per day), horseback riding ($6.50 first hour), skeet, sailboats for rent.

P.S. Peak season is spring, quietest fall and winter (except for Christmas and New Year); some conventions in winter.

The King and Prince Hotel
St. Simons Island, Ga.

This Spanish *palacio,* by the edge of a splendid beach on the largest of Georgia's Golden Isles, opened its doors in a classic feat of bad timing, on July 4, 1941. It didn't get into its stride until after the war, when it became one of the traditional spots for vacations in these parts; now it seems to be holding its own under new ownership and management. Most of the gracious atmosphere has been retained (in some cases by popular demand—when central heating and air conditioning were installed, regular guests insisted that the old blade fans be retained, which they have, even if some of them no longer work). The Sidney Lanier Room is still a sunny, elegant lounge with Queen Anne and Chinese Chippendale furniture; the patios have been replanted with oleanders and azaleas; dining is still a pleasant experience surrounded by the stained glass of the Delagal Room. A covered walkway has been converted into eight cabana suites with sunken living rooms and entrances directly onto the beach. The remaining eighty-odd rooms are spread over three floors, all with private bathrooms, air conditioning, room phones, color TV, and those operative or inoperative ceiling fans. There's an unusual Bridal Tower (room #300), a pink-and-green circular room at the top of a spiral stairway, with a semiprivate entrance to the beach and an almost-360-degree panoramic view of the ocean.

The new management has just completed a new sports facility, the St. Simons Island Club, which has a golf course, saunas, and exercise rooms, plus an additional dining room and veranda for cocktails. Even so, a prince and count rather than king and prince.

NAME: The King and Prince Hotel

INNKEEPER: Edward B. Brophy

ADDRESS: 201 Arnold Road, St. Simons, Ga. 31522

DIRECTIONS: By car, follow U.S. 17 or U.S. 341 to Brunswick, then follow the causeway to the island and follow the signs to the K&P; by air, to Brunswick (scheduled flights) or to McKinnon Field on the island; by Amtrak to Thalmann (30 miles away).

TELEPHONE: (912) 638-3631

ROOMS: 94 rooms, 4 suites

RATES 1978: EP, $24 to $55 all year; plus 3% state and 3% county tax on total bill.

MEALS AND ENTERTAINMENT: Breakfast 8–10, lunch 12–2, dinner 6:30–10 (approx. $14 to $20 for two); room service during dining-room hours; appropriate casual dress; piped music or live music in the Frederica Tavern. No liquor on Sunday.

DIVERSIONS: Outdoor freshwater pool, beach, tennis (3 courts, no lights, $1 per guest per hour); at the hotel's Island Club, about 10 minutes away, golf (18 holes, $10 per round), sauna and exercise rooms; horseback riding and bicycles nearby.

P.S. A summer resort primarily, but open all year and a welcome break in winter if there are no conventions in the
house.

Greyfield Inn
Cumberland Island, Ga.

Cumberland Island is not of this world. It exists somewhere
between Atlantis, Bali Hai, and the Garden of Eden, eighteen
miles of wilderness, of sea oats, marsh grass, forests of wi-
zened live oaks, and beaches a couple of hundred yards wide.
Alligators wallow in the marshes, wild boars snuffle around
among the trees, and wild horses canter through the fields,
their manes flowing in the wind, like pent-up poodles let off
the leash in the park. The island's human population is
twelve; you can walk a hundred yards here, pick out a sheltered dune, and slip out of your swimsuits without having to
crane your necks every five minutes. This is pure escapism.
You can reach Cumberland only by ferry or chartered plane.
Fly over and you'll get a bird's-eye view of the gray-green,
gray-white island as you come in to land. Your pilot circles
the inn to alert the innkeeper that a guest is arriving; you
approach the vague landing strip, and hope the boars will get
out of the way before you land. A few minutes later, Elizabeth Blount comes jouncing along in a beat-up jeep and
jounces you back along overgrown lanes, and across the
dunes to the inn.

If Greyfield didn't exist, Tennessee Williams or Somerset
Maugham would have invented it: a slightly decaying, peel-
ing, three-story plantation mansion in a grove of live oaks,
with a flight of stairs rising from the hitching posts up to the
veranda. There's a spooky quality to the garden, and inside,
the inn is creaky and ancestral.

Guests are welcomed in a parlor brimming with family clutter—ivory-inlaid chairs, rolltop desks, a shell collection, silver candlesticks, bulky scrapbooks with yellowed curling pages. But these are no ordinary family heirlooms: it's a Carnegie silver pot your tea is poured from, and it's a Carnegie sofa you're sitting on.

Greyfield was built in 1901 as a summer home for the family of Thomas Carnegie, brother and partner of Andrew, and it's been in the family ever since. In 1966, Lucy Ferguson, the current head of the clan and granddaughter of Thomas (you may meet her, and she has some tales to tell), decided to invite paying guests from their wide circle of friends. It's still pretty much a family affair, but they now take in a few guests from beyond their immediate circle. In fact, you may be asked to send references with your reservation. Send them; Greyfield is worth a ten-page résumé. There's nothing like this anywhere else along the entire coast.

To their undying credit, Carnegie's descendants haven't tried to jazz up the old home. The rooms are still those of a well-to-do family's beach home, and the rooms still have the names the family gave them—"Statesman's Choice," "Mr. Buzzer," "The Artist's Room." Some of the rooms have private baths, most of them don't. There's no television, no pool, no tennis court, no golf. Not even a bartender; when you want a drink you go and mix it yourself, and pay for it on the honor system.

ROAST SUCKLING PIG AND QUAIL. You dine family style off the Carnegie mahogany table. The meals don't try to be gourmet; the kitchen makes do with what's around the island—oysters, clams, mullet, flounder, shrimp, occasionally roast lamb or roast beef. One evening you may have roast suckling pig, another the island's unique quail. Before dinner, retire to the snug library and skim through a volume from the collected works of Abraham Lincoln; after dinner, sip a nightcap out on the veranda beneath the moon.

It's strictly a back-to-nature existence on Cumberland Island. Digging for clams. Building sand castles. Kicking the surf at each other. Swimming, sunning, shelling, surfing. Riding in a one-horse shay. But on an island as serene as this, lovers don't need prompting; they know what to do, and they have all the time in the world to do it.

Maybe.

"Cumberland Island is the nation's foremost example of an unspoiled wilderness island," said Georgia's governor, with the best of intentions. All the property on the island is owned by only a few families, and when one landowner tried to sell off some lots, the state stepped in and had the island declared a National Seashore. Now 70 percent of Cumberland Island is owned by the National Parks Service, which plans to preserve the nation's foremost example of an unspoiled wilderness island by introducing ferry services for an anticipated 10,000 beer-can-tossing trippers *a day* ("currently three hundred a day and that's bad enough," sigh Cumberland Island fans). The only people allowed to stay overnight on the island will be campers, and Greyfield, as an inn, may join the other Carnegies as a pleasant memory. Hurry.

NAME: Greyfield Inn

INNKEEPER: Elizabeth Blount

ADDRESS: P. O. Box 878, Fernandina Beach, Fla. 32034

DIRECTIONS: On Cumberland Island, Ga., a few miles off shore; get there by National Park Service boat out of St. Mary's, Ga., by the R. W. Ferguson ferry or Greyfields ferry out of Fernandina Beach, Fla., by private boat to private dock (inn guests only); by charter plane or helicopter and put down in a field.

TELEPHONE: (912) 496-7503 (mobile phone)

ROOMS: 12, including 1 suite, plus 2 cottages

RATES 1978: AP $100 year round; plus 15% for gratuities, and 3% tax on total bill.

MEALS AND ENTERTAINMENT: Breakfast 8:30–9:30, picnic

style lunch, hors d'oeuvres (at the bar, on the house) 6, dinner 6; no room service; dress at dinner "from sports coats to jacket and tie, but no blue jeans."

DIVERSIONS: Beach, dunes, croquet, shelling, tours of mansions and graveyards, fishing, biking, hiking and (maybe) horseback riding.

P.S. Spring and fall are the best times to be here.

Amelia Island Plantation
Amelia Island, Fla.

The plan here is to check into a Pool Villa. In the morning, you step from bed, tiptoe across the wall-to-wall, push aside the glass doors, and plop into a private pool. Forget about swimsuits; palmettos and sabal screen you from the marsh and the wild ducks and ospreys. After your wake-up dip, you can breakfast *au naturel* on your private screened patio; there's no room service here, but you have a complete kitchen at your disposal. If you'd prefer to wake up to glistening vistas of dunes and ocean, check into one of the inn rooms. These would be attractive love nests even if they were looking into the parking lot: contemporary colors and paintings, stylish resort furniture, four-bladed ceiling fans (and air conditioning), wet bar and refrigerator, separate dressing area and bathroom *and* toilet, *plus* a sun deck or balcony with live seascapes beyond. You could also choose from dozens of townhouses and villa suites, because Amelia Island Plantation, in case you haven't already guessed, is another of those planned communities that make an honorable effort to respect and enhance the environment. Wooden walkways weave through a sunken forest of live oak and laurel oak; observation decks stand watch at strategic locations so that you can admire the wildlife (half of this 1800-acre plantation has been set aside for conservation). Step across the walkways to the beach and you can walk a mile or two in either direction without passing a building higher than the trees. (Unfortunately, not everyone in these parts has the same respect for the environment; the county allows motor vehicles on the beach, so you may share your morning jog with a camper truck or beat-up old Chevy. Fortunately, when the tide's out it's a wide, wide beach.)

BEAUTIFUL RACQUET CLUB. One of the outstanding features of Amelia (its *raison d'être,* even, if you happen to be tennis players) is the beautiful Racquet Club run by All-American Sports. Its nineteen composition courts are spaced in clusters of two or three among a grove of oak trees; the sunken center court with timber bleachers avoids the usual eyesore of tubular scaffolding; the clubhouse is designed in the contemporary cedar-and-cypress vogue, and it's all so pleasant you may just sit on its verandas all afternoon, watching the sun filter through the foliage. If you're here between September and May, you can polish up your game at one of the highly praised All-American clinics (one pro to every four students, working on each individual's existing game). There are special three-day programs for people who don't want to dedicate their annual vacations to tennis, and court time is free, when available, for players enrolled in the clinics. *If* you're here from September through May, a word of warning: don't put in a hard day on the courts and then rush back to your Pool Villa before checking to see whether your pool is *heated.* Brrr.

NAME: Amelia Island Plantation
INNKEEPER: Bill Elvins
ADDRESS: Amelia Island, Fla. 32034
DIRECTIONS: Take Interstate 95 to Fernandina Beach/Yulee exit, go east on A1A and Amelia Island Parkway, a distance of 29 miles from Jacksonville; by air to Jacksonville, where you can rent a National car and drop it off at

the plantation without a drop charge (which works out less than limousine service).

TELEPHONE: (904) 261-6161; toll-free outside Florida (800) 874-6878

ROOMS: 24 in inn, plus 275 rooms and suites in villas and townhouses

RATES 1978: EP, from $65 to $102 through May 26, $57 to $87 March 27 through November 15, $52 to $82 November 16 through February 28; plus 15% service charge on food and bar bills, and 4% tax on total bill.

MEALS AND ENTERTAINMENT: Breakfast 7–11, lunch 11:30–2:30, dinner 6:30–10 (approx. $20 to $25 for two), snacks at beach club and golf club house; no room service; jackets in the dining room in the evening; occasional live music, piped music in the dining room, a large TV in the inn lobby/lounge.

DIVERSIONS: Outdoor freshwater pool at beach club (plus a dozen other pools on plantation), sauna, exercise room, therapy pool, 5 miles of walking trails (mostly boardwalk, including a sunken forest), fishing in lagoons; tennis (19 composition, no lights, $4 per person per hour, pro shop, viedotape, ball machines, clinics run by All-American Sports Tennis Academy), golf (27 holes, Pete Dye design, $12 per round), bikes ($1.50 an hour), horseback riding ($10 an hour, on trails or beach), hayrides.

P.S. Open all year, busiest in spring, rainiest in July; some groups at other times of the year.

The Breakers
Palm Beach, Fla.

Walking into The Breakers' lobby you get something of the soul-soaring lift opera buffs get when they walk into the Met. All that marble. All those frescoes. All that gilt. All those glis-

tening, glittering, scintillant chandeliers. It's enough to make you launch into a duet from *Tosca*.

Oddly enough, Tosca and Cavaradossi and other lovers from the realm of opera might feel at home here, because the architect commissioned to design The Breakers way back in the twenties got so carried away with its oceanside location that he decided that the only thing to do it justice would be an Italian palazzo. But what he finally put together was a pastiche of Italian palazzi: the twin towers and arches of the exterior were inspired by the Villa Medici in Rome (which is rather like saying the Washington Monument was inspired by the Campanile in the Piazza San Marco); the ornate ceiling in the Gold Room was copied from the Palazzo Ducale in Venice; the frescoes in the lobby are based on those in the Palazzo Carega in Genoa; and so on, marble column after marble gilt column and frescoed ceiling after frescoed gilt ceiling. It may not add up to a true palazzo but it certainly is quite a place to show off your latest Puccis.

FROM MANSE TO MANSION. The Breakers is, in fact, a memorial, built by the trustees of the Flagler estate and dedicated to the creator of the Flagler millions. Henry Morrison Flagler was a poor boy who figured there had to be a better way of life than his minister father could offer in Hopewell, New York; so at 14 he left the family manse, went into business, and after a series of ups and downs joined forces with a man called John D. Rockefeller; together they formed a company that went on to prosper as the Standard Oil Company of New Jersey. Many years and many, many millions later, Flagler built railroads to the South that ultimately brought him to Palm Beach, and with remarkable vision was able to foresee that that expanse of swampland could become America's answer to Europe's Riviera. Everywhere his railway went, Flagler built a hotel; in Palm Beach he built two, both of which disappeared, but to commemorate the great man, the Flaglers built The Breakers in 1926. It's still owned and operated by the family.

How do you pass the charmed hours in surroundings of such opulence? Slip into your beach Pucci and shuffle down to the private beach. Or sample the hotel's beach club, said to be one of the most modern in the world: carpeted dressing rooms, sauna, massage, and your choice of pools—outdoor saltwater, indoor freshwater. The outdoor pool is surrounded by an outdoor restaurant with sky-blue patio furniture, the indoor pool by a restaurant with yellow patio furniture beneath a tent of tinted glass and hanging plants (a beautiful room—the Medicis would have loved it).

For something less languorous, try tennis or golf, water skiing, snorkeling, sailing or fishing; or take a bike and go riding through gardens filled to tropical excess and looking like nature's answer to all the gilt and marble indoors.

In the evening, dress up and treat yourselves to a slap-up dinner in the Rotunda—a great circular dining room reaching for the heavens in a dome of glass above a gigantic Venetian chandelier, and surrounded by mirrors, crystal and frescoes that make most other dining rooms look like pizza parlors. Then, if you've had the foresight to reserve a room in the new oceanside wing, you can top the evening off with

brandy on the balcony looking down on the real breakers—
the kind that lull you to sleep.

*And you certainly won't lose any sleep thinking about
the bill if you come to The Breakers in summer: this palatial
splendor, which will set you back at least $100, Modified
American Plan, in winter, will cost you only $34 (without
meals) in summer or early fall.*

Ah, but what's the weather like in Palm Beach in summer? Average maximum temperatures between June and
October range from 85 to 91 degrees. Perfect temperature for
a Pucci (and don't worry if it's not an original—the palazzo
isn't an original either).

NAME: The Breakers

INNKEEPER: John F. Clifford

ADDRESS: South County Road, Palm Beach, Fla. 33480

DIRECTIONS: From Interstate 95 or U.S. 1 go east on Palm
    Beach Lakes Boulevard or Okeechobee Road; by air to
    Palm Beach (30 minutes away by limousine) or by Am-
    trak to West Palm Beach.

TELEPHONE: (305) 655-6611

ROOMS: 600 rooms, 42 suites

RATES 1978: EP only in summer (June 1 to October 1), from
    $34 to $48; MAP only in fall (October 1 to December 1),
    from $80 to $110, and winter (December 1 to April 1),
    from $100 to $140; plus service charge of $9 per double
    room in spring, fall, and winter, and 4% tax on room and
    service charge.

MEALS AND ENTERTAINMENT: Breakfast 7–10, continental
    breakfast 10–11, lunch 11:30–3, dinner in two seatings
    at 6 and 8:30 (expensive); room service 7 a.m. to 10
    p.m.; jacket and tie at dinner; live music in Alcazar
    Lounge, dancing in the dining room.

DIVERSIONS: Indoor (freshwater) and outdoor (salt) pools,
    beach club, walking trails, lawn bowling, putting green,
    bicycles, movies, bingo, bridge, backgammon, tennis (12

courts, $3 per person per hour, pro shop), golf (2 18-hole courses, $15 per round).

P.S. Open all year, a beehive of millionaires in winter, an uncrowded, unhurried bargain in summer.

Boca Raton Hotel and Club
Boca Raton, Fla.

The *Saturday Evening Post* once called this "Florida's flossiest hotel," and Frank Lloyd Wright called its architect "little more than a scenic designer." Both critics have gone, but the Boca Raton keeps getting bigger and bigger.

The original 1926 hotel had a hundred guest rooms built in the style of a cloister around formal gardens; in 1928 the inn was bought by a tycoon named Clarence H. Giest, who had a penchant for wandering through the lobby in his bathrobe, and who added 300 more rooms; more recently another 257 rooms have been tacked on, in a twenty-six-story tower just east of the original cloister, on the edge of Lake Boca Raton, overlooking the Intracoastal Waterway. The hotel is no longer a quiet little hideaway, flossy or otherwise, but it's still true to the original affluent concept.

Many of the original antiques are still there—priceless then, more priceless than ever now: the wooden beams and carved wall brackets from the University of Seville, a splendid refectory table, a massive seventeenth-century credenza and gold-embossed mirror from Spain, countless artifacts from country churches in Guatemala. You'll dine here in a salon whose columns are covered with fourteen-carat gold leaf.

PLEASURE DOMES. If its architect was little more than a scenic designer, the story of its creation was downright horse opera. Addison Mizner had come to Palm Beach in 1918 in failing health, planning to spend his few remaining weeks or months on earth in one of earth's balmier corners; there he encountered another invalid ready to breathe his last, Paris Singer, the son of the Singer who invented sewing machines. Singer was not only prepared to breathe his last but also to spend his last, and together they concocted plans for the ultimate pleasure domes. Since neither of them died as soon as expected, they went on to build some of their dream palaces and Mizner became the most demanded architect in Florida. The Boca Raton is one of the offshoots of this strange partnership. It was originally called the Cloister Inn, and when it opened on February 6, 1926, there was such a dazzling array of tycoons, movie stars, and royalty on the doorstep that the hotel still keeps the guest register of that auspicious evening under glass in the main lobby.

But never in their wildest dying dreams did Singer and Mizner conceive something like the present-day Boca Raton Hotel. When you come here to please yourselves in this pleasure dome, you'll find a thousand acres of semitropical paradise with secret places among the angel trumpet, creeping gif, gumbo limbo trees, monkey apple, golden dewdrop, Spanish bayonet, screw pine, and shaving-brush trees. This being a millionaires' resort, you have everything at your fingertips. Tennis? Twenty courts. Golf? Four courses. Sunning? A mile of beach and a cabana club. Bikes? Bikes. Fishing? Boats and tackle and bait. Polo? Every Sunday afternoon from January through April.

But at $80 a day minimum you may prefer to spend most of your time in your own room, and that's not such a bad idea either: love nests don't come much plusher than this. Rooms #220, #221 and #222 in the original inn are probably still the most romantic in the hotel, but if it's grand gesture time, the celebration of a year-old affair or consummation of a day-old one, rent one of the executive suites in the new tower ($400-plus a night), or take over the entire Presidential Suite, with its private elevator, grand piano, step-down bath of Italian marble, and a leopard-skin chaise positioned to give you a dramatic view of the ocean and the feeling that you're king and queen of the castle.

If you want to be away from the mainstream, rent a villa alongside the golf courses—bedroom, parlor, kitchen, and balcony, within walking distance of the hotel.

NAME: Boca Raton Hotel and Club

INNKEEPER: L. Bert Stephens

ADDRESS: Boca Raton, Fla. 33432

DIRECTIONS: On the Inland Waterway, 45 miles north of Miami, between Ocean Highway (A1A) and U.S. 1, and between Palmetto Park Road and Camino Real; by scheduled air service to Fort Lauderdale or private/charter flight to Boca Raton Airport; by Amtrak to Deerfield Beach.

TELEPHONE: (305) 395-3000

ROOMS: 460 rooms, 40 suites, 200 villas

RATES 1978: MAP $110 to $175 to April 30, $80 to $175 from October 1 to December 16, special summer rates and EP rates on request; plus $10 per room per day service charge, and 4% tax on total bill.

MEALS AND ENTERTAINMENT: Breakfast 7–11, lunch 11:30–2:30, dinner 6:45–10; room service to 3 a.m. in winter; jackets for dinner; piano, 3 orchestras, and strolling minstrels every night.

DIVERSIONS: 3 pools, therapy pool, sauna, exercise rooms, parcours jogging track, putting green, fishing, skeet shooting, tennis (20 clay courts, 6 lighted, $5 per person per *day*, pro), golf (3 18-hole courses, $12 per day), cabana club on Atlantic (5 minutes from hotel) with ½-mile private beach.

P.S. Peak season from January 3 through Memorial Day, lots of conventions at other times.

Pier House
Key West, Fla.

"Long, boozy breakfasts," promises David Williams Wolkowsky, the Pier House's owner. Fresh tropical fruits, eggs
benedict, maybe a soufflé, served from seven in the morning
to three in the afternoon, beneath the lazy, long-bladed fan
and palm-frond roof of the new Tiki restaurant right on the
beach.

This beach is more or less the spot where the old Havana
ferry used to set sail for Cuba, which places the Pier House
right at the end of the Overseas Highway, in the very heart of
Old Key West, a shuffle away from the shrimp boats, Sloppy
Joe's, and other haunts of Ernest Hemingway. To get to the
Pier House, you have to cross a car park, but then to get to
the beach, you almost have to push your way through a garden of hibiscus, oleander, and coconut palms—none of which
prepares you for what is, as René D'Harnoncourt of New
York's Museum of Modern Art noted, "the most unusual
motel design in America." It's a modern habitatlike structure
of painted cinder blocks (not the most romantic material but
useful to have around you in a tropical storm) that gives
every room a patio or balcony, and almost all of them a view
of a multihued sea at the very spot where the Atlantic
caresses the Gulf.

The hundred rooms (no two are identical, but they all
have patio or balcony, color television, and air conditioning)
include a couple of duplex apartments and a penthouse built
over the Gulf, where you feel as if you're on a cruise ship,
with the sea lapping the pilings below the balconies. The
newest buildings are constructed around an indoor tropical
garden, giving you the feeling of being outdoors even when
you're in. Wolkowsky's own favorites are in the section
known as the Old Navy Officers' Quarters, which he has had

moved in as a part of his complex; there are six units here, including two on the second floor with two bedrooms each and a long porch running the length of the building and overlooking the pool, the gardens, and the Gulf.

The Pier House's facilities include a private beach, fresh-water swimming pool, rental boats, a lounge (the Chart Room). It has some features like free coffee and doughnuts in the morning and coin machines for soft drinks, ice, and snacks; it's also filled with all manner of surprises—an original watercolor by Tennessee Williams in the lobby, a glass case with a huge collection of birds dating back to the Audubon period, and a huge figurehead handcarved in Switzerland in the 1800s and rescued by Wolkowsky from a ship about to be scuttled.

The figurehead is not the only thing David Williams Wolkowsky has saved from scuttling or decay; he restored Captain Tony's (Key West's oldest bar, which had been owned by his grandfather and frequented by Hemingway), and helped preserve and develop Pirate's Alley, a picturesque old street of boutiques, cigar factories, restaurants and craft shops. All interesting spots to visit—if you ever finish breakfast.

NAME: Pier House

OWNER/INNKEEPER: David Williams Wolkowsky

ADDRESS: 5 Duval Street, Key West, Fla. 33040

DIRECTIONS: Keep driving until you run out of America; scheduled flights, more or less hourly, direct from Miami by Air Sunshine (currently $50 round trip, but check with National about special fares from New York, just $9 one-way more than Miami, with luggage checked all the way through).

TELEPHONE: (305) 294-9541

ROOMS: 101, about 20% of them suites

RATES: EP, $30 to $44 from mid-April to mid-December, $44 to $55 remainder of year; plus 4% tax.

MEALS AND ENTERTAINMENT: Breakfast to midafternoon, dinner 6–11 (approx. $20 to $30 for two) in a Victorian house 200 feet offshore; room service; informal dress (if you wear a jacket here, people may think you're from the Secret Service); junkanoo band on the beach 2 or 3 times a week, piano nightly in the lounge.

DIVERSIONS: Beach, pool; bikes, snorkeling gear, boats to reef; tennis and golf nearby.

FROM THE GREAT LAKES TO THE GULF

And when Love speaks, the voice of all the gods
Makes heaven drowsy with the harmony . . .

SHAKESPEARE

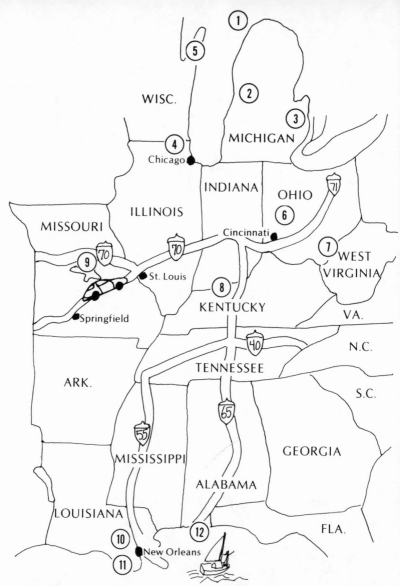

1. Grand Hotel (Mackinac Island)
2. Shanty Creek Lodge
3. Dearborn Inn Colonial Homes and Manor Houses
4. The Whitehall
5. White Gull Inn
6. The Golden Lamb
7. Wells Inn
8. The Inn at Pleasant Hill
9. Lodge of the Four Seasons
10. Hotel Maison de Ville and Audubon Cottages
11. The Saint Louis Hotel
12. Grand Hotel (Point Clear)

Grand Hotel
Mackinac Island, Mich.

The Grand is grand in every way. It's the world's largest summer-only hotel, with the world's longest veranda overlooking one of the world's longest suspension bridges. It flies more than a dozen rippling flags, is bedecked with boxes and boxes of marigolds and geraniums, and is surrounded by more than twenty-five thousand flowering plants and groves of cedar. You can sleep beneath a tear-drop chandelier in an outrageously spacious room, dine lavishly in a 250-foot mirrored ballroom with a view of the sparkling clear waters of Lake Huron, and enjoy the sort of service your great-aunt swore had disappeared.

Mackinac (pronounced Mackin-*aw* despite the final C) is America's Bermuda. A sparkling summer island ("open" mid-May to mid-October only), it's lush and hilly, dotted with bright white eighteenth- and nineteenth-century homes, a Revolutionary War fort, and remnants of John Jacob Astor's fur-trading operations.

It's accessible only by ferry or private plane, and transportation on Mackinac is *exclusively* by horse-drawn carriage or self-powered bicycle. When you arrive at the island you'll see your bags, and ten or twelve others, piled high on a bicycle basket to be skillfully pedaled up the hill to the hotel by a bright-eyed college student while you board a waiting phaeton to be driven there by a gallant top-hatted coachman. By day Mackinac is chock-a-block with day trippers buying moccasins and chocolate fudge (which seems to be the island's principal export item), taking pictures of the world's longest porch, and counting their traveler's checks to see if they can

afford the Grand's magnificent ten-table buffet lunch. But come evening, when the hotel sends one of its liveried door-men halfway down the hill to enforce the "after six" dress rules, it's then the grandeur of the Grand emerges. The sun takes a long time to set on this little island at 46 degrees North Latitude, where evening breezes are cool and laden with the scent of flowers. You join the after-dinner strollers on the porch as violins and a delicate piano invite you to dance in the Terrace Room. A carriage waits to take you on a sunset ride through the now quiet village, or you may choose to travel in a Palm Beach rolling chair or simply to sit and watch the stars come out from one of the little benches on the sloping lawn. Later, you'll wander to the gazebolike Grand Stand bar near the golf course, drawn there by the scent of fresh-brewed espresso and the possibility of sam-pling a liqueur-laced Grand Café. But there's no hurry as you stroll along, hand in hand; you pause a moment to greet the spirit of Isabel Archer returning from her evening walk with Phileas Fogg.

L.E.B.

NAME: Grand Hotel

INNKEEPER: Joseph M. Grantham, Jr.

ADDRESS: Mackinac Island, Mich. 49757 (from October to April, 222 Wisconsin Avenue, Lake Forest, Ill. 60045)

DIRECTIONS: By ferry, as many as 70 a day in midsummer, between Mackinaw City and the island; private and charter flights can land at Mackinac Island Airport, but the nearest commercial airfield is at Pellston, Mich., and from there you can take an air taxi service to connect with the ferries at Mackinaw City.

TELEPHONE: (906) 847-3331; or (312) 234-6540 from October to April

ROOMS: 262, including 2 large suites, the Governor's and the President's

RATES 1978: AP $82.50 to $130, May through September (closed rest of year); plus 15% service charge and 4% tax.

MEALS AND ENTERTAINMENT: Breakfast 8–9:45, buffet lunch 12–2, dinner 7–8:45; room service during meal hours, with snacks to 1 a.m.; "In accordance with Grand Hotel traditions, guests are requested to observe the following customs of dress; after six in the evening ladies are dressed in their loveliest for the enjoyment of many social activities; for gentlemen, sportswear and shirts with collars are most acceptable in all hotel areas during the daytime; after six in the evening neckties and jackets are required in all areas of the hotel. Leisure suits are permitted after six, but ties must be worn with such attire." Other entertainment besides dressing up includes piano bar, combos, dinner-dance orchestra, and occasional cabaret acts.

DIVERSIONS: Heated serpentine pool, sauna; tennis (4 courts, $5 per court per hour), golf (9 holes, $6 a day), bikes; riding, sailing, waterskiing, hiking, and fishing nearby.

Shanty Creek Lodge
Bellaire, Mich.

Shanty Creek is sports. Golf, tennis, skiing, fishing, swimming, water skiing, sailing, snowmobiling, canoeing, hunting, hiking, riding, boating, cycling, skeet shooting, mushroom hunting in the spring, berry picking in the summer, bowling, roller skating, badminton, croquet, horseshoes, volleyball and—some romance at last—dinner-dancing, sleigh rides, and saunas. Shanty Creek says it has The Whole World Waiting For You and bills itself as The Total Destination Resort. That may stretch a point, but this *is* a Caribbean resort and a Colorado ski area keeping company on a mountaintop in northern Michigan.

Originally, in the 1950s, Shanty Creek and its 1200-plus acres were paced off with the idea of creating a private club, an exclusive sports retreat for a select group of one hundred members. But inflation barked at the heels of the project; club became hotel and now chunks of the land are being sold as woodland home sites (with the result that suburban bungalows and pseudo-chalets are popping up like those spring mushrooms around the golf course and along the road to the trout pond).

Now, about the lodge. It's not an easy thing to say about a place that tries so hard to show you a good time, but you may find yourselves partaking of more of those out-of-the-room activities than you planned because Shanty Creek rooms just aren't romantic. Spacious, yes, with two big beds and a convenient dressing area with separate sink; but frankly, they're Holiday Inn-ish. Maybe it's just that a nice notion went wrong. You see, every room in the lodge—and the nearby Windcliff Lodges—has a sliding door picture window and private balcony; but if you don't have the front drive just below, or a phalanx of rooms on the wing directly opposite, you'll be facing the curious stares of the day trippers on the ski lift.

Except at night. When the place is finally quiet after the fresh-faced young entertainers have sung their last set in the lounge, when the moon is coming over the mountain and you can look down from your perch nearly a thousand feet above Torch Lake, Shanty Creek isn't hopeless. It's time for sports again.

L.E.B.

NAME: Shanty Creek Lodge
INNKEEPER: John Meeske
ADDRESS: Bellaire, Mich. 49615
DIRECTIONS: Off Mich. 88, between Bellaire and Mancelona, and well signposted; from Interstate 75 take Grayling exit and travel west on Mich. 72, north on County 571 to Mancelona (or, if arriving from the north, exit at Gaylord and follow County 42 west to 131 south to Mancelona); from Traverse City Airport, U.S. 31 northeast to Mich. 72, east to County 593, north along Torch Lake to County 620, east to Bellaire and from there south on 88 to the hotel. Phew!
TELEPHONE: (616) 533-8621; or toll-free in Michigan (800) 632-7118
ROOMS: 123, including 17 Lodge Suites and 32 double rooms in the Windcliff Lodges
RATES 1978: EP, $30 and $40 from March 15 through June 14, $36 and $55 from June 15 through October 14, $30 and $40 again from October 15 to December 14, $30 to $60 from December 15 through March 14; plus 4% tax.
MEALS AND ENTERTAINMENT: Breakfast 7:30–11 (to 10:30 on Sunday), lunch 12–2:30 (to 3 for Sunday brunch), dinner 6–9 weekdays, 6–10 Friday and Saturday (approx. $12 to $20 for two); room service during meal hours, beverages and sandwiches available "most of the time"; "at the evening meal jackets for gentlemen are not required but are desired, dresses and pant suits are the desired attire for ladies"; live music and dancing

nightly except Sunday in summer, mostly weekends in winter.

DIVERSIONS: Beach or pool swimming, hiking; tennis (2 courts, $1 per person per hour), golf (18 holes, $10 per round), skeet shooting, bikes; in winter, downhill and cross-country skiing, ice skating, snowmobiling, and ice fishing.

Dearborn Inn Colonial Homes and Motor Houses
Dearborn, Mich.

Rabbits hop round the corners of tidy Colonial cottages, gentlemen read the *Wall Street Journal* in wing chairs in the lobby, and children are dressed in starched pinafores and school blazers. The doors are solid mahogany and the hand-painted wallpapers and bargellolike carpets have lasted—and stayed bright—for more than forty years. This is a gracious inn, created by a remarkable man.

Henry Ford I built the Dearborn Inn in 1931 for the convenience of executives and dignitaries visiting Ford Motor Company. Here he expressed his love for the elegance of early American Georgian architecture and decoration and, by reproducing the Colonial homes of five famous Americans as additional accommodation space, found another outlet for his penchant to preserve America's historic buildings (best exemplified by his Greenfield Village across from the Inn).

But a hotel is only as good as its management, and Adrian de Vogel (or "Dutch" as he is known to some) is a manager in the best European tradition, having served in several of the world's finest hotels and passenger liners, prior to his twenty years at Dearborn. He's the one who *maintains* the graciousness and efficiency of the Dearborn Inn, who personally supervises the blending of every Colonial hue used in repainting and the subtle lighting that highlights the gracious decor. His menus are so American—in fact, so Michigan—you'd think the man in the front office came from Ann Arbor instead of Amsterdam.

Take any room available at Dearborn Inn (except those in the uninteresting Motor Houses), but try your darnedest to get one of the thirty-three rooms in the five Colonial Homes. They're charmers. You'll have a latch key to the front door and your room will be your own Colonial sitting room, with a mantelpiece, perhaps, a sofa or set of wing chairs and a reproduction of Oliver Wolcott's nightstand, Barbara Fritchie's fourposter, or a writing table like Edgar Allan Poe's. Unfortunately, you'll have a color TV anachronistically staring you in the face, but you'll have much more fun if you watch the frisky rabbits and squirrels out on the lawn.

L.E.B.

NAME: Dearborn Inn Colonial Homes and Motor Houses
INNKEEPER: Adrian A. de Vogel
ADDRESS: 20301 Oakwood Boulevard, Dearborn, Mich. 48123
DIRECTIONS: Dearborn is a suburb southwest of Detroit, halfway between downtown and Metropolitan Airport; once you reach Detroit area, follow signs for Greenfield Village, the Inn's neighbor on Oakwood Boulevard.
TELEPHONE: (313) 271-2700
ROOMS: 181, including 6 suites and 33 rooms in five Colonial Homes
RATES 1978: EP $33 to $40 all year; plus 4% tax.
MEALS AND ENTERTAINMENT: Breakfast 6–11:30 (7–12 Sunday), lunch 11:30–2 (Sunday brunch 10:30 to 6), dinner 5–10 weekdays, 5–11 Friday and Saturday (from $7 to $35 for two); room service during dining-room hours; informal dress; piano in the dining room weeknights, combo for dinner-dancing Friday and Saturday.
DIVERSIONS: Heated pool, shuffleboard, two free tennis courts; public golf course nearby. (Children have a separate play yard.)

The Whitehall
Chicago, Ill.

Here's a hideaway right in the heart of the Windy City that manages elegantly, seductively, and lavishly to combine the grandeur of a grand hotel with the intimacy and attentiveness of a small hotel. There's a refrigerator in every room, scales in every bathroom; the marble is Italian, the soap English, the plumbing American. A large bowl of apples and an all-knowing-but-never-tattling concierge greet you in the lobby; the chambermaid turns down your bed and leaves goodnight mints on the pillows; room-service waiters are on call around the clock. Sneak away to downtown Chicago. Take the phone off the hook, settle in, and live off room service.

Check into a Petite Suite and you may not even bother to switch on television, because the room dividers are floor-to-ceiling mirrors. Check into one of the four tower suites; in the Contemporary Suite even the canopy bed is chrome, and the white-and-silver wallpaper in the bathroom seems to have been inspired by a *Playboy* centerfold. Royalty would probably feel more at ease in the English Suite, with oriental rugs, parquet floors, and an antique geographer's globe that opens up to reveal a mini-bar. Katharine Hepburn reportedly raved about her $400-a-day apartment with its own kitchen, formal dining room, and roof terrace (where, if you prefer, the waiters will set your formal table for dinner, overlooking the lights of Chicago).

You don't have to go quite that far. Just check into any room, and make sure you call ahead to have the champagne chilling in your refrigerator.

L.E.B.

NAME: The Whitehall
INNKEEPER: Kevin Lloyd Malloy

ADDRESS: 105 East Delaway Place, Chicago, Ill. 60611
DIRECTIONS: On Chicago's elegant Near North Side, just off North Michigan Avenue (the Miracle Mile), one block from the Hancock Building, 3½ blocks from the lake.
TELEPHONE: (312) 944-6300
ROOMS: 226, including suites
RATES 1978: EP, $84 to $95 for rooms, $100 to $345 for suites; plus 8.1% tax.
MEALS AND ENTERTAINMENT: Breakfast 7–11, lunch 12–3, dinner 6–11 (approx. $30 to $35 for two); room service around the clock; jacket and tie in the dining room.
DIVERSIONS: Wallowing.

White Gull Inn
Fish Creek, Wisc.

This is probably the closest you'll find to a Cape Cod inn west of Detroit. Nothing fancy, mind you; and small. But cozy, clean, and very American.

On the front porch are two settees, an old cider press, and a bulletin board covered with local notices. Out back is a flagstone patio where any Monday or Thursday you can mingle with Fish Creekers at the Early American Buffet, sampling such old-fashioned fare as turkey dumpling soup, corn and clam pie, maple-baked carrots, glazed ham, and scalloped potatoes. Or join the throngs who book weeks in advance for the Door County Fish Boil dinners featuring Lake Michigan catch-of-the-day, boiled potatoes, homemade coleslaw, and home-baked cherry pie. Top that off with a frothy Milwaukee beer and you've had yourself a good helping of old Wisconsin hospitality.

After a pleasant meal in the coolness of a Door County evening, take a stroll around the trim little village of Fish Creek, down to the dock or over to Sunset Park. Sit by the fire in the parlor or retire to your little room that opens onto the second-story porch. There's a simplicity and quiet about Door County, and Fish Creek, and the White Gull Inn in particular. Let the rest of the world drift away on the evening breeze while you cuddle up together in a white iron bedstead like Grandma and Grandpa used to have.

L.E.B.

NAME: White Gull Inn
CO-OWNERS/INNKEEPERS: Andrew and Jan Coulson
ADDRESS: Box 175, Fish Creek, Wisc. 54212
DIRECTIONS: From Sturgeon Bay, gateway to Door County, take Route 42 to Fish Creek; go left at the bottom of the hill (Main Street) and the inn is across from Sunset Park.
TELEPHONE: (414).868–3517
ROOMS: 12, including 9 in the lodge and 3 in cottages, plus a 2-bedroom housekeeping cottage
RATES 1978: EP, from $17 to $22 in the lodge (with a weekly rate of 7 nights for the price of 5); cottages $35 a night, housekeeping cottage $145 a week (Saturday to Saturday only); plus 4% tax on room.
MEALS AND ENTERTAINMENT: Breakfast 7:30–11, lunch 11:30–2, dinner 6, 7, and 8 (fish boils $10.50 for two, Early American Buffet $11 for two); no room service; informal dress.
DIVERSIONS: Beach nearby.

The Golden Lamb
Lebanon, Ohio

¢

This is Ohio's oldest. Since it opened its doors in 1815, The Golden Lamb has hosted ten presidents (including U. S. Grant and John Quincy Adams), several writers (Charles

Dickens for one), and statesmen (De Witt Clinton and Henry Clay, among others). But when *they* stayed here they didn't have great trucks growling past the window at three o'clock in the morning. If the Lamb were out in the fields, it would be an ideal nook for lovers; as it is it's right smack in the middle of town, so it can only be recommended as a pleasant place to spend a night on the way to somewhere else. The rooms are charmers—all done in period furniture, many of them with private bathrooms, some with big fourposter beds and rag rugs, most of them with TV and air conditioning. Beware: people who drop in for dinner are invited to take a look at the guest rooms when the doors are open, so remember to keep yours closed (and to be on the safe side, keep it *locked* when you're using it). All the rooms are named for notables who've visited the inn, and even if you've never heard of Ormsby Mitchell ask for his room; it's pink and pretty with a pencil post bed, and it's on the quiet side away from the main street.

Diners at the Golden Lamb seem to outnumber staying guests by a thousand to one, and dining used to be a hassle, but now overnight guests get priority dinner reservations. The dining rooms are attractive in a ye-olde-tavern sort of way (apart from the intrusive piped music that does nothing to enhance the nineteenth-century atmosphere); the food is hearty and tasty, and the menus feature curiosities like Shaker sugar pie and prune and butternut fudge pie.

Right inn, wrong place.

NAME: The Golden Lamb

INNKEEPER: Jackson B. Reynolds

ADDRESS: 27 S. Broadway, Lebanon, Ohio 45036

DIRECTIONS: Halfway between Cincinnati and Dayton, 7 miles east of Interstate 75, 3 miles west of Interstate 71, and right in the heart of a 6000-population town.

TELEPHONE: (513) 932–5065

ROOMS: 18

RATES 1978: From $18 to $26 EP, year round; plus 4½% tax on total bill.

MEALS AND ENTERTAINMENT: Breakfast Sunday only, 8–10, lunch 11–3 (Monday to Saturday), dinner 5–9 Monday to Thursday, 5–10 Friday to Saturday, 12–8 Sunday; jacket and tie required in dining room; live music Friday and Saturday, 8–midnight.

Wells Inn
Sisterville, W. Va.

I can't think of any reason in the world for you to take a lover to Sisterville, but if by some disaster of navigation you find yourself driving along the eastern banks of the Ohio River, past the power plants and charcoal factories south of Wheeling, take heart. Before long you'll come to the Wells Inn, an oasis of tasteful Victoriana, where you can drink a grateful toast to Ephraim Wells, who built the inn in 1894, and to John Wells Kinkaid, who restored it a few years ago.

Sisterville is an old oil town, which once boasted 2500 wells, an opera house and a great deal of vice. That's what *was;* what *is* is a dreary little backwater of a town that happens to have a delightful little hotel filled with antique brass cuspidors, grandfather clocks, mahogany woodwork, flock wallpaper, and chandeliers. The thirty-six bedrooms have all been restored in period style—and there's nothing at all in town to keep you from tumbling into bed at seven o'clock in the evening.

If you're slipping off for a secret tryst, Sisterville is probably a good place to go—no one would dream of looking for you here.

NAME: Wells Inn
INNKEEPER: Max Taylor
ADDRESS: 316 Charles Street, Sisterville, W. Va. 26175

DIRECTIONS: On W. Va. 2, in the center of town.

TELEPHONE: (304) 652-3111

ROOMS: 36, with 4 suites

RATES 1978: $24 to $28 EP all year; plus 3% tax on room, food, and bar.

MEALS AND ENTERTAINMENT: Breakfast 7–10:30, lunch 11–3, dinner 5–8:30 (approx. $10 to $15 for two); dress informal; no room service; music in the lounge on Friday and Saturday.

DIVERSIONS: one 9-hole golf course nearby, by appointment only.

The Inn at Pleasant Hill
Shakertown, Harrodsburg, Ky.

This is an ironic choice for a lovers' hideaway—the restored village of a religious sect that banned sex, where boys and girls were never allowed to be alone together, and where the houses had not only separate dormitories for each sex but separate doors and stairs. Not surprisingly, the sect is all but extinct ("celibacy contributed to their undoing," as one commentator put it) but their village remains as a placid anachronism, a freeze-frame in the movie of history.

First, the location. Pleasant Hill is about twenty miles southwest of Lexington, which puts it right on the edge of Bluegrass Country, along a winding fence-lined lane. This, they say, is the only historical village in the country where you can spend a night in the original houses (not inns, but houses). Spooky? Only if total silence punctured by rattling windows and creaky floorboards turn you to Jello; if they do, just make a grab for each other.

The twenty-odd clapboard or birch houses in Shaker-town are neatly lined up on either side of an unpaved street which in turn is lined by picket-and-plank fences and mulberry trees.

RAG RUGS, TRUNDLE BEDS. The main lodge, Trustees' House, has been putting up guests since Shaker times, but you can also spend the night in, say, the Ministry's Workshop, or the East Family Sisters Shop (above the spinning and weaving rooms), or the East Family Brethrens' Shop (above the carpenters' tools and broom-making equipment). All the guest rooms feature the ascetic, precise, well-proportioned Shaker decor (it's like living inside a painting by Mondrian); plain walls trimmed with wood in brown or blue, plank floors with handwoven rag rugs, curtains in the Shakers' traditional "dogwood" pattern, stout twin beds (some of them trundles). The Shakers draped everything over wall pegs—sconces, clothes, mirrors, even chairs—and that's the way it is at Shakertown. (Note, by the way, that this creates a resonant acoustic, so take it easy or you may keep the neighbors awake, wondering if they're hearing the spirits of the former inhabitants at one of the "shaking" parties from which they got their name.) Concessions to the twentieth century include tiled bathrooms, air conditioning, fire sprinklers, and television sets (which are as jarring in this setting as a naked body must have been to a Shaker).

MARSHMALLOWS IN YOUR APPLE SAUCE. The Trustees' House has four dining rooms, including a summer porch with tall windows overlooking the garden, bare brick walls, and scrubbed wooden tables. The waitresses are dressed in authentic Shaker checked dresses, and Mrs. Kremer's menu is a combination of Shaker and Kaintuck cooking. Village hot breads and the relish tray come automatically. Thereafter you have a choice of four appetizers (including eggs in aspic on anchovy toast), five entrees (say, pork tenderloin, which comes accompanied by piles of fresh vegetables from the village garden, and applesauce with marshmallows). The five choices of dessert include chess pie and Shaker lemon pie—

which leave you feeling that at least the Shakers got *some* pleasure out of life.

There are no frivolities here like swimming pools and saunas. Instead you can go for long walks through the fields, or long drives through the Bluegrass Country; but spend at least one morning or afternoon visiting the village exhibits, buying Shaker-inspired gewgaws, and getting to learn something about these remarkable people. In some ways they were ahead of their time. They were pioneers in organic foods and the medicinal use of herbs; they invented several of the labor-saving devices we take for granted—the washing machine, for one; they were pacifists, women's libbers (they believed Christ would appear the second time as a woman), and in a sense they were doing something about the population explosion long before everyone else awakened to its threats. They themselves expected to survive by conversions and adoptions; but since they also had the work ethic with a vengeance, in the end they didn't have much to offer the younger generation. But they left quite a legacy here at Shakertown.

NAME: The Inn at Pleasant Hill
INNKEEPER: Ann Voris
ADDRESS: Route 4, Harrodsburg, Ky. 40330
DIRECTIONS: On U.S. 68, about 20 miles southwest of Lexington, about 8 miles from Harrodsburg.
TELEPHONE: (606) 734-5411
ROOMS: 60 rooms, 2 suites
RATES 1978: EP, from $21 to $35 all year; plus 5% sales tax on room and food.
MEALS AND ENTERTAINMENT: Breakfast 8:30–9:30, lunch 12, 1, and 2, Sunday 12:30, 1:45, 3:15, and 6, dinner 6 and 7:15 (approx. $14 to $18 for two); no room service; informal dress.
DIVERSIONS: Walking, sightseeing.

Lodge of the Four Seasons
Lake of the Ozarks, Mo.

There's only one place to stay in these parts and this is it. (The Lake of the Ozarks, for the record, is a manmade body of water surrounded by manmade honky-tonk.) Everything you could ask for on a vacation is a five-minute walk from your bed—an outdoor pool in a Japanese garden, and an indoor pool; a spa with saunas, whirlpool baths, massage, exercise rooms; sightseeing boat trips on the lake, boats for rent; golf, including a brand-new eighteen-hole Robert Trent Jones course; tennis, fishing, riding, hiking, water skiing, archery, games room; a private 680-acre shooting preserve; a Jerry Lewis movie theater. There are ample dining facilities—a lakeside coffee shop and a lavish circular restaurant called the Toledo Room, hosted by a maitre d' who'd be a credit to most restaurants in New York. After dinner you can whoop it up in the discotheque or nightclub with live entertainment.

LANAIS AND CASAS. The lodge's 220 rooms are spacious, comfortable, and equipped with telephones, television, and individually controlled heating and air conditioning. They're spread out through a four-story lodge, two four-story motel wings known as the Casadero, lanai rooms facing the pool and Japanese garden, and lakeside casas. The quietest rooms are the casas (except during the boating season, because they're right above the marina), or the Casadero rooms (which also have good views, and balconies for enjoying them).

This is a much better hotel than most people would expect to find out there in the Ozarks among all those hillbillies; in fact, you'd expect a colorful resort like this in Miami or San Juan rather than Missouri, and you may find yourself wishing that there was just a touch more of the hillbilly about the place. Even that the persistent piped music could be coaxed into playing Bluegrass now and again.

NAME: Lodge of the Four Seasons

INNKEEPER: G. Frederick Davis

ADDRESS: P.O. Box 215, Highway HH, Lake Ozark, Mo. 65049.

DIRECTIONS: 170 miles southwest of St. Louis; from Interstate 70, take U.S. 63 or U.S. 65 south, following the signs for Lake of the Ozarks and Bagnell Dam, then drive west 2½ miles from Business 54 to County HH; by air, from Kansas City or St. Louis to Lee C. Fine Airport, Lake of the Ozarks.

TELEPHONE: (314) 365-2381

ROOMS: 220 rooms, 7 suites

RATES 1978: MAP $390 to $570 per week all year (EP rates by the day are available on request); plus 15% service charge and 4% tax on total bill.

MEALS AND ENTERTAINMENT: Breakfast 7–11, lunch 12–3, dinner 5:30–10:30; room service; jacket and tie at dinner; live music and dancing in the nightclub.

DIVERSIONS: Heated outdoor pool, hiking trails, bowling, archery, trap shooting, bikes for rent, horseback riding ($4 an hour), tennis (6 courts, 2 with lights, $4 per court per hour, pro, ball machines, clinics), golf (18- and 9-hole courses, $12 per 18), sailing, waterskiing—all on the premises.

Hotel Maison de Ville and Audubon Cottages
New Orleans, La.

Even if you've never been there, you probably know from photographs what the typical Vieux Carré townhouse looks like—two-story facade with wrought-iron balconies, and a courtyard with slave quarters at the rear. The slave quarters at 727 Rue du Toulouse date from 1783 and may be among the oldest buildings from the days of the Spanish grandees; the elegant main house was rebuilt in the early eighteenth century, and was at one time the home of M. A. A. Peychaud, the ingenious apothecary who is said to have invented the cocktail. You could almost be persuaded that M. Peychaud still lived behind this grandly carved door and cut-glass window if it weren't for the gleaming brass nameplate announcing Hotel Maison de Ville.

Inside you step back a century or two to the days of the Spanish and French beau monde, into a miniature palace filled with antiques—a Biedermeier love seat in crushed velvet, an eighteenth-century bombe commode, a carved Louis XV trumeau. You may while away your nights of bliss in a Chippendale bed draped with French silk, or a double bed covered with a Belgian sable spread trimmed in black velvet, or twin beds with brass headboards for curling your toes around.

Three of the double rooms are in the slave quarters, connected by a careworn wooden staircase to the courtyard—a leafy, sun-dappled pocket park with a three-tiered cast-iron fountain trickling into a fish pond. This is pure Vieux Carré,

and to crown it all you can enjoy several felicities of service:
you get your shoes polished when you put them outside your
door; you have a concierge to attend to details—like reserving
a table for two at Brennan's; ice, mixers, soft drinks, and
newspapers are on the *maison;* breakfast arrives in your
room on a silver tray—freshly squeezed orange juice, freshly
brewed New Orleans coffee, freshly baked croissants. There
are only fourteen rooms in the hotel; it's no place to be if you
like spacious lobbies and roomy rooms, but if you like gems,
here's one.

Recently the gem acquired a new facet: a secret courtyard with half a dozen bungalows dating from the eighteenth
century, in "Santo Domingo" style, each with pastel stucco
walls, trim gardens, patios, and fountains. John James Audubon lived and painted here in 1821, hence the name—
Audubon Cottages. Each cottage has been carefully restored
and furnished with antiques, and has acquired a modern
kitchen stocked with wines, mixers, and fresh fruit from the
nearby French Market. The cottages are ideal for two or more
couples, but you can, if you prefer, reserve just one bedroom.

NAME: Hotel Maison de Ville and Audubon Cottages
INNKEEPER: William W. Prentiss
ADDRESS: 727 Toulouse Street, New Orleans, La. 70130
DIRECTIONS: In the heart of the Vieux Carré, a leisurely stroll
    from everything (but, for all that, quiet and secluded).
TELEPHONE: (504) 523-1189
ROOMS: 14 rooms, 3 suites, 5 cottages
RATES 1978: EP $55 to $70 all year, suites from $90, cottages
    from $100, including continental breakfast, morning and
    afternoon papers, afternoon tea or coffee, mixers and soft
    drinks, parking in an enclosed garage; plus 7% tax on
    room.
MEALS AND ENTERTAINMENT: Breakfast only, 7:30 to noon;
    room service 7 a.m. to 11 p.m. for drinks, snacks, and
    meals from nearby restaurants.
DIVERSIONS: Pool, sauna; bikes, tennis, boating nearby.
P.S. Open all year, quietest in summer; special rates for
    Mardi Gras and other events.

The Saint Louis Hotel
New Orleans, La.

A count might have lived here a century ago, greeting lovely crinolined ladies in the courtyard by the fountain. The fact is, there was a bottling plant here until a few years ago when William H. Henderson, a local entrepreneur who had always wanted a hotel like the Ritz in Paris, pulled the plant down and built this hotel. He spared few expenses—least of all in "aging" the facade to make it look like the sort of place a count might have entertained in a hundred years ago. The predominant color is cantaloupe (or "a melon-smoked-salmon shade" as one of the designers calls it), which is the color theme used in bed linen and table linen. The lobby looks like the salon of a Parisian townhouse, dominated by a century-old gilt mirror; beyond it French doors lead through to the inner courtyard (which, by a directive of the New Orleans Vieux Carré Commission, must represent 30 percent of any property).

Begin your stay at the Saint Louis in this delightful spot. Find a table beneath a slowly turning blade fan, order a cool drink, hold hands, and admire the banana palms, the golden rain tree, and the baby weeping willow. Then trot upstairs and ease into the cuddly terry towel bathrobes hanging in the dressing room. The eighty bedchambers are luxurious—furnished in the style of Louis XV or XVI, Empire or Directoire (reproductions, alas, but then people in cuddly terry towel bathrobes shouldn't expect everything). All the rooms have air conditioning, color TV, electric shoe polisher, and bidet. If you want to fork out $150 a night you can have the Presidential Suite—all the above plus a log fire, spacious patio, kitchen, dining room, two baths, and a bedroom with mirrored closets.

CANDLELIGHT AND PROFITEROLLES. One problem with New Orleans is that it has so many fine restaurants, and you feel you *must* eat in the legendary Galatoire's, Antoine's, or Brennan's; which is a shame because Le Petit Restaurant in the Saint Louis is a cozy nook with brick walls, blade fans, candlelight, and that lovely cantaloupe table linen. Specialties include pompano de chef, noisettes d'agneau, paupiettes de veau, and freshly baked *profiterolles* and *tarte aux pommes* (dinner here will cost you about $8 a head without wine—which is also reasonable, like $6 for a bottle of Mouton Cadet).

NAME: The Saint Louis Hotel
INNKEEPER: Carolyn L. Hughes
ADDRESS: 730 Bienville Street, New Orleans, La. 70130

DIRECTIONS: In the Vieux Carré, 2 blocks from Canal Street, and 3.5 minutes from Preservation Hall and its Dixieland jazz.

TELEPHONE: (504) 581-7300

ROOMS: 66 rooms, 11 suites

RATES 1978: EP, from $60 to $75 through spring and summer.

MEALS AND ENTERTAINMENT: Breakfast 7–10:30, lunch 11:30–2:30, dinner 6:30–10:30 (approx. $35 to $40 for two); room service; jacket and tie at dinner.

DIVERSIONS: New Orleans.

P.S. June through early September are the quiet months, weekends are quiet most of the year; there may be small groups in residence in winter, and you'd better book at least one year in advance for Mardi Gras.

Grand Hotel
Point Clear, Ala.

The Point is a giant V formed by two long strips of white sand beach surrounded by turquoise sea. Within the V you have 500 acres of pines, live oaks, and gardens, and, somewhere among it all, the Grand Hotel. There's an air of quiet elegance about the place, luxury without ostentation. The buildings are muted gray, with brick-and-timber interiors; the fifty bed-sitting rooms have wall-to-wall carpeting, color television, and terraces or balconies facing the gulf or the gardens.

What do you do on a sunny day in Alabama? Just about everything. You can plunge into the freshwater swimming pool (it's enormous—140 feet in diameter); suntan on the white sands; water ski; sail on the bay (there are Rhodes 19 daysailers for rent); play tennis; or ride a horse or tandem through the five hundred acres of pines and live oaks. In the evenings you can stroll over to Julep Point and enjoy the view, or a julep, or a seafood luau. If you have any energy left after the day's activities you can even do a spot of dancing under the stars. Take an after-dinner stroll on the white sands, sniff the soft air, and you could be in the Caribbean.

NAME: Grand Hotel

INNKEEPER: Jim Pope

ADDRESS: Point Clear, Ala. 36564

DIRECTIONS: Point Clear is 23 miles south of Mobile via Battleship Parkway and U.S. 98, and 49 miles west of Pensacola, Fla.; limousines will meet your plane at Mobile Airport on request; private planes can land at Fairhope Airport, 4 miles away.

TELEPHONE: (205) 928-9201

ROOMS: 170, with 25 suites, 10 villas

RATES 1978: Not available at press time, but expect them to be around $75 to $85 MAP in spring and summer; plus 15% service charge and 4% tax on total bill.

MEALS AND ENTERTAINMENT: Breakfast 7:30–9:30, lunch 12–2, dinner 7–9; room service during meal hours; jacket and tie at dinner; live music and dancing.

DIVERSIONS: Freshwater pool; tennis (10 courts, $2.50 per person per hour, pro, ball machines), golf (three 9-hole courses, $9 a day), bikes for rent, waterskiing ($12 an hour); horseback riding nearby.

P.S. Open all year, most popular in spring and fall, but the weather is not too warm in summer, not too chilly in winter, so consider those seasons also; small groups in winter.

IN AND AROUND THE ROCKIES

Trip no further, pretty sweeting,
Journeys end in lovers meeting,
Every wise man's son doth know . . .
SHAKESPEARE

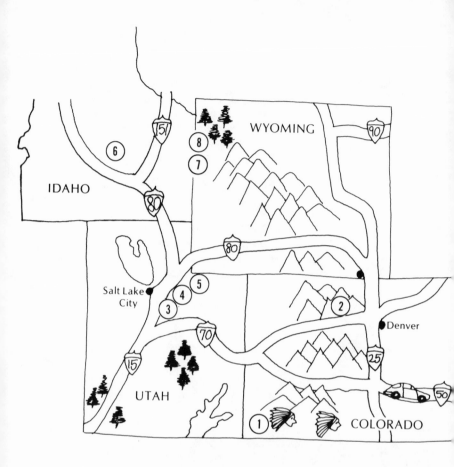

IDAHO

WYOMING

Salt Lake
City

Denver

UTAH

COLORADO

1. Strater Hotel
2. C Lazy U Ranch
3. Sundance
4. The Lodge at Snowbird
5. Alta Lodge
6. Sun Valley Lodge
7. Jenny Lake Lodge
8. Jackson Lake Lodge

Strater Hotel
Durango, Colo.

Here's another pleasant Victorian Revival in a town that's nowhere near as romantic as its name or history. Still, there's a lot to explore in the surrounding countryside, where four states (Colorado, New Mexico, Arizona, Utah) meet, so keep the Strater in mind as a refuge if you happen to be in this part of the world, any time of the year except perhaps April and early May.

This red-brick-with-white-trim hotel recently celebrated its ninetieth birthday but it's a spruce and spry nonagenarian, refurbished to re-create the elegance of its early years when miners and merchants fought in the saloon, and some fabled poker games took place in a back room that's now the accountant's office. Through the years its guest list has included luminaries such as Will Rogers, Lowell Thomas, and JFK.

Of the hotel's hundred TV-and-phone-equipped rooms, sixty-seven are Victorianized (the others are basic motel/hotel, because that's the way businessmen like them, and businessmen are a major part of the clientele). The pinnacles of opulence are suites #333 (king-size bed, writing desk, modern bathroom, TV nook with elegant Victorian sofa) and #322 (where you can play Victoria and Albert in an enormous hand-carved, half-tester bed or in a real old-time, free-standing, four-legged bathtub).

MELODRAMA AND OLIO. The Strater has its own Diamond Circle Theater, a 300-seater establishment where $10 will buy you a pair of tickets for a three-act show of melodrama, olio, and vaudeville. *Time* magazine called it one of the three best shows of its kind in the country—and you'll have to take *Time*'s word for it unless you make a reservation for the theater (open from Memorial Day to Labor Day only) when you reserve your room. Likewise if you want a ride on the other attraction that brings five thousand visitors per summer day to Durango—the hair-raising, breathtaking, mountain-clinging ride on the narrow-gauge Denver and Rio Grande Railway. Don't say you weren't warned—five thousand visitors a day. That's a good crowd if you're a Will Rogers looking for an audience or a JFK looking for votes, but if what you have in mind is a quiet, romantic little nook you'd better reroute your trip.

NAME: Strater Hotel

INNKEEPER: Earl A. Barker, Jr. (general manager), Patrick Gleason (resident manager)

ADDRESS: 699 Main Avenue, Durango, Colo. 81301

DIRECTIONS: The town is on U.S. 160, the so-called Navajo Trail, and the hotel is on the main thoroughfare, a couple of blocks from the railroad station; scheduled air services to La Plata County Airport.

TELEPHONE: (303) 247-4431

ROOMS: 94, with 3 suites

RATES 1978: EP, $22 to $30 from May 16 through October 16, $20 to $28 remainder of year, special ski packages; plus 5% tax on total bill.

MEALS AND ENTERTAINMENT: Breakfast 6–11, lunch 11–5, dinner 5–10 (approx. $12 to $20 for two), with some seasonal variations; room service during dining-room hours; dress optional; honky-tonk piano in the saloon, singing waiters and waitresses in the Opera House Restaurant in summer.

DIVERSIONS: No sports facilities in the hotel, but in the neighborhood there are tennis courts, golf courses, bikes and horses for rent, and skiing at Purgatory, 30 miles north of town.

C Lazy U Ranch
Granby, Colo.

What this ranch has going for it is its lazy-making setting—a sheltered valley of meadows and pines and streams, eight thousand feet up in the Continental Divide.

It's a real-life working ranch, and in June you can watch the roundups; at other times you can attend nearby rodeos and county fairs. Most people come here, however, for the riding, since it's free. There's a horse for every guest, and once you pick a mount to suit your skills, it's your personal horse all the time you're there. If you can afford to ignore the fact that you're paying for horses but still don't want to ride, you'll find plenty of other pastimes to keep you occupied—a heated pool, Ping-Pong, fishing, a skeet range, horseshoe pitching, a jogging track, and a couple of new tennis courts. There are miles of walking trails to lonely groves, and unlimited spectacular sightseeing if you want to go for a drive. If you're here in the snowy months you'll find winter horseback riding, ice skating, snowshoeing, sleigh rides, and hot buttered rum before the big fire in the main lodge.

The ranch consists of a big red-roofed lodge facing a lake and flanked by smaller guest cottages. The six rooms in the lodge are the originals, and the most charming. The other rooms are spacious and decked out with "custom-built functional furniture," but they have little personality. (The Mobile Guide consistently gives C Lazy U a five-star rating and calls it luxurious; the Ritz in Paris is luxurious, the Santa Barbara Biltmore is luxurious, but the C Lazy U Ranch is comfortable and pleasant—which is really all you ask of a working guest ranch.)

What happens in the evenings? You seem to spend most of the time eating wrangler-sized meals; but the ranch prides itself on its friendly, first-name atmosphere, and if you feel like mixing you'll find conviviality, cocktails, and a Baldwin grand piano. Forget the conviviality, get to bed early, and get up early to enjoy the mountains and the meadows. Or just B lazy old U.

NAME: C Lazy U Ranch

INNKEEPER: Wright M. Catlow

ADDRESS: Box 378, Granby, Colo. 80446

DIRECTIONS: From Denver, take Interstate 70 and U.S. 40 to Granby, continue a couple of miles to Colo. 125, then go north for 8 miles; from Rocky Mountain National Park, take U.S. 34 to Granby, then go west on Colo. 125; $50 charge (for two) if you're picked up in Denver.

TELEPHONE: (303) 887-3344

ROOMS: 12 rooms, 24 suites

RATES 1978: AP by the *week*, $650 in June and September, $750 in July and August (check with the ranch for specific dates, and rates at other periods); plus 10% service charge and 3% tax on total bill.

MEALS AND ENTERTAINMENT: Breakfast 7:30–9, lunch 1, dinner 7; no room service; dress optional; occasional square-dancing evenings in summer.

DIVERSIONS: Horseback riding and tennis (2 courts) included in rates, heated outdoor pool, sauna, hiking trails, skeet, fishing, table tennis, pool; golf, skiing, sailing, and waterskiing nearby.

Sundance
near Provo, Utah

Shangri-la is Chinatown at rush hour compared to this: a grove of quaking aspen and pines serenaded by a babbling brook, watched over by the Wasatch National Forest and towering Timpanogos Mountain. You wander along pathways lined with kinnikinnick, drink fresh spring water, and share 4300 acres of wilderness with inquisitive deer and pot guts (Rocky Mountain ground squirrels). Since there are only nine houses on the estate, you can go from breakfast to dinner without seeing another human.

If you want to know precisely how ravishing Sundance is before you go barreling out to Utah, see *Jeremiah Johnson*. It was filmed there. (And just for the record, the resort was known as Sundance long before Robert Redford made *Butch Cassidy and the Sundance Kid*, and he and his buddies bought up the place.)

The place is a marvel of unspoiled tranquility, partly because of the setting, partly because when Redford and his posse rode in they laid down firm laws: chop one tree, plant two; hide all buildings among the trees; no hunting, ever.

Until six years ago, there wasn't much here except a short ski tow, thousands of trees, and the pot guts; there still isn't much. So what is Sundance? Hard to say. It's sort of a ski resort, but it certainly isn't a hotel—to stay there, you rent one of the nine private vacation homes (cabins, they modestly call them) dotted among the trees. There are no hotel services, except daily maid service.

BOSKY LOVE NESTS. All nine "cabins" are different, and there's no way of knowing which one will be available when you get there. When you arrive, ask Brent Beck to take you on a tour to show you which homes are free. With luck he'll offer you the Magelby Home. This one is named for a local artist who traded his artistic skills for a plot of land, and then built himself a Hansel-and-Gretel cabin of rough-hewn timbers and filled it with stone fireplaces, wood paneling from an old barn, a couple of cuddly bedrooms (one with a fireplace), and antiquey things like old ice skates, a retired bear trap, and an antiquated pedal organ. It's positively the most romantic spot in Utah, and if you hurry you may be able to rent it for $50 a night (in summer).

A slightly larger house higher up the hill belongs to an

anonymous Hollywood person, who designed it and even did a lot of the chopping and sawing himself. A labor of love for love's labors: all pine and glass, with wrap-around veranda, a kitchen the size of the entire Magelby Home, two bedrooms, bathrooms, and sauna. As if that weren't enough, he then erected a crow's-nest balcony halfway up the living room, padded it with carpet, and installed a hi-fi and a sofa where you can lounge yourself into euphoria just looking at the trees and listening to the music, but chances are you'll think of lots of other things to do at that idyllic elevation. Also $50 a night in summer.

Although Sundance is basically a ski resort, there's plenty to do here in summer and fall. For a start, those 4300 acres are great for walking and picnicking. There's a stable with thirty-five horses ($4 an hour), and you can go trotting off on your own without taking a wrangler along—or with a wrangler, on an overnight pack trip into the backwoods. There's no pool (but you can drive to one of the lakes in the neighborhood for swimming and waterskiing), and no tennis (although sixteen courts are promised).

Otherwise, Sundance has a main lodge that includes a village store, snack bar, and restaurant. The snack bar's most gobbled lunch is a giant hunk of freshly baked bread smothered with melted butter and honey. It costs twenty-five cents apiece, and has enough calories for an entire meal, and if you're not careful you may end up looking like a pot gut. Dinner is served in the Tree Room, which has a Douglas fir growing through the roof, Navajo rugs, and stills of *Jeremiah Johnson* on the wall. The steaks and seafood are so good here, people drive over from Salt Lake City for dinner—and the Sundance outdoor theater.

BORDELLO BANDITO. The irrepressible people who run Sundance have built themselves an unusual open-air theater, where they put on plays and musicals which they compose, write, design, and produce themselves. A recent hit was called *Bordello Bandito,* but you might also be there for an afternoon of rock or a moonlight recital of chamber music. Sundance is nothing if not surprising.

It will soon have a complete Ghost Town, assembled from the remains of several old mining towns around Utah. They're installing a new ski lift to the top of the mountains, so that Robert Redford can enjoy championship skiing without having to drive over to Snowbird. (It's enough to make you want to be a movie star.) They also plan to hide Sundance. The parking lot, now the first thing to greet you, is being shunted off to a tree-screened location behind the lodge, and the forecourt will be landscaped with more trees. *More* trees? Shangri-la never had it so good.

NAME: Sundance
INNKEEPER: Brent Beck
ADDRESS: P.O. Box 837, Provo, Utah 84601
DIRECTIONS: Take Interstate 15 to the Provo or Orem exit, then follow U.S. 189 about 10 miles into the canyon to Utah 80, where you go left (for its seclusion, it's surprisingly accessible); by air to Salt Lake City; by Amtrak to Ogden.
TELEPHONE: (801) 225-4100
ROOMS: 9 mountain homes
RATES 1978: EP all year, from $50 a night April to November, from $125 a night December to March; plus 4¾% tax on room and food.
MEALS AND ENTERTAINMENT: Breakfast 9–11, lunch 10–2, dinner 5:30–10 (approx. $10 to $30 for two); no room service; dress optional; occasional live music.
DIVERSIONS: Outdoor pool, hiking trails, skiing, cross-country skiing (bring your own gear); horseback riding ($4 an hour); tennis (free), golf ($3 a round), sailing, and waterskiing nearby.

The Lodge at Snowbird
Snowbird, Utah

Utah has some of the most good-God-will-you-look-at-that scenery on the face of the earth, but until recently the only places to stay were run-of-the-mill motels. New ski resorts are changing all that. The most spectacular of these resorts is Snowbird, six years old and created from scratch eight miles inside Cottonwood Canyon, which is so narrow you can almost throw snowballs from one side to the other. From the skier's point of view the Snowbird statistics are as thrilling as a slalom: 3000 feet of vertical rise, an average snowfall of 450 inches a year (more than Aspen and Vail *together*), and an aerial tram that hoists 1200 hopefuls an hour to the top of the runs.

Your first view of the Lodge at Snowbird from the road is a two-story structure of rough-cast concrete and cedar trim, snug with the side of the canyon, and so diffident about its majestic surroundings that you have to peer twice to see the name plate. In the lobby you're confronted with duplex floor-to-ceiling windows framing a stunning view of the slopes, and when you step out onto the terrace you realize you've seen only two of the lodge's seven stories. The other five go *down* the hillside. Seven stories of concrete and a mammoth aerial tram may not sound like the best thing that could happen to a lovely, virgin canyon, but in fact Ted Johnson and Dick Bass, the founder and funder respectively of Snowbird, seem to have been at great pains to preserve and protect the environment. Item: of the total of 860 acres owned by the duo, only twenty acres will actually have buildings (hooray for the high-rise); item: no private land is being offered for sale, so they keep control of all the architecture; item: the 150,000 square feet (the equivalent of three and one-half acres) of the Lodge at Snowbird were sited in such a way that only four evergreens had to be removed.

GRANITE FIREPLACES, BENTWOOD ROCKERS. Now for the lodge itself. It has 160 condominium rooms, in three types of accommodations—bedroom, studio, and suite. The suites are Playboy Seductive, with granite fireplaces, enough logs for a protracted seduction, stylish leather-and-teak Scandinavian sofas and chairs; a kitchen for mixing wicked drinks; and a loft with queen-size beds and bentwood rockers. Each suite's two floors of window open onto that spectacular mountain view, but since the terrace outside the window runs the full length of the lodge and people can pass to and fro, keep the lights low when you're admiring the view if you're admiring each other at the same time. The studios are similar to the suites, but without the loft bedroom; the bedrooms are spacious, motel-type rooms with two queen-size beds. All the rooms have modern bath/showers, television, room telephones. (Note: the adjoining sixty-eight-room Turramurra Lodge has identical accommodations, same rates.) The only problem at Snowbird is the one you have in most ski resorts: the staff is full of enthusiasm—for skiing rather than housekeeping. Otherwise, a nice place to be, especially in summer when the last skier has gone clomping and stomping off with his zombie boots, and tranquility reigns once more.

All of Snowbird Village's facilities are operating in summer—ten restaurants, shops, delicatessen, an unusual bar built around the exposed workings of the giant aerial tram. The tram itself is slowed down from its regular six-minute ride for impatient skiers to a twelve-minute ride for leisurely sightseers, from 8100 feet at the plaza to 11,000 at Hidden Peak. And even if it hauls up a full load of 125 people there are still plenty of out-of-this-world spots among the trees and the peaks.

NAME: The Lodge at Snowbird
INNKEEPER: Ed Pilkerton
ADDRESS: Snowbird, Utah 84070
DIRECTIONS: Take Interstate 15 to the Sandy exit, about 20 miles south of Salt Lake City, then go east another 12 miles or so on Utah 210; or take Interstate 80E to Interstate 125 Belt Route to Wasatch Boulevard, follow the boulevard to Little Cottonwood Canyon (Utah 210), then up 7 miles to Snowbird. By air, to Salt Lake International Airport; by Amtrak, to Ogden.
TELEPHONE: (801) 742-2222 or, for reservations, 742-2000
ROOMS: 160 (plus an additional 410 at three other resorts in Snowbird)
RATES 1978: EP, $30 to $64 through October, higher in fall and winter; plus 8% room tax, 5% on food.
MEALS AND ENTERTAINMENT: Breakfast 7–11, lunch 11–4, dinner 6–10 (approx. $5 to $35 for two), plus ten other restaurants in the resort; no room service; informal dress; live music, dancing, disco, wine-and-cheese parties, symphony concerts, craft fairs, etc.
DIVERSIONS: Heated outdoor pool, therapy pool, sauna, hiking trails, tennis (3 indoor, 3 outdoor, with lights, $7 per court per hour, pro shop, clinics); skiing, cross-country skiing, ice skating; horseback riding nearby.

P.S. This hotel has been claiming to have been "named one of the 10 most romantic spots in the U.S. by *Esquire* magazine." This is based on an article carrying my byline and featuring, not 10, but 13 excerpts from *Lovers' Guide to America.* For the record, nowhere in the article were these 13 hotels named as *the* most romantic spots, merely as a selection of romantic spots; the Lodge may be one of the *110* most romantic spots, but certainly not one of the top 10.

Alta Lodge
Alta, Utah

Alta is one of the granddaddies of ski resorts, one of the first in the U.S. to hoist skiers up the mountain with a chair lift; but originally it was discovered by people who were more interested in getting *into* rather than up the mountain—would-be miners with the same gleam in their eyes that you see in skiers' after the first snowfalls of the season. Some people made fortunes in silver up here, and in the last part of the nineteenth century Alta had a population of five thousand. When you go walking in the woods you can still stub your toes on the remains of their homes and mines. Today the population is reduced to a few dozen in summer, nature lovers and the like—hiking, bird watching, picnicking, savoring the fresh mountain air.

Several of the resort's ski lodges remain open throughout the year, and the most popular is also one of the oldest, the Alta Lodge. Its fifty-six rooms include a few dormitories and some luxurious bed-sitting suites. Most of the latter are in a new chrome-and-glass wing tacked on to the side, with wall-to-wall carpeting, king-size beds, and picture windows, and a few of them also have fireplaces and balconies facing the

High Rustler Slope; but some of the most popular rooms are the old-style pine-paneled nooks in the chaletlike main lodge. Compared with Sundance, say, or Sun Valley, it's not exceptional, but its off-season rates ($24 to $30) make it a more-than-agreeable spot for a relaxed summer or fall vacation in the heady mountain air, 8600 feet above sea level, surrounded by the pines and firs of the Wasatch National Forest.

NAME: Alta Lodge
INNKEEPER: Bill Levitt
ADDRESS: Alta, Utah 84070
DIRECTIONS: Take Interstate 15 to the Sandy exit, about 20 miles south of Salt Lake City, then go east another 12 miles or so on Utah 210, and continue for a couple of miles past Snowbird; by air to Salt Lake International Airport, by Amtrak to Ogden.
TELEPHONE: (801) 742-3500
ROOMS: 56
RATES 1978: EP June 8 to October 1 $24 to $30, MAP November through April $56 to $94; plus 15% service charge and local taxes—8% on the room, 5% on the dining room.
MEALS AND ENTERTAINMENT: Breakfast 8–9:30, lunch 12–1:30, dinner 6:30–9:30 (approx. $20 to $30 for two); coffee in the lobby all day; no room service; dress optional.
DIVERSIONS: Tennis, hiking trails, skiing, cross-country skiing (with rentals) nearby.

Sun Valley Lodge
Sun Valley, Idaho

I think I know why so many celebrities vacation in Sun Valley: no one pays the slightest attention to a passing princess or shah because everyone is so engrossed. There's just so much to do here. The listing below is only part of the story: most winter resorts have cross-country skiing, but few of them have thirty instructors; many resorts rent bicycles but not many give you a choice of standard or three-speed or ten-speed or tandem; and while several resorts have activities for the mind as well as the body, not too many have a Center for Arts and Humanities with workshops in yoga and tai chi chaun, ceramics, and photography.

The way Averell Harriman conceived it, back in the thirties when he was a youthful chairman of the board of Union Pacific Railroad, Sun Valley would be a winter resort in the wilderness—but with an air of sophistication. It soon became the most fashionable, most successful resort in the Rockies; it has been through two new owners and major developments since then, and the original lodge and its sibling inn are now surrounded by acres of condominiums. But the location is probably as invigorating as ever—a natural bowl in the mountains, a vale of aspen and pine and sagebrush, with dazzlingly green fairways and Hemingway's favorite trout stream winding through the foothills.

The lodge itself is set off by trim lawns and duck ponds and masses of flowers. The new owner has decided to replace its distinctive thirties furnishings with contemporary lines and fabrics, and color television has been installed in each room; for anyone who never knew the lodge in the old days the new styling will probably be just fine. Certainly it's comfortable. Several of the suites in the main lodge have fireplaces, a few of them have *two* terraces—one facing the lawns, the other overlooking the ice-skating rink where so many Olympic medalists have been trained. In addition to the lodge, Sun Valley offers you almost as many options in types of accommodations as there are diversions—Lodge Apartments (spacious suites with fireplaces and kitchens, adjoining the lodge), condominiums in all sorts of configurations, beside the pool and tennis courts, in the foothills of the mountains, between the creek and the fairways, right at the base of the ski lifts. How do you choose? For good value, an Atelier Studio (murphy bed, TV, kitchenette, but no view) rents for just $33 in spring; for a few dollars more you can have a tri-level studio in Villager One; a few more dollars and you get a one-bedroom suite with loft bedroom and full kitchen in Villager Two. If you're a skier, you can ski right to the door of the one-bedroom suites in the Snow Creek condominiums.

Yet with all the activity going on around you, twosomes can still go off on their own and be romantic. The obvious: renting a tandem and cycling the mile into the village of Ketchum for lunch, or renting horses and trotting off through lonesome canyons for a quiet picnic beneath cottonwood trees by the edge of a mountain stream. The unusual, too. In winter, you can hire a horse-drawn cutter and driver, wrap yourselves in blankets, and skim across the snow to wine and dine in a log cabin. And for a grand gesture, how about this: rent the Lodge's glass-enclosed swimming pool for the evening, call room service, and have the waiters bring over champagne and dinner. Just the two of you. No one will pay any attention—they'll assume you're just another shah and princess.

NAME: Sun Valley Lodge

INNKEEPER: Wally Hoffman

ADDRESS: Sun Valley, Idaho 83353

DIRECTIONS: By car, Interstate 80N to Twin Falls, then go north for an hour on U.S. 93 (that's the simplest route, but from Boise you can also take I-80 to Mountain Home, then State Highway 68 across the windy mesa to U.S. 93, and from Yellowstone and points north, take Interstate 15 to Blackfoot, then U.S. 26 past Craters of the Moon National Monument to U.S. 93). By air, to Twin Falls (where you can be met by bus or limousine), or by Key Airlines from Boise and Salt Lake City to Hailey, 12 miles south of the lodge.

TELEPHONE: (208) 622-4111

ROOMS: 140 rooms in the Lodge, plus Lodge Apartments and hundreds of condominium apartments

RATES 1978: Very complicated, because of the nature of the place, but basically from $33 to $70 EP in the lodge and

Lodge Apartments in spring and fall; higher rates in summer and winter, in larger condominiums, and there's a variety of special packages available; plus 3% tax on total bill.

MEALS AND ENTERTAINMENT: Breakfast 8–10, lunch (indoors or outdoors) 12–6, dinner 6–9:30 (maybe later, approx. $22 to $25 for two), plus several restaurants in all price ranges in the valley and nearby Ketchum; room service during dining-room hours in lodge and Lodge Apartments; dress informal, but usually jackets at dinner in the main dining room; combo in the lounge, lots of entertainment in the neighborhood.

DIVERSIONS: 3 heated outdoor pools (glass-enclosed lodge pool open year round), sauna, hiking trails, fishing, kayaks and rowboats, archery, trap and skeet shooting, pool room, bowling alley, ice skating year round; Arts and Humanities Center with workshops in karate, ceramics, dance, photography, etc.; tennis (26 courts, no lights, $8 doubles per hour, pro shop, clinics, automated ball machines), golf (18 holes, $9 a round, other courses nearby), bikes for rent; horseback riding (indoors in winter), float trips, helicopter trips, soaring nearby; in winter, 58 downhill runs, cross-country trails, sleigh rides, *no* snowmobiles.

P.S. Busiest in summer and winter, lots of groups (but they tend to keep to themselves); special playschool, ski school, and pool for children.

Jenny Lake Lodge
Grand Teton National Park, Wyo.

Think, for one soul-refreshing moment, of the classic Rockies setting—craggy peaks, gouged by glaciers, permanently frosted, soaring above stands of birch and pine. Think of the classic Western homestead—a forest encampment of snug log cabins surrounded by meadows of wildflowers. Think of serenity—no cars, no jets, no jangling telephones, no television, no mobs. Think of mountain streams and elk and trumpeter swans, think of days in the saddle and wide open spaces. Now put all these dreams together and you begin to have an inkling of what Jenny Lake is all about.

This is another of those remarkable Rockresorts that so adroitly blend the wonders of the wilderness with just the right degree of civilized comforts. Here they have some of the most spectacular mountain scenery in the world, a range of rugged peaks leaping right up out of the plain; a mile or two in either direction will bring you to the haunts of elk and moose, and occasionally a deer or young bear will wander into the garden to see what's cooking. One of the cabins dates from the original Jenny Lake settlement (in the twenties), and they're all furnished in the manner of pioneer days—braided rugs, chairs with hide seats, headboards of wood lashed with rawhide; even with the addition of bathrooms, ceiling fans, electric blankets, leather ice buckets, umbrellas, and flashlights, these cabins still give you a real feel of the Old West. It's not until you sit down in the rustic, raftered dining room that you realize the Old West was never like this: maitre d', award-winning German chef, seafood Bengali, chateaubriand with sauce bearnaise, *Schwarzwalderkirschtorte,* and a Sunday buffet that stacks the groaning board with more than a hundred different dishes.

Jenny Lake is not for everyone (some people can't figure out why there's no wall-to-wall carpeting, air conditioning, television, and room phones—considering how much it costs to stay there), but for others, this is the ideal combination of wilderness and civilization, like having your *Schwarzwalderkirschtorte* and eating it too. For nonequestrians, it's a shame that horseback riding is included in the rate, because there's contentment enough just sitting on your patio, shaded by birch and pine, surrounded by clumps of choke-

cherry and Indian paintbrush, admiring the towering Tetons.
It's a grand sight.

NAME: Jenny Lake Lodge

INNKEEPERS: Bernard F. Iliff (general manager), Phil Breede-
love (resident manager)

ADDRESS: Grand Teton Lodge Company, P.O. Box 240,
Moran, Wyo. 83013

DIRECTIONS: In Grand Teton National Park. By car, take any
of five U.S. highways—26, 89, 187, 189, or 287 (if you
can, arrive or leave via Yellowstone National Park, next
door); by air, daily flights by Frontier to Jackson Hole
Airport (14 miles away, each flight is met by the lodge
bus); by Amtrak to Rock Springs, Wyo.

TELEPHONE: (307) 733-4647

ROOMS: 30 rooms, in individual log cabins

RATES 1978: MAP only, including horseback riding and bicycles, $110 for 1-bedroom cabin, $165 for 2-bedroom
cabins with fireplace, from June 15 through Labor Day
(closed rest of year); plus 4% tax on room and meals.

MEALS AND ENTERTAINMENT: Breakfast 7:30–9, lunch
12–1:30, dinner 6:30–9, gargantuan buffet dinner on
Sunday, trail-ride breakfasts; room service for continental breakfast; informal dress; liquor service; chamber
music once a week.

DIVERSIONS: Unlimited horseback riding, bicycles, fishing,
hiking (informal or guided, full day or overnight); golf,
tennis, and heated pool at Jackson Hole Golf and Tennis
Club, 14 miles away; raft trips down Snake River.

P.S. Reserve early, certainly before the end of April; no
groups, few children, one baby bear.

Jackson Lake Lodge
Grand Teton National Park, Wyo.

This is Rockresort's democratic version of *Jenny* Lake Lodge, an opportunity for the average traveler to enjoy the splendors of the Tetons in better-than-average comfort and style. Your anticipation may falter, though, on arrival: the parking lot may be cluttered with camper trucks, and the ground-level lobby is almost institutional. But once you climb the stairs to the main lounge, once you get your first glimpse of its vast windows rising three stories, like vertical Cinerama, and your first view of Mount Moran reflected in the lake, your spirits will soar anew. And stay up there. The lodge sits on a bluff above Willow Flats, and there's a large terrace that becomes a promenade when guests gather at sunset to scan the Flats for a glimpse of elk and moose heading for their waterholes; at any time of the day you have an awesome panoramic view of the entire landscape—flats, lake, and the full range of Tetons, constantly changing form and texture as the sun crosses the sky. You could simply sit here all day admiring the scenery, without ever hopping into your car and going for tours. The lodge has all the facilities you need: that impressive lounge, a morning-to-night coffee shop, a rather grand dining room decorated with murals of the Old West, and the Stockade Bar, decorated with authentic artifacts from the surrounding settlements. The guest rooms are dispersed among the main lodge, one-story Patio Suites, and two-story motor-lodge wings at one end. Since The View is the attraction, that's what you pay for: the least expensive rooms are just fine if you plan to be out-of-doors most of the day, but if you insist on a view, ask for a room on the west side of the main lodge, or a motor-lodge room numbered 580 to 594, where you'll have a private balcony or patio to watch the elk and moose amble across Willow Flats.

NAME: Jackson Lake Lodge

INNKEEPERS: Bernard F. Iliff (general manager), Ms. Dorris Stalker (resident manager)

ADDRESS: Grand Teton Lodge Company, P.O. Box 240, Moran, Wyo. 83013

DIRECTIONS: A few miles beyond Jenny Lake Lodge.

TELEPHONE: (307) 733-2811

ROOMS: 385, including 42 in the main lodge, the remainder in bungalow and motor-lodge units

RATES 1978: EP, from $34 to $53 (for rooms with mountain views) from early June through late September (closed rest of year); plus 4% tax on room and meals.

MEALS AND ENTERTAINMENT: You can eat in the coffee shop from 6 in the morning to 10:30 at night, in the main dining room during regular meal hours (prices from a few dollars to $20 for two); room service breakfast only (7:30–10); dress informal, although you might feel out of place wearing cut-off jeans in the main dining room; cocktail piano nightly, occasional Indian dances, square dancing, movie shows, and lectures.

DIVERSIONS: Heated outdoor pool, sun deck, hiking trails, bikes and horses for rent; raft trips, golf, tennis, and boating nearby. Yellowstone National Park is 20 miles to the north.

P.S. Busiest July and August, a few groups other months; lots of children.

THE DESERT RESORTS OF THE GREAT SOUTHWEST

It is the hour when from the boughs
The nightingale's high note is heard;
It is the hour when lovers' vows
Seem sweet in every whisper'd word . . .
BYRON

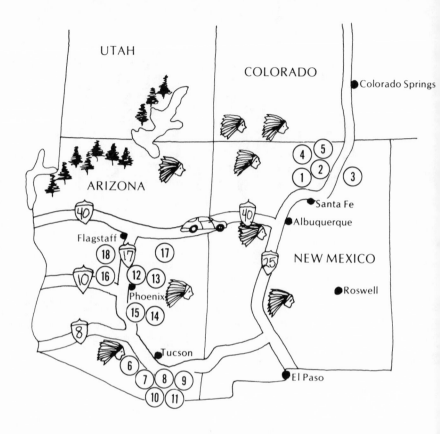

1. The Bishop's Lodge
2. Rancho Encantado
3. Tres Lagunas Guest Ranch
4. Sagebrush Inn
5. Hacienda de San Roberto
6. Arizona Inn
7. Hacienda del Sol
8. Westward Look Resort
9. Tanque Verde Ranch
10. Wild Horse Ranch Club

11. Sundancer Saddle
    and Surrey Ranch Resort
12. Arizona Biltmore Hotel
13. Marriott's Camelback Inn
14. John Gardiner's Tennis Ranch
15. Hermosa Inn
16. The Wigwam Resort
17. Carefree Inn
18. Wickenburg Inn

The Bishop's Lodge
Santa Fe, N.M.

Here's a resort that owes its existence to an apricot tree. About a century ago, Archbishop Lamy was wandering through the Little Valley of the Tesuque when he discovered an old apricot tree with particularly succulent fruit. He liked the fruit, and the valley, so he built himself a small hilltop retreat and an adobe chapel with belfry steeple and hand-painted "stained glass" windows. The chapel is still there, and the apricot tree, now a gnarled 350 years old, still welcomes you to the lodge.

At the turn of the century the archbishop's estate was bought by newspaper tycoon Joseph Pulitzer, who built a couple of villas for his daughters; Jim Thorpe's family, in turn, bought it almost sixty years ago and converted it into a resort in 1919—which probably makes it the oldest resort in the Southwest.

IDEAL LOCATION. The location is ideal: a five-minute drive from the bustle of downtown Santa Fe, yet sheltered from the rest of the world, a valley in the foothills of the Sangre de Cristo Mountains, a private estate of eleven hundred acres with five miles of frontage on the Santa Fe National Forest, 7300 feet above sea level, almost in the desert but shaded by cottonwoods, mountain poplars, crepe myrtle, lilac, Castilian roses—and fruit trees planted by the archbishop. Days are warm and sunny up here most of the year, but even in midsummer the nights are cool and you'll want to snuggle under a blanket.

The resort consists of the main lodge, with lounge, dining room, and cocktail lounge, all with Southwest decor, the two Pulitzer villas, and a couple of new wings put up in the past ten years: sixty-five guest rooms and suites in all, and most of them are in authentic Southwest/New Mexico/Mexico decor, or something very close to it. For the record: the dreamiest is room #8, all adobe, with chunky beams, flagstone floor, Navajo rugs, fireplace and Mexican hand-carved bed; suite #1 is a corner room with patios facing Colorado, plus a small lawn out front, cozy bedroom, fluffy carpets, fireplace, and viga (or rough-hewn beam) ceiling; suites #21 and #22, in the old Pulitzer House, have fireplaces, huge bathrooms with Mexican dressers, parlors (they're both $80, but #22 is probably the better buy because it has *two* fireplaces and a small garden). But all the Bishop's rooms are comfortable and/or charming, and eighteen of them have fireplaces.

OLD WOODCUTTERS' TRAILS. Riding is the big thing at the Bishop's. The half dozen wranglers handle sixty to sixty-five horses in summer (and they're all the lodge's own horses), and if you can prove to the wrangler you know your way about he might let you go off on your own. There are miles of trails in and around the estate, but you can also follow old woodcutters' trails through the forest all the way to Colorado. Better take a picnic lunch along.

But you don't have to be an equestrian to enjoy the lodge. There are five new Laykold tennis courts, a big heated pool with saunas and a Jacuzzi, fishing and trap shooting. You can lie back and do a spot of bird watching (forty-four species at last count), or you can drive off and visit some of the Indian pueblos around Santa Fe. This is one of the most fascinating corners of America—and the Bishop's Lodge is perfectly located for local excursions.

Evenings at the lodge usually begin with a drink in El Charro, a manly sort of place with saddles, sombreros, and spurs to remind you of *el charro*—the legendary cowboy of Mexico. The food is a mixture of continental and American—mignonettes of beef, Rocky Mountain trout, boeuf à la Deutsch, Pacific red snapper; the main dining room has a

Mexican feel to it, with notched off-white beams, copper chandeliers, murals of Indian ceremonies, "cantina" furniture, and hand-beaten tin doors. On warm evenings you can dine on the terrace and sniff the perfumed air that lured the archbishop here in the first place.

NAME: The Bishop's Lodge
OWNER/INNKEEPER: James R. Thorpe, Jr.
ADDRESS: P.O. Box 2367, Santa Fe, N.M. 87501
DIRECTIONS: Three miles north of Santa Fe Plaza on Bishop's Lodge Road (via Washington Avenue from Plaza, via Camino Encantado from U.S. 285/64/84); by air to Albuquerque (an hour and $45 a couple away by lodge limousine); by rail via Amtrak to Lamy ($17 per couple by lodge limousine).
TELEPHONE: (505) 983-6377
ROOMS: 65 rooms and suites in five lodges
RATES 1978: EP in spring and fall, from $42 to $123; AP only in summer, from $76 to $192; closed November through February; plus 12½% service charge and 4½% tax.
MEALS AND ENTERTAINMENT: Breakfast 8–9:30, lunch 12–1:30 (Sundays 11:30–2), dinner 7–8:30 (to 9 in summer), approx. $20 to $40 for two; room service during meal hours; jacket and tie for dinner.
DIVERSIONS: Heated outdoor pool, therapy pool, sauna, stocked-pond fishing, badminton, croquet, table tennis, all free; tennis (5 courts, $4 per court per hour, pro shop, ball machine, clinics, special tennis packages), horseback riding ($10 per ride, 1½ to 2 hours), skeet-trap shooting; bicycles for rent nearby.
P.S. Special programs for children during summer; small conventions in spring and fall.

Rancho Encantado
near Santa Fe, N.M.

Beautiful. No, enchanting, like it says. By day there's desert as far as the eye can see; by night, there are stars as high as the eye can see; and there are interiors filled with art, artifacts and antiques.

The ranch's 168 acres are surrounded on three sides by the Tesuque Indian Reservation and on the fourth by the Santa Fe National Forest; to the east are the Sangre de Cristo Mountains, to the west (away to the west) the Jemez Mountains. The grandeur of the setting and the charm of the ranch have corraled the likes of Nelson Rockefeller, Henry Fonda, Kirk Douglas, Gregory Peck, the Duchess of Argyll, and Prince Rainier and Princess Grace of Monaco. Some posse.

The ranch got its start back in the early thirties when a young lady who learned her innkeeping at The Bishop's Lodge decided to branch out on her own; she chose this spot and had her brother-in-law put up the buildings (he also made a lot of the furniture, some of it still there in the lobby). But the ranch's present name and personality are the creation of its present owner, Betty Egan, a widow from Cleveland, who started a new life here six years ago with her four teenagers. Among them, and with the imagination and taste of their interior designer, Donald Murphy, they've created the sort of guest ranch you always hope a desert ranch will look like.

The lobby's quarry tile floors and raftered ceiling set the tone; the lounge is a casually elegant room with a huge adobe fireplace, cowbells, a skylight above the fire, rawhide tables and lamps, decorative tiles, and hand-woven cushions. The dining room is three tiers of white adobe, decorative tiles, and quarry tile floors, with most of the tables command-

ing a view through tall windows and across the terrace to unending, unspoiled desert. There are lots of neat little touches about the place—like a wall plaque with nineteen (*19*) types of barbed wire, and a hand-carved armoire concealing a cigarette machine.

The twenty-eight guest rooms are equally enchanting—all in southwestern style, with Franklin stoves or adobe fireplaces, antique lamps, raftered ceilings, tiled floors, Indian rugs and wall hangings, *retablos,* and so forth. The quietest rooms are in the cottages (they also have fireplaces), but the prettiest is probably #8, up a beautiful tiled stairway to the second floor of the main lodge. All the rooms have private bathrooms with tub/showers, but no television (you can have one installed if you're gauche enough to ask for it).

Despite all this luxury, Rancho Encantado is an outdoorsy sort of place. One of its earliest horseriding guests, a Mrs. Sage Underwood, used to turn up with her own cowboy; today she'd probably be happy to rely on wrangler Don Olson. His stable has ten frisky horses and a somnolent buffalo named Lucille. (Horses rent for $6.50 an hour, and you'll probably have to be accompanied by a wrangler.) There's also an elevated swimming pool with sun terraces and a stunning view across the desert. Sharpshooters will find the trap range across the road; tennis buffs can while away the time between sets playing pool or having a beer in the Cantina Lounge, next to the courts.

It would be a shame if the ranch's meals were a letdown for its lovely dining room. They're not. At lunchtime try a snack called The Bread Board, which is just that—a wooden bread board with bread, slices of apple, Dutch cheese, and a glass of red wine ($2). For dinner you can go Mexican with a Tesuque Special (enchiladas, tamales, tacos, guacamole, tostadas, and home-made sopaipillas with honey—$4.50) or carne asado (steak marinated with chili strips—$7.25); or go cowboy with steaks (8-, 10-, 12- and 14-ouncers) and butterfly porkchops cooked in beer ($6.50). Top that off with something that's neither Mexican nor cowboy, just sinful—a concoction called a Flower Pot ($2.50 worth of ice cream and goodies). Wines? Everything from Paul Masson's Cabernet Sauvignon at $4.50 to Château d'Yquem at a Rockefellerish $20. If it means the difference between staying here and not staying here, settle for the Paul Masson. Or a glass of beer. Or even a glass of water.

NAME: Rancho Encantado
INNKEEPER: John T. Egan
ADDRESS: Route 4, Box 57C, Santa Fe, N.M. 87501
DIRECTIONS: In Tesuque, 8 miles north of Santa Fe, on State Highway 22, off Rte. 285.
TELEPHONE: (505) 982-3537
ROOMS: 28 rooms, 9 suites
RATES 1978: Not available at press time, but probably a dollar or two higher than in 1977—from $57 to $62, May through September; may be closed for a few months in winter; plus 4½% tax on room and food.

MEALS AND ENTERTAINMENT: Breakfast 8–10:30, lunch 12–2:30, dinner 6–9, or 5:30–10 during the opera season (approx. $12 to $20 for two); room service 7 a.m. to 10 p.m.; informal dress; recorded and live music.

DIVERSIONS: Heated outdoor pool, archery, hiking trails, game room, parlor games, tennis (3 courts, no charge), horseback riding ($6.50 an hour); bicycles, skiing, sailing nearby.

P.S. Make your reservations far in advance, especially during the opera season.

Tres Lagunas Guest Ranch
Pecos, N.M.

Another side to New Mexico—a Maine-like setting of log cabins dwarfed by Ponderosa pines and firs, with a bubbly mountain stream, between Willow Creek and Holy Ghost Creek. Besides the natural glories of the Pecos Wilderness area, Tres Lagunas has a stable of quarterhorses (you can go riding off by yourselves); a heated pool; three trout-stocked lakes and a private mile-long stretch of the Pecos for fishing; and mile after mile of walking tracks, along the stream and up the road (it goes nowhere so it's never crowded).

The cabins look just rustic and right in this all-embracing greenery, but you don't have to rough it. They have stone fireplaces, bathtubs in wood-walled bathrooms, Navajo rugs, and porches. Socializing takes place in the main lodge, an oversized frontier cabin with a comfy lounge, library, and three oversize fireplaces; meals are served in the wonderfully woodsy Waterfall Room overlooking the Pecos River and the Ponderosa pines.

NAME: Tres Lagunas Guest Ranch

INNKEEPERS: Bob and Paula Johnson

ADDRESS: Route 2, Box 100, Pecos, N.M. 87552

DIRECTIONS: Leave Interstate 25 at the N.M. 63 Pecos/Glorieta exit (16 miles east of Santa Fe); the ranch is 12 miles north of Pecos, still on N.M. 63; by air to Albuquerque, by Amtrak to Lamy, pickup by ranch limousine.

TELEPHONE: (505) 757-6194

ROOMS: 5 rooms, 9 cabins

RATES 1978: AP only, May 31 through Labor Day, from $67 to $88 (closed rest of year); plus 4% sales tax.

MEALS AND ENTERTAINMENT: Breakfast 7–9, lunch 12:30–2, dinner 6:30–8:30 (approx. $14 to $40 for two); no room service; informal dress.

DIVERSIONS: Heated outdoor pool, hiking, fishing in three stocked lakes, horseshoes, pinball, pool, table tennis; horseback riding ($4.50 per hour).

Sagebrush Inn
Taos, N.M.

This is the sort of inn you hope to find in a place like Taos, with its clusters of terra-cotta adobe buildings, its cherished southwestern ambiance, and its love affair with Indian, Mexican, and Western art. The Sagebrush is shaded by cottonwoods and filled with the works of local artists. It's slightly ramshackle—but even that's part of the Taos charm. The main lounge is an authentic hacienda room—viga ceilings and a massive adobe piñon-burning fireplace, Navajo rugs, handcarved *santos* and handpainted *bultos,* rare pottery, and paintings by some of the old masters and some of the not-so-old and not-so-masterful artists who live in and around Taos. Las Maracas, the cocktail lounge, is as snug as a pub, with an open fire and rawhide and wicker furniture, and a folk singer strumming through a repertory of Spanish, Mexican, and flamenco songs; the dining room is colorful Mexican—wicker chairs and wooden tables, candles and paintings—and a popular spot with the poets, artists, musicians, and assorted dilettantes who've been here long enough to call themselves *taosenas*.

The guest rooms are grouped around a courtyard at the rear and linked by a shady ramada—except for a few rooms in the second story of the main building, and one rather drafty room in the penthouse of the mission-style tower. They're also in southwestern style, and some of them have adobe fireplaces in the corner (they're the most popular buys, because you may think you're out in a blazing desert in Taos but in fact you're 7000 feet up and it can get chilly there, even in midsummer). Unfortunately, there's nothing very Taosy or romantic in the inn's setting—plunk by the side of the highway like any common or garden motel; and the South Santa Fe Road only proves that the main drag into a cultured, historic spot like Taos can be as dreary as any other main drag. So use the Sagebrush Inn as a base for exploring the art galleries, boutiques, restaurants, old churches, that marvelous multi-story Indian pueblo just north of town, and the other sights of this extraordinary corner of the United States. Otherwise don't leave your cozy little Sagebrush room except to lounge in the lounge, drink in Las Maracas, or replenish your energy in the dining room.

NAME: Sagebrush Inn

INNKEEPER: Ken Blair

ADDRESS: P.O. Box 1566, Taos, N.M. 87571

DIRECTIONS: Two miles south of Taos and just north of Rancho de Taos, on the South Santa Fe Road (U.S. 64).

TELEPHONE: (505) 758-2254

ROOMS: 26, including 4 suites

RATES 1978: AP year round, $30 to $50 (EP on request); plus 4% sales tax.

MEALS AND ENTERTAINMENT: Breakfast 7:30–10, lunch 11:30–2:30 (June through September only), dinner

6–10 (approx. $10 to $24 for two); no room service; informal dress.

DIVERSIONS: Heated outdoor pool; tennis (2 courts, $3.50 per court per hour).

P.S. Busiest July and August, and weekends during the skiing season.

Hacienda de San Roberto
El Prado (near Taos), N.M.

This is the alternative to the Sagebrush if you want lots of local charm but prefer not to be next to the highway. The Hacienda has five suites, and that's it. Just five two-room suites, each with an adobe fireplace handmade by Taos Pueblo Indians and a porch with spectacular views across the valley to the gambel oaks, piñon, and junipers of the Carson National Forest. It was built in 1966 by a wealthy Ohioan for other wealthy Ohioans, or at least for well-to-do types who wanted to get away from it all without having to sacrifice creature comforts—other than radios, telephones, television, and air conditioning. The new owners go along with the no-phone-no-TV concept, "the better to hear the wind in the pines." Or the stellar jays fluttering among the bushes, or the deer browsing on the lawn.

The dining room (Spanish Rustic decor, adobe fireplace, half a dozen tables) is a lovely spot. The terrace usually offers dazzling sunsets at the Margarita hour, but there's a lot to be said for trotting off to your own suite, having dinner sent over, and settling down for an evening before your own piñon fire—perfect spot for lovers.

NAME: Hacienda de San Roberto
INNKEEPERS: Norm Seim and Marcia Kennerly
ADDRESS: P.O. Box 449, El Prado, N.M. 87529

DIRECTIONS: Follow I-64 5 miles north from Taos, then go right on N.M. 150 through Valdez; the Hacienda is a few miles beyond that, just before you go into the canyon that takes you to Taos Ski Valley.

TELEPHONE: (505) 776-2630

ROOMS: 5 two-room suites

RATES 1978: EP, $40 May through November, AP only in winter—about $88; plus 4½% tax on room and food.

MEALS AND ENTERTAINMENT: Breakfast 7:30–9:30, skiers' lunch in winter only, dinner 6:30–9 (approx. $15 to $30 for two); room service to 10 p.m.; informal dress; live music on weekends.

DIVERSIONS: Heated indoor pool, therapy pool, sauna, hiking trails, table tennis; indoor and outdoor tennis, golf, horseback riding, and winter sports nearby.

Arizona Inn
Tucson, Ariz.

Lawns everywhere. Beds of violets and poppies. Anchor doves flitting among the palo verde, poplars, bottlebrush, and longneedle pine. Eight gardeners silently trimming, weeding, watering. You could easily fool yourself into thinking you're out in the country. In fact, you're smack in the middle of suburbia, and the Arizona Inn is merely a cocoon coddling you from the real world.

It wasn't always that way.

When it first opened forty-odd years ago, the Arizona was indeed away out in the middle of the desert, but then the almost perfect climate of Tucson lured more and more vacationers to the area, and then more and more residents, and slowly the city besieged the inn. You'd never guess that from inside the inn, and there's no reason to leave. You have everything you need for unwinding right there within the pink stucco walls of this fourteen-acre oasis.

You have a private patio for sunbathing; an uncrowded swimming pool with a sun terrace on one side and a leafy arbor on the other; a couple of Har-Tru tennis courts (floodlit for evening play) and a pro shop; a croquet lawn and a putting green; and a pampering staff.

STRAWBERRIES, FIGS, AND BAKED WINESAP APPLES. Goodness, how you'll be pampered. Morning paper waiting at your door. Breakfast on your patio (anything from muffins, strawberries, apricots, and figs to hot clear bouillon, kippered herring, and baked winesap apple). Lunch by the pool. Dinner by the fire in your room. Fresh flowers and finger bowls in the dining room.

This is the sort of place where personal service still means *personal* service. The poolside waiter gets quite upset if he can't remember your name when you order your second round—and the fact that he's been remembering names correctly for over thirty-seven years doesn't console him. Almost half the staff have been at the Arizona Inn for twenty years or more (not too many hotels can make a claim like that), which is probably one reason why so many of the guests have been coming back year after year since the inn was surrounded by desert. They're not only loyal, they're a pretty distinguished group, too—from Winston Churchill and assorted English lords to Salvador Dali and Cary Grant. John D. Rockefeller liked it so much here he kept a cottage for his permanent use. And apparently the inn still gets the patricians, because the registration card includes space at the bottom for the names of your chauffeur and maid.

This special place came into being in a rather unusual way. Shortly after World War I, a local lady by the name of Miss Greenway (the first congresswoman from Arizona) started a plan to help veterans adapt to postwar conditions: they made furniture by hand, their wives decorated it, Miss Greenway bought it. They must have been eager beavers because after a short time Miss Greenway had more furniture than she could use. So she built an inn out in the desert.

But don't get the idea that the Arizona Inn is a rickety place filled with old handmade furniture. It isn't. Miss Greenway added some of her own family heirlooms, and regional decorations made from copper and cactus. It's a luxurious place, with a full-time decorator on the staff to make sure everything stays immaculate. The lounge is fit for a Spanish grandee—dark wooden ceiling and rafters, stately furniture grouped around a huge fireplace, and custom-designed carpets handwoven in Morocco. The rooms are equally comfortable, with armchairs, desks, coffee tables, card tables, walk-in closets, hand-blocked linen spreads, original paintings, air conditioning for the summer months, television (they finally gave in), private patios—or, in some cases, private gardens, patios within patios.

NAME: Arizona Inn

INNKEEPER: Robert Minerich (manager), John S. Greenway (owner)

ADDRESS: 2200 East Elm Street, Tucson, Ariz. 85719

DIRECTIONS: Leave Interstate 10 at the Speedway Boulevard exit, go east on Speedway to the University of Arizona, turn left on Campbell, drive 5 blocks, turn right and you're on East Elm, almost at the entrance; also scheduled air and Amtrak service.

TELEPHONE: (602) 325-1541

ROOMS: 85 rooms, 8 suites, 3 private homes

RATES 1978: EP, from $32 to $45 May 1 through December 31, $62 to $88 January 1 through April 30; plus 7% tax on room, 6% on food and bar bills.

MEALS AND ENTERTAINMENT: Breakfast 7–9:30, lunch 12–1:45, dinner 6:30–8:30 (approx. $18 to $22 for two); room service during dining-room hours; jacket and tie for dinner in winter.

DIVERSIONS: Heated outdoor pool, putting green, croquet,

badminton, tennis (2 Har-Tru courts with lights, no charge for guests, pro); golf, horseback riding nearby.

P.S. Open all year, peak months (mostly elderly clientele) January through April; small groups during the summer.

Hacienda del Sol
Tucson, Ariz.

The well-to-do of Tucson are taking to the hills these days, to the foothills of the Catalinas, but the Home of the Sun beat them to it. Its knolltop perch will probably stay unspoiled for years to come, too, because the owner of this swatch of desert lives on the neighboring knoll and he likes the view just as it is. You're welcomed to the hacienda by a mission gateway, and a gently splashing blue-tiled fountain and a pathway shaded by orange and grapefruit trees lead you inside to a cloisterlike cluster of adobe casitas, all arches and red-tiled roofs. Very Mexican, very Spanish.

The hacienda was built originally as a girls' school, back in 1929, and transformed into a guest ranch in 1946; when the Hartmans took over about eight years ago, they moved in their personal collection of Mexican and Indian art—Aztec suns, gods' eyes, hand-painted chairs, hand-beaten tin screens and chandeliers. The dining room is roofed by heavy carved beams, highlighted by silver lamps and sconces; the lounge has a blue adobe fireplace and a collection of Navajo rugs and Kachina dolls. It's the Southwest with style and taste.

It's a wonderfully detached, soothing place, up there above the city. You can lounge in the courtyard beneath the orange and grapefruit trees or in the glass-enclosed therapy pool with a view of the Catalinas. At tequila time you can pull up a chair by the windows of the Casa Feliz, look down on

Tucson's sprawling lights, and pretend they're moonlight shimmering on a lake; then a leisurely dinner in that beautiful dining room (the hacienda's chef was recently invited to spend a summer cooking aboard the Norwegian royal yacht); afterward, a stroll around the garden before turning in for the night. If you want something to read, the hacienda's library fills two walls (one of the country's leading publishers spends a few weeks here every year).

Despite all this charm and style, the hacienda is really a ranch; it has its own stable and its own string of fifteen horses, and its friendly wranglers will take you riding up beyond the foothills of the Catalinas to Piñon Canyon and Finger Rock.

NAME: Hacienda del Sol
INNKEEPER: Robert E. Hartman
ADDRESS: Hacienda del Sol Road, Tucson, Ariz. 85718
DIRECTIONS: Follow Campbell Drive from the University of

Arizona to River Road; turn right, drive until you come to Hacienda del Sol Road, and stay with it all the way (about 8 miles from downtown Tucson).

TELEPHONE: (602) 299-1501

ROOMS: 31 rooms, 7 suites, 5 villas

RATES: AP only, $75 to $90 for rooms, $100 to $125 for suites, November 1 to May 1 (closed rest of year); plus 15% service charge, 4% tax on total bill.

MEALS AND ENTERTAINMENT: Breakfast 8–10, lunch 12:30–1:30, dinner 6:30–7:30; room service during meals; jacket at dinner; occasional movies and games in evening.

DIVERSIONS: Heated outdoor and indoor pools, therapy pool, exercise room, hiking trails, putting green, tennis court—all free; horseback riding ($5 an hour).

P.S. Quietest times are first two weeks in November, first three weeks in January, but relaxing at any time.

Westward Look Resort
Tucson, Ariz.

From the distance, it looks like a Greek village, a terraced hilltop of dining room and tennis courts, swimming pool and therapy pool, and a cluster of townhouse suites on the lower tier, the whole held together by well-tended gardens and winding pathways. The surrounding acres of desert may look scraggly and bleak, but if you were to spend an afternoon walking around and counting the different types of plant and flower you'd have enough names to fill a foolscap page— everything from periwinkle to cow's-tongue cactus. These acres of desert also serve to isolate the Westward Look from its neighbors, which gives it its quiet, unhurried air. It's probably the best of these Tucson hideaways for tennis buffs, even though its altitude (3200 feet) exposes the courts to occasional gusts of wind that play havoc with lobs; the tennis complex is captained by Norm Peterson, a genial pro who manages to match up the right twosomes and foursomes.

The so-called Posada rooms are standard-sized, standard-equipped units, grouped around the swimming pool and therapy pool; the townhouse, or Fiesta, rooms have an extra dining area, kitchen, and refrigerator. Some have better views than others, but don't lose any sleep on that point because Tucson is not the most exciting cityscape in the land. In any case, if you want to admire the twinkling city lights you can do that from the dining room, the Gold Room no less, which has floor-to-ceiling windows and soft lights. You may be grateful here for something to look at, other than the parchment menu, because the service confirms that old rule of thumb about waiters: the fancier the shirt, the chancier the service. A shame, because the resort managed to land a first-rate chef, John Simic, formerly executive chef of the Swedish America Lines; and it's not every resort where you can play a few sets of tennis, soothe your muscles in a therapy pool, then settle down to boula-boula (that's clear turtle soup topped with pea soup), escalope de veau Oscar, or scampi Bretonne, followed by slices of mango flamed with Martinique rum. If you want to enjoy your boula-boula without suffering the ineptness of frilly-fronted waiters, stay in your room and have your dinner carted down (or up) the hill. It's *faster* that way.

NAME: Westward Look Resort
INNKEEPER: Joe Darling
ADDRESS: 245 East Ina Road, Tucson, Ariz. 85704
DIRECTIONS: Take Interstate 10 to Ina Road exit, go east on Ina Road; the resort is ½ mile beyond Oracle Road (U.S.80/89).
TELEPHONE: (602) 297-1157
ROOMS: 93 rooms, half of them poolside, half of them townhouse-style semisuites (and 9 rustic casitas adjoining the tennis courts)
RATES 1978: EP $27 to $48 in summer (through Septem-

ber 30), $38 to $80 in fall (through December 31), $41 to $99 in winter (through May 15); plus 3% tax on room, 4% tax on food and liquor.

MEALS AND ENTERTAINMENT: Breakfast 7–10, lunch 11:30–2:30, dinner 7–10 (approx. $20 to $40 for two); room service during meal hours; jacket for dinner in winter; combo every evening except Monday in the stygian Lookout Lounge.

DIVERSIONS: Heated outdoor pool and therapy pool; tennis (8 courts, 3 lighted, pro shop, ball machines, clinics), horseback riding ($3.50 an hour); a selection of golf courses nearby.

Tanque Verde Ranch
Tucson, Ariz.

Many desert moons ago, the Tanque Verde's owner was strung up by the neck over the rafters of what is now the Reading and Card Room. Not by irate guests, but by outlaws out for his petty cash. That was back in the days when the ranch was a stagecoach stop on the San Pedro run, and it had its fair share of Injun raids and cattle rustling. Nowadays, the posses heading out of the corral are harmless and wobbly tourists, and the ranch is one of the most peaceful spots in Arizona.

It could hardly be anything else, given its location. It's 2800 feet up in the foothills of the Tanque Verde Mountains; its eastern border is 1,385,307 rugged acres of the Federal Coronado Forest Preserve, and its southern border is the 63,000-acre Saguaro National Monument. Tucson is twelve miles and twenty-nine dips away along the Speedway Boulevard. All that wilderness shuts out the rumbles of civilization and you're left with the cry of the coyote and the assorted

chirps, warbles, cries, and whistles of the red-shafted flicker, LeConte's thrasher, the bridled titmouse, Williamson's sapsucker, and the lesser scaup. There's a birdbath in sight of every room, so you can sit on your porch and watch the cavortings of the common bushtit, black phoebe, boat-tailed grackle, and Inca dove. Look farther and you may spot a bald eagle. More than 196 species have been spotted here. (There's a bird-banding every Thursday, and guests are invited to join in.)

Most people don't come here, though, to watch the birds. They come to ride over desert trails, past giant saguaro, and up into the mountains to *Campos Americanos* and the *Puerto de Cabeza de la Vaca* (the Cow-headed Saddle). This is very much a horse-and-wrangler type of ranch—and you can take your pick from a string of eighty palominos, appaloosas, sorrels, and buckskins. Unlimited riding (but only with escort) is included in the rate, so most people ride. But if you get saddle sore, don't despair. There's plenty to do down on the ranch (see listing).

The oldest part of the ranch, dating from 1862, is now the office/lounge, alongside a low-ceilinged wing of adobe rooms sheltered by an authentic ramada of rough-hewn timbers topped by a roof of ghost saguaro. Hammocks dangle between the timber pillars. Antique Mexican pottery dots the garden, among the eucalyptus, pepper, and wild orange tree (if you're lucky you may even sample a wild orange pie some evening at dinner).

Across the garden is the old adobe bunkhouse, which has gone through a few transformations and become the Dog House Bar—a bottle club with flagstone floor, adobe fireplace, rawhide chairs, and pictures of Wild Bill Hickok, Wyatt Earp, Luther Patton, and that notorious Wild West dog-kicker, W. C. Fields. This is the gathering place after a day riding the range. Here, or up on the sundeck above the Sonora Health Spa and Recreation Center. The spa is where you'll find Tanque Verde's indoor pool, sauna, and exercise rooms. Unlikely items on a dude ranch? But this is no ordinary dude ranch.

THE PHD AND THE STEWARDESS. How could it be with a manager who speaks fluent French, Chinese, and Japanese, and earned his PhD with a thesis entitled "A Russian Agronomist's Influence on Japanese Agriculture"? DeeDee Cote was a stewardess who used to come here between flights to ride her favorite horse, Champ, before she realized she was really coming because she was in love with the manager. So they got married.

And where else will you find a dude ranch with one German and one French chef, and a pastry chef from Berlin? So you won't have to settle for chuckwagon food. Some evenings you'll find German dishes, other evenings Polynesian or Mexican.

Tanque Verde's sixty patio lodges and cottages all have private baths, individual thermostat controls for heating and air conditioning, and room phones, but no TV. Many of the rooms have log-burning fireplaces, many have private patios. No two rooms are alike, so take a peek and pick the one that suits you before you move in. Room #7, for example, is a suite with adobe fireplace, fitted carpet, wood walls; suite

#22 has corner windows facing the sunset, a garden patio and fireplace; and if you're more interested in riding than in comfort, you can have a small "ramada" room (only $79—but remember that includes all meals *and* riding).

NAME: Tanque Verde Ranch
INNKEEPER: Bob Cote
ADDRESS: Route 8, Box 66, Tucson, Ariz. 85710
DIRECTIONS: Follow East Speedway east until it goes no farther—15 miles from the center of Tucson.
TELEPHONE: (602) 296-6275
ROOMS: 47 rooms, 13 suites
RATES 1978: AP only (including unlimited horseback riding), $79 to $106 January 1 through April 30, $69 to $89 the rest of the year; plus 12% service charge, 4% tax on room.
MEALS AND ENTERTAINMENT: Breakfast 8–9, lunch 12:30–1:30, dinner 6:30–8; no room service; informal dress; occasional movies and square dancing in the Bottle Club.
DIVERSIONS: Heated outdoor and indoor pools, therapy pool, sauna, exercise rooms, hiking trails, shuffleboard, bird banding, pool, table tennis, horseback riding, tennis (4 courts, 1 lighted for night play)—all free.
P.S. Busiest season December through April.

Wild Horse Ranch Club
Tucson, Ariz.

They say you can still find Indian relics within walking distance of this ranch (Cochise and his braves used to scout these parts); and don't be surprised if deer, wild pigs, or coyotes cross your path, because the land around here is part of a wildlife preserve.

Some of the riding trails may even look familiar because nearby Box Canyon popped up frequently on TV shows like *High Chaparral* and *Bonanza;* and if you can remember all the way back to Hollywood's epic *Arizona,* you may recognize the covered wagon that welcomes you to the ranch.

The Wild Horse Ranch Club is located twelve miles northwest of Tucson, in the foothills of the Tucson Mountains. It's been a guest ranch since the twenties, with just the right modern touches to make it comfortable without stifling the Old West atmosphere.

KACHINA DOLLS AND KUMQUATS. The public rooms, particularly, put you right in the mood. Throughout the ranch, you'll see a fine selection of early paintings of the Old West by artists like Ray Strang, Dale Nichols, and Carolus Verhaeren. The Branding Iron Room, the bar, was inspired by the Old Trading Post at Ganado (now a national monument). The unstuffy library is decorated with Navajo rugs and Kachina dolls—a pleasant spot to rest up between rides, and bring yourself up to date on the lore of the pioneers. The dining room is brightly Mexican, with an indoor-outdoor garden that makes you less reluctant to come in out of the greenery outside—a stampede of joshua trees, date palms, ironwood, sweet-scented jasmine and bougainvillea, pomegranates, olives, kumquats, and over a hundred types of cactus. Every few yards you come across bird feeders that lure whitewing doves and orioles and quail. Somewhere in the midst of all this nature are the cottages. With a build-up like that garden, they turn out to be a bit disappointing. Spic-and-span, *sí;* southwestern, Mexican, ranchlike, *no.*

If you want to spend most of your time in bed, this isn't the place for you; but if you want to spend some time by a pool, ride horses, stroll along nature trails, play tennis, or look for the head of a tomahawk—then consider the Wild Horse.

NAME: Wild Horse Ranch Club
INNKEEPER: Randolph J. Spiett
ADDRESS: P.O. Box 5505, Tucson, Ariz. 85703

DIRECTIONS: Leave Interstate 10 at Ina Road exit, north of Tucson; turn left for 2 miles, then follow signs.

TELEPHONE: (602) 297-2266

ROOMS: 40 rooms, 6 suites

RATES 1978: AP $48 to $88, October 15 to December 14, $58 to $98 December 15 to May 1 (closed rest of year, EP rates on request); plus 12% service charge, 3% local tax on total bill; rates include horseback riding and tennis.

MEALS AND ENTERTAINMENT: Breakfast 6:30–9, lunch 11:30–1, dinner 6–8; room service during meal hours; informal dress.

DIVERSIONS: Horseback riding, tennis (2 courts, pro), heated outdoor pool, hiking trails, shuffleboard, putting green— no charge.

P.S. Quietest months are early fall and early spring.

Sundancer Saddle and Surrey Ranch Resort

Tucson, Ariz.

Only thirty guests can bunk down here at one time, and since horseback riding is included in the room rates and the ranch is surrounded by a 100,000-acre wildlife refuge, most of those thirty people spend as much time in the saddle as their flesh will allow. Their enthusiasm makes for a clubby atmosphere, helped along by the rawhide-and-blue-tiled cantina, a bottle club where wranglers and riders get together after their days in the sagebrush and saguaro. Helped along, too, by the *Patron Grande* and his wife Colette, now in their twenty-fifth season at the ranch.

Jack Jackson's etc. etc. Resort is an informal, easy-going sort of place, casual as a cowpoke; no jacket or tie for dinner here (but you are expected to be in their Mexican-style dining room ready to sit down to a family-style meal at seven o'clock pronto). After dinner, you can pull up a chair before one of the fireplaces; or dodge the color TV in the lounge and play a few games of billiards in the raftered game room; or join a square dance on the terrace. More likely, you'll want to slip off to bed and get a good night's sleep to prepare you for tomorrow's breakfast ride up into the Tucson Mountains.

NAME: Sundancer Saddle and Surrey Ranch Resort

INNKEEPER (or *Patron Grande*): Jack J. Jackson

ADDRESS: 4110 Sweetwater Drive, Tucson, Ariz. 85705

DIRECTIONS: Leave Interstate 10 at Grant Road exit; drive west 1 mile to Silverbell Road, north 2½ miles to Sweetwater Drive, west 1¼ miles on Sweetwater. If you're coming by air, they'll pick you up at the airport.

TELEPHONE: (602) 743-0411

ROOMS: 14 casitas

RATES 1978: AP only, $84 to $108 through May 1, $78 to $96 October 1 through December 15 (closed in summer); plus 15% service charge and 4% tax.

MEALS AND ENTERTAINMENT: Breakfast 7:30–9, buffet lunch 12:30 by the pool, dinner 7 (served family style, bring your own wine); room service available; informal dress; live music and dancing on the terrace, Sunday evening barbecues, cookout rides.

DIVERSIONS: Heated outdoor pool, Aqua'ssage hydrotherapy pool, hiking trails, horseback riding, sunbathing tower, shuffleboard, putting green, billiards, backgammon, tennis (1 court)—no charge; and "any mixed doubles team that can beat Jack and Colette Jackson in two out of three sets will be offered a free day's stay on their next visit."

Arizona Biltmore Hotel
Phoenix, Ariz.

The lobby, lounge, and dining room have ceilings of pure gold leaf; Frank Lloyd Wright had a hand in the design, and the master's touch can be seen in murals and chandeliers, and in the texture and motifs of the unique facade. No ordinary resort this. But it may be heading that way.

Phoenix now has the Biltmore in a half-Nelson, and some of the sense of spaciousness has gone; and that splendid driveway sweeping from 24th Street to Cloud Nine is no longer lined with groves of orange trees but with more and more homes (classy homes, true, but hardly as pleasing to the soul as trees). To top it all off, the third owner in five years has just taken over (the Four Seasons group of Canada), and presumably they'll continue to put more emphasis on group business.

Still, the Arizona Biltmore *is* one of a kind, and it does offer at least some of the style of a resort in the grand manner: room service comes with all the trimmings, including white gloves on the waiters, and guests still dress to the nines for sumptuous dining beneath the gold leaf.

The Biltmore's 314 guest rooms are classics in the Frank Lloyd Wright manner, revivified with pastel colors and geometric wall hangings. The most romantic rooms are in the fifteen cottages behind the main building, facing acres of lawns and beds of snapdragons and calendula. The new Paradise Wing (constructed at great expense to match the texture and color of the original buildings) have biggish boudoirs with deep-pile carpeting, armchairs, and color TV; rooms on the first and fourth floors have patios (the rooms on the top are smaller, but you have more privacy on your patio), and you'll have a view either of the famed blue-tiled pool or the gardens and Squaw Peak.

Other new features include more tennis courts, more fairways, and the spectacular new Orangerie Café, dripping with long Art Deco chandeliers, and a new terrace café with blue-and-white patio furniture. The gardens are still one of the delights of the Biltmore: 388 acres of flowers, fan palms, and weeping bottlebrush trees, cholla and saguaro cactus. You can step from your room, reach up, and help yourself to an orange or grapefruit. No apples, but Eden enough. Especially if you didn't know the Biltmore in the old days.

NAME: Arizona Biltmore Hotel

INNKEEPER: Cecil Ravenswood

ADDRESS: 24th Street and Missouri, Phoenix, Ariz. 85002

DIRECTIONS: Just off 24th Street, between Camelback Road and Lincoln Drive, 15 minutes from the airport, interstates, and Amtrak depot.

TELEPHONE: (602) 955-6600

ROOMS: 263 rooms, 36 suites and 15 villas

RATES 1978: EP, $40 to $75 in spring and summer, $55 to $95 in winter; special tennis and gold packages; plus 5% tax on total bill.

MEALS AND ENTERTAINMENT: Breakfast 6:30–10:30, lunch 11:30–2:30 (indoors, on the patio, by the pool), dinner 6:30–10:30 (approx. $25 and up for two); room service 6 a.m. to 11 p.m.; jacket and tie for dinner (informal dining in the Mexican-style Adobe Clubhouse); live music and dancing nightly.

DIVERSIONS: Heated outdoor pool, therapy pool, sauna, exercise rooms, hiking trails; tennis (20 courts, lighted, $2.50 per person per hour, pro shop, ball machines, videotape, clinics), golf (36 holes, $10 per round), bikes for rent; horseback riding nearby.

P.S. Spring and fall are the best times to be there (from the point of view of climate and crowds), but check for conventions.

Marriott's Camelback Inn
Scottsdale, Ariz.

This sand-colored enclave blends into sixty-five acres of desert (and concrete) in the foothills of Mummy Mountain, across the way from Camelback Mountain. Its most distinctive features, the circular Chaparral Restaurant and Cantina Lounge, look like enormous cupcakes, and behind the cupcakes adobe-style casitas encircle a giant pool and a dazzlingly colorful garden, planted, in springtime, with a thousand daffodils and forty-five hundred ranunculus and anemone bulbs. The Camelback guest rooms, too, are larger than usual (they're five hundred square feet, for the record), and color TV, wet bars, and separate dressing areas come as standard equipment. The most unusual Camelback lodgings are the five-sided rooms inspired by the Indians' ceremonial *kivas* (beamed ceilings, oversize beds, rainbow headboards), but many of them are in a heavy-traffic location between the driveway and the tennis court; for privacy, the quietest rooms are closest to the mountain, but a good hike from the hub of the complex. To compensate for that, several of the suites up here have fireplaces, complete kitchens, and their own pools. If you can, check into one of the twenty-five Aztec Patio Rooms, on the second floor of the casitas, with secluded decks for intimate sunbathing.

But your problem in Phoenix may not be so much deciding which *room* but which *hotel*—Camelback or Biltmore. Each has its loyal following, but for those who have yet to sample the luxuries of either, here are a few comparisons. Many people find the informality of the Camelback more relaxing, whereas the Biltmore's grandeur tends to put some people on their Sunday-best behavior; at the Camelback, you can park your car almost at your doorstep, which gives you an added degree of privacy, if that's a consideration (but in turn that accounts for the extra concrete—you can't have it both ways); at certain times of the year the Camelback is cheaper (but since each hotel has its own pattern of seasons you'll have to study dates closely); if you plan to play a lot of tennis, court time is free at the Camelback; at dinnertime, you can choose between the Biltmore's European-style elegance and the Camelback's pseudo-sophisticated, red-plush cupcake Chaparral with waitresses in skimpy shorts and black tights.

It's a tough choice, unless you happen to be a thrifty tennis player who fancies black tights; the only sane solution is to spend a few days at each resort.

NAME: Marriott's Camelback Inn

INNKEEPER: Dave Rolston

ADDRESS: P.O. Box 70, Scottsdale, Ariz. 85252

DIRECTIONS: On East Lincoln Drive, the main east-west road on the north side of Camelback Mountain; about 10 minutes from Scottsdale, 20 minutes from downtown Phoenix, Sky Harbor Airport and the Amtrak depot.

TELEPHONE: (602) 948-1700

ROOMS: 413 rooms and suites

RATES 1978: EP, $56 to $65 through May 31, $25 and $35 June 1 through September 14, $64 to $73 September 15 through December 31; plus 3% tax.

MEALS AND ENTERTAINMENT: Breakfast 6:30–11:30, lunch 11:45–2, dinner 6–10:30 (approx. $20 to $30 for two, although you can eat much more cheaply in the inn's attractive coffee shop); room service 7 a.m. to 10 p.m.; jackets requested in the Chapparal Room.

DIVERSIONS: Two heated outdoor pools, two therapy pools, hiking, shuffleboard, table tennis, tennis (10 courts, 4 lighted) free of charge; golf (18 holes, $12 per round in winter, $5 in summer), pitch-and-putt golf ($2.50), bikes ($5 a day); horseback riding nearby.

P.S. Lots of conventions, but note those summer rates.

John Gardiner's Tennis Ranch
Scottsdale, Ariz.

From the main road you can barely pick out the ranch, so neatly does it blend in with the foothills of Camelback Mountain, but once you get there the statistics are impressive. Tennis courts? Two dozen of them, and if you rent the Casa Ken Rosewall you'll have a private court on your roof. Pros? thirty-six. Swimming pools? A total of nine, including six private casa pools. If you join one of the famed clinics, you'll be on the courts for three and a half hours a day, battling it out with a computerized ball machine that pops out three thousand balls an hour. Everyone takes his or her tennis seriously here, but there are enough duffers and fluffers to keep the great Rosewall and his pros wincing; and whatever the state of your game you can enjoy the luxury of John Gardiner's Ranch.

Most of the accommodations are in forty-odd casitas—each with beamed ceilings, open fireplace, spacious patio, air conditioning, but, oddly enough, a square tub/shower rather than the stretch-out-in kind of bathtub you'd probably welcome after all that dashing around on the courts. The casas offer really deluxe accommodations, with fieldstone fireplaces, color TV, private therapy pools; six of them have private pools and private tennis courts. Most spectacular of the bunch is Casa Rosewall, which has beds (and bathrobes) for eight guests ($500 a day, but divide that by eight and it's not prohibitive).

What sets the Gardiner Ranch apart is not only the thoroughness of its clinics and the luxury of its rooms, but the thoughtful touches. Orange juice, coffee, and a newspaper appear on your doorstep every morning before you join the clinic; your room comes stocked with setups, coffee, and tea; your MAP rate includes buffet lunch rather than dinner, on the theory that tennis players are more likely to want to have lunch at the ranch, then dress up in the evening and sample the scores of good restaurants in the neighborhood. Finally, on the rare occasions when rain stops play and everyone is fidgeting to get back on the courts, John Gardiner pops open the champagne and fills everyone's glass. On the house. That's the sort of hospitality that has attracted such budding Rosewalls as Elton John, David Frost, and Art Buchwald.

NAME: John Gardiner's Tennis Ranch
INNKEEPER: Mr. Vik Jackson
ADDRESS: 5700 East McDonald Drive, Scottsdale, Ariz. 85253
DIRECTIONS: Between Scottsdale Road and 44th Street, one block south of Lincoln Drive.
TELEPHONE: (602) 948-2100
ROOMS: 105 rooms, in various casitas and casas
RATES 1978: MAP only from $90 through June 1, closed June through September; 15% service charge, 4% tax; Tennis Clinic Package $700 per person per week (22 hours of instruction), including service charge and tax.
MEALS AND ENTERTAINMENT: Breakfast 7:30–10:30, lunch 12:30–3:30 (buffet), dinner 7:30–10:30; room service (limited) 11 a.m. to 7 p.m.; jacket and tie at dinner; occasional live music and dancing.
DIVERSIONS: 3 heated pools, 2 therapy pools, tennis (24 courts, no charge, 36 pros, no lights, ball machines, clinics), golf, horseback riding nearby.

Hermosa Inn
Paradise Valley, Ariz.

Here it is—the desert equivalent of a small country inn in New England. Just twenty-eight rooms, hidden away somewhere between the Arizona Biltmore's estate and Camelback

Mountain, across a canal, near a small white church with a big black cross, surrounded by cactus—and silence.

The Hermosa is a low white hacienda—a paella of Spanish, Mexican, and Indian. The tiny lobby has a pair of open fires that fill the cool desert evenings with the smell of burning mesquite. An archway leads through a quiet courtyard to a colorful dining room, all beams and gleaming table linen. The guest rooms are brick pueblos, nestled among seven acres of trees and cactus, decorated in what's usually called "Mediterranean style," with bare brick walls, soft light, wooden furniture, boldly patterned spreads and carpets. All rooms have radio, TV, and individual controls for heat and air conditioning. The inn's seven acres of grounds include a small heated pool, tennis court, and shuffleboard. *Hermosa:* beautiful, handsome. Hermosa it is.

NAME: Hermosa Inn

INNKEEPER: Jacqueline Louis

ADDRESS: 5532 North Palo Cristi Road, Paradise Valley, Ariz. 85253

DIRECTIONS: Drive along Camelback Road to 32nd Street, then go north; at Stanford Drive turn right, at the white church, turn left.

TELEPHONE: (602) 955-8660

ROOMS: 41 rooms and suites in four villas

RATES 1978: EP, from $42 to $55 in spring, from $38 to $48 in fall, special summer rates on request; plus 4% tax on room, 5% on food.

MEALS AND ENTERTAINMENT: Breakfast 7:30–9:30, lunch 11:30–2, Sunday brunch 11–3, dinner from 6 (approx. $15 to $25 for two); room service for breakfast; jacket requested at dinner; occasional live music.

DIVERSIONS: Heated outdoor pool, 3 tennis courts (no charge), bikes for rent.

The Wigwam Resort
Litchfield Park, Ariz.

Back in World War I the United States needed Sea Island cotton fast for revolutionary new tires. So the Goodyear Tire and Rubber Company rolled to the rescue and went into the cotton plantation business on a stretch of desert seventeen miles west of Phoenix. To keep its uprooted executives happy, the company built a guest house, known as the Organization House, which became so popular that it was converted into a resort in 1929. That may seem an unpromising beginning for a resort inn, but you just try to get a reservation here in February or March. The only signs of the ownership are occasional fly-overs by the Goodyear blimp, and the name of the resort's golf course—the Goodyear Golf and Country Club. Even a B. F. Goodrich stockholder couldn't be offended.

The Wigwam is surrounded by a garden suburb, Litchfield Park, which in turn is surrounded by a 14,000-acre operating ranch that branched out from the original cotton to alfalfa, grains and melons; but several of these 14,000 acres are still native desert where the inn's wranglers will lead you along cactus-lined riding trails.

CASITAS AND EUCALYPTUS. The inn itself is a series of one- and two-story pink stucco casitas sheltered by palms, eucalyptus, and bougainvillea, or flanked by the velvet fairways of Robert Trent Jones's masterful golf courses.

The 205 rooms are divided into five types of accommodations—something for everyone. Even the simplest rooms give you space to stretch out, and they all have TV, refrigerators, and individually controlled heating.

The Wigwam probably has more lounges than any other hotel anywhere, with all sorts of quiet nooks and crannies, fireplaces, potted plants, and magazines. But with winter weather like Arizona's, you'll probably prefer to do your lounging around the pool, or on the rooftop solarium. The Goodyear Golf and Country Club, besides forming a lovely background for the inn, is also one of the most famous golf clubs in the Southwest, with two superb golf courses. Until recently it was golf that lured visitors to the Wigwam, but in 1973 the resort opened a new tennis club, with eight Plexi-pave courts, a pro shop, and four practice alleys with automatic ball pitching machines to give your strokes a workout. The Organization House has come a long way.

NAME: The Wigwam Resort
INNKEEPER: Reade Whitwell
ADDRESS: Litchfield Park, Ariz. 85340
DIRECTIONS: 17 miles west of Phoenix on West Indian School Road.
TELEPHONE: (602) 935-3811
ROOMS: 220 rooms, 16 suites, in groups of casitas and villas
RATES 1978: AP only, $82 to $88 April 9 through May 28, closed May 28 to October 1, $86 to $92 October 1 through January 28; plus 4% tax on total bill.
MEALS AND ENTERTAINMENT: Breakfast 7:30–9:30, continental breakfast 9:30–11, lunch 12–2, dinner 6:30–9:30; room service 7 a.m. to 11 p.m.; jacket and tie at dinner; dinner-dancing nightly, live music in lounge nightly, occasional fashion shows and square dancing.
DIVERSIONS: Heated outdoor pool, therapy pool, sauna, walking trails, badminton, shuffleboard, volleyball—all free; tennis (8 courts, 6 lighted, $5 per court per hour, pro shop, ball machine, clinics), golf (3 18-hole courses, $11 per day, carts $11 per round), horseback riding ($10 for 2½-hour ride), bikes ($5 per day), trap and skeet shooting.
P.S. The big push is during February, March, and the first week of April, when the regulars move in for weeks at a time and you'll be lucky to get a reservation for less than a week; small groups at other times.

Carefree Inn
Carefree, Ariz.

Take a bike ride in the desert. Chase a roadrunner through the cactus. Hunt for white-speckled quartz. Walk down to Cave Creek, push through the swing doors of a saloon, and have a drink with real cowboys. Explore the neighborhood for ghost towns, old gold mines, Hohokan ruins and Indian petroglyphs. Up there in Carefree you're closer to the desert than in Phoenix or Scottsdale. But hurry. Carefree isn't exactly car-free, and it's getting more built up every day.

Carefree is a new town, a planned community that has some respect for the desert. It's 1400 feet higher and thirty-five miles northeast of Phoenix. Up here the sun shines smoglessly nine days out of ten; and some people will swear it's the most beautiful spot on earth when the palo verde blooms yellow in the spring, or when summer showers turn the ocotilla crimson.

The inn itself looks like a motel—a pair of two-story wings embracing a pool surrounded by rocks and cacti. There are also a few casitas with kitchens, wet bars, and sunken tubs, and some new townhouse-style units across the parking lot. The rooms are oversize, the beds are oversize, the closets are oversize, and they all have balconies, refrigerators, electric blankets, electric alarms, color TV, and room phones. Nothing exceptional—just very roomy and very comfy, and recently refurbished to the tune of $1000 a room.

But you're not going to be indoors much, especially with the lights on. Most of the time you'll be playing tennis (six Laykold courts, five floodlit, all free), riding horses over old territorial trails to Bronco Butte or Apache Peak, or playing golf on two of the most spectacular courses in the Southwest.

In the evenings you can dine formally or informally (some folks drive all the way up from Phoenix for dinner here); and if you want a change of cuisine, you can drive over to Carefree town and dine beneath the stars in the patio of a Spanish restaurant.

Note the summer rates. They're a steal. And don't let the heat put you off: temperatures average 84.5 degrees in July, 87.8 in August, but the average relative humidity is 10 percent to 20 percent. That shouldn't stop you taking a bike ride in the desert—especially if you go by tandem.

NAME: Carefree Inn

INNKEEPER: Dick Osgood

ADDRESS: Box 708, Carefree, Ariz. 85331

DIRECTIONS: About 20 minutes north of Scottsdale; keep driving on Scottsdale Road until you see the signs for Carefree; air-conditioned limousine service to and from Phoenix Airport, about 40 minutes.

TELEPHONE: (602) 488-3551

ROOMS: 200 rooms, including 86 suites, plus villas

RATES 1978: EP all year, $50 for rooms, $100 for one-bedroom suites from May 1 through 31, $26 and $52 from June 1 through September 14, $50 and $100 from September 15 through January 14; plus 3% tax on room, 4% tax on food and bar bills.

MEALS AND ENTERTAINMENT: Breakfast 7–11:30, lunch 11:30–5, dinner 5–10 (approx. $20 to $25 for two); no room service; informal dress; live music and dancing.

DIVERSIONS: Heated outdoor pool, tennis (6 courts, lighted, free in summer, $1.50 per person per hour at other times, pro shop, clinics), horseback riding (165 to 200 horses, $4 an hour, $8 on cookout rides, also overnight pack trips), bicycles (standard, 3-speed, 10-speed for both men and women, by the hour or day), golf (two 18-hole courses nearby, $10 a round in winter, $5 in summer), trap and skeet shooting, hiking trails, trail rides by 4-wheel "Jackrabbits," charter flights to Grand Canyon, etc.

P.S. Open all year, busiest in winter, great bargain in summer (remember, it's cooler here than in Phoenix), but check for conventions.

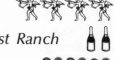

Wickenburg Inn Tennis and Guest Ranch
Wickenburg, Ariz.

The ranch hand who drove me to my casita in a golf cart pointed to the pile of mesquite on the porch: "Let me know if you want a fire set, either in the parlor or up on the roof." The roof, up a spiral stair, is a private deck for sunbathing by day or star-gazing by night, with a small adobe-style fireplace in one corner. The Wickenburg Inn, I decided, is what a desert resort is all about.

The owners, Chicago businessmen Jean Kempner and Warren Jackman, set out to create "the most beautiful desert resort in the country," and for my money they come very close. Everything possible has been done to preserve the character of the desert. A dirt road bounces you through the scrub to the parking lot, but from there on you get around on foot, horseback, or golf cart. A naturalist-in-residence keeps the staff on its toes to make sure the ecology is not disturbed, but he's also eager to tell guests about the one night of the year when the spade toad comes out after rain; bird feeders encourage the hummingbird and mountain bluebird to pay a call and sing a song. The riding and walking trails go on for mile after desert mile, but the owners have spared a thought for the saddle-sore and built an arts and crafts center where guests can indulge in macramé, stone-grinding, and other old-style crafts.

BOOKS, FRUIT, WINE. Apart from ten rooms in the main lodge (perfectly adequate, if you don't take a peep at the casitas), accommodations are in dust-colored casitas that hug the dust-colored hillsides. They're built in the adobe brick-and-beam manner, furnished with comfortable seats and sofas (with at least one antique per room), bathrooms with modern fixtures and rustic decor; each room has a shelf or two of

books, and the casitas have small refrigerators and the makings for tea and coffee (regular *and* decaffinated). Arriving guests are welcomed with a tray of fruit and a half-bottle of wine; beds are turned down every evening when you're at dinner. The inn's cooking is ranch-style hearty without frills, but the culinary highlight of the week is the cookout on Eagle Flats, a mesa setting of sagebrush and yuccas and chollas. You don't have to be a John Wayne to get to Eagle Flats; half the guests get there on horses, others by haywagon, and the unrepentant dudes by golf cart. Steaks are cooked over mesquite, accompanied by cowboy beans and beer biscuits; when the last deep-dish apple pie has been gobbled up, everyone gathers around the campfire and Ed Cheek and his wranglers get out their guitars and strum through a few Western ditties. With some style, too. The party usually continues back at the lodge, but there, alas, with amplification. Time to duck out, follow the lanterns up the hillside to your casita, uncork that half-bottle of wine and, if you're smart enough to have a deluxe casita, climb to your rooftop deck, light the fire, and toast the stars.

NAME: Wickenburg Inn Tennis and Guest Ranch

INNKEEPER: Ed Cheek

ADDRESS: P.O. Box P, Wickenburg, Ariz. 85358

DIRECTIONS: By car, 1½ hours north of Phoenix; from the town of Wickenburg, take Highway 93 a mile or so north of town, then go northeast on U.S. 89, and the entrance to the inn is a couple of miles away on the right (but you have to watch carefully to spot the sign); the inn's limousine can be alerted to pick you up at the airport or Amtrak station in Phoenix, and there's an airfield for private planes at Wickenburg.

TELEPHONE: (602) 684-7811

ROOMS: 51 rooms (10 in the main lodge, the remainder in hillside casitas, including deluxe suites)

RATES 1978: AP only, $60 to $88 from May 1 through November 16, $82 to $124 from November 16 through December 16 and from January 3 through February 5, $96 to $136 from December 17 through January 2 and February 6 through April 30; plus 15% service charge and 4% sales tax.

MEALS AND ENTERTAINMENT: Coffee and rolls 7–11, breakfast 8–9:30, lunch 12:30–1:30, dinner 7–9; cookouts twice a week, with country and western music.

DIVERSIONS: Heated outdoor pool, tennis (11 courts, pro shop, ball machines, clinics, no lights), horseback riding, arts and crafts center, wildlife study—all free; 9-hole golf course nearby.

P.S. "During major holidays, children are expected to join their peers . . . under the supervision of trained counselors." October and November are ideal months.

SUNNY SOUTHERN CALIFORNIA

The sweetest hours that e'er I spend,
Are spent amang the lassies, O!
BURNS

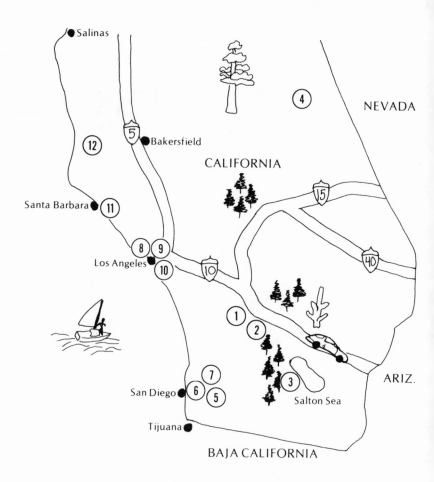

1. Ingleside Inn
2. La Quinta Hotel
3. La Casa del Zorro
4. Furnace Creek Inn
   and Ranch Resort
5. Rancho Bernardo Inn
6. La Valencia Hotel

7. The Inn at Rancho Santa Fe
8. Beverly Hills Hotel
9. Beverly Wilshire Hotel
10. Bel-Air Hotel
11. Marriott's Santa Barbara Biltmore
12. Alisal Guest Ranch

Ingleside Inn
Palm Springs, Calif.

I imagine this is how movie stars live: a lovely old hacienda with red-tiled roof, a cool veranda facing a lawn and pool, a pillared patio at the rear with a cherubic fountain among the flowers; the San Jacinto Mountains provide a backdrop just beyond the garden gate, Saks Fifth Avenue is one convenient block away in the other direction. Coming from Saks with your bundles of Puccis, you enter Ingleside through elegant gateposts, along a curving driveway strewn with Rolls-Royces, Aston Martins, and Cadillacs. (But no Pierce-Arrows, although the hacienda began life as the estate of the heirs to the Pierce-Arrow millions.) In the thirties through fifties it became a very chic, very exclusive hideaway for Samuel Goldwyn, Howard Hughes, Liz Taylor, Cyd Charisse, and a galaxy of other celebrities. Now the inn has come full cycle, having been bought up three years ago by Mel Haber, who also made his millions or whatever from automobiles, marketing what is politely referred to as "automotive novelties." In other words, those tacky little dolls and animals that wink at you from rear windows. Treat them with new respect from now on, because they enabled this Brooklyn entrepreneur to pour something like half a million dollars into rehabilitating Ingleside, in the process creating one of the most delightful, most unusual inns in the country. Unusual because on one hand it's unabashedly indolent, on the other it's congenial and "with it." Mel Haber himself is a walking birthday party, and this has become *the* place for the stars, starlets, and statesmen of Palm Springs. They flock to the Casablanca Lounge to imbibe, in an environment of wicker and rattan, ceiling fans with brass filigree, a grand piano with a copper lid; then to the glass-enclosed terrace of Melvyn's Restaurant to dine. Darryl Zanuck is said to eat here three or four times a week, Frank Sinatra held his prewedding dinner here, movie stars are married on the front lawn. Into the bargain, the food is first rate, the dapper waiters are not at all star-struck and, so far as I could tell, everyone seemed to be getting proper attention.

If you want to observe the people parade, spread out on one of the luxuriously padded leather loungers beside the pool. But if you want to escape, simply retire to the leather-and-marble library and have a game of backgammon, or head for the tranquil patio and read a good book beside the fountain. It's another world. Most of the guest rooms and suites are grouped around this patio, each one a boudoir fit for a star, furnished with antiques and objects carted over from Europe by the Pierce-Arrow clan. My suite had a Limoges cigarette lighter and ashtray on a Louis XVI night table and jade doodads on a Chippendale chest of drawers; every suite comes equipped with steambath, stocked refrigerator, and matches with your initials emblazoned in gilt. I'm told that Lily Pons came here for a few nights and stayed for thirteen years; you may want to do the same.

NAME: Ingleside Inn

INNKEEPER: Melvyn (Mel) Haber

ADDRESS: 200 West Ramon Road, Palm Springs, Calif. 92262

DIRECTIONS: Corner of West Ramon Road and Belardo Street, between Palm Canyon Drive and the San Jacinto Mountains; ask for directions to either the Ingleside Inn or Melvyn's Restaurant.

TELEPHONE: (714) 325-1366

ROOMS: 26 rooms and villas

RATES 1978: EP, October–May: $65–$95, double bedrooms; $80–$165, villas; $75–$130, penthouses; $125, mini-suites.

MEALS AND ENTERTAINMENT: Complimentary continental breakfast in your room, on the veranda, or beside the

pool; luncheon 12–3; dinner 6–11; champagne brunch
Saturdays and Sundays 9–3; room service from 7 a.m. to
midnight; refrigerators in every room stocked with beverages and light snacks (complimentary). Dress—informal, but "stylish" informal; piano bar in the Casablanca,
strolling violinist on weekends.

DIVERSIONS: Pool, luxurious loungers, therapy pool, private
steam baths in every room, croquet and shuffleboard;
tennis, golf, and horseback riding nearby.

La Quinta Hotel
La Quinta (near Palm Desert), Calif.

It gets its name from stagecoach days when journeys took a
breather on the fifth day, *la quinta,* for refreshment and,
when the passengers were compatible, revelry. This La
Quinta came along in the twenties, an oasis at the base of the
Santa Rosa Mountains—forty Spanish-style bungalows
spread over twenty-eight acres of trim gardens. All the accommodations are bungalows with two or three bedrooms,
furnished in tasteful southwestern style, each with a private
entrance somewhere among the tangerine and grapefruit
trees, or the palms growing dates for the chef's homemade
date ice cream and date cake. La Quinta's kitchen staff is a
mini-United Nations—Italian, French, Mexican, two Danish
chefs—and Steen Weinold, who's been manager here for
fourteen years, is a member of the Confrérie de la Chaîne des
Rôtisseurs. Their boast is that even when their guests stay at
La Quinta for three weeks they'll never be offered the same
menu twice. Dinner here runs to six courses, and might
include poached salmon court bouillon, veal sauté Marengo,
and roast rack of lamb.

WESTERN WHITE HOUSE. La Quinta is part of a larger, eight-hundred-acre estate, and both the landowners and the hotel's "distinguished clientele" are top drawer. During Eisenhower's presidency, La Quinta frequently served as his Western White House. The lure was obviously the estate's exclusive golf course, where a round will set two players back almost $70, including carts, which are obligatory. Forget it. There's plenty to enjoy here besides golf, and a staff of 110 to pamper just 150-odd guests. They're a friendly group too, despite the top-drawer clientele—just the sort of people you'd be happy to see on *la quinta*.

NAME: La Quinta Hotel

INNKEEPER: Steen Weinold

ADDRESS: La Quinta, Calif. 92253

DIRECTIONS: On Highway 111, about 20 miles south of Palm Springs, 7 each from Palm Desert and Indio; by air to Palm Springs, by Amtrak to San Bernardino (about 69 miles away), and you can arrange to have the hotel pick you up at the airport or station.

TELEPHONE: (714) 564-4111

ROOMS: 76 rooms, plus cottages with 2 to 6 bedrooms

RATES 1977/78: AP only, from $110 to $135 for rooms, to $251 for suites from October 1 through January 20; slightly higher rates January 21 through May 15, closed remainder of year; plus 15% service charge, and 6% tax on total bill.

MEALS AND ENTERTAINMENT: Breakfast 8–10, lunch 12–2 (indoor or outdoor), dinner 6:30–8:30; room service during dining-room hours; jacket and tie at dinner; trio six nights a week.

DIVERSIONS: Heated outdoor pool, masseur, tennis (6 courts, no lights, free to guests, pro shop, ball machine, and backboard), golf (at La Quinta Country Club, $25 a round plus $18 for carts—but then this is the scene of the Bob Hope Desert Classic), horseback riding (24 horses, desert and mountain trails, $6.50 an hour).

P.S. Special playground and pool for children.

La Casa del Zorro
Borrego Springs, Calif.

Back in the thirties, Zorro was known as the Desert Lodge, an adobe-style hideaway for Hollywood adventurers who wanted a taste of the desert. That's certainly what they found in the Anza-Borrego wilderness, the largest state park in the nation, mile after moonscape mile of seemingly lifeless, bewitching desert. Yet Borrego Springs is only an hour and a half by car from Palm Springs, a little over two hours from San Diego. It huddles beneath the eight-thousand-foot peaks of the Santa Rosa Mountains, a mere hamlet with a few shops, a restaurant, a bar or two, golf course, landing strip, and the Casa del Zorro.

The Casa is half-hidden in an oasis of tamarisk trees and roof-high oleanders—the original, refurbished lodge, a motel-style wing of rooms, and eighteen individual cottages in the garden at the rear. The lodge's dining room recalls its pioneer heritage with original paintings of old California and the Butterfield Stagecoach, which used to pass nearby; the bar is hung with antique copper and brass, but the guest rooms lack any special charm, spacious and comfortable though they are (each has air conditioning, a phone, and color TV). The chief attractions here are the rates (a one-bedroom cottage with kitchenette for as little as $30 a night) and, of course, the solitude. You can drive from the Casa across the desert to the Salton Sea and pass maybe a couple of other people along the way. The Salton Sea (234 feet below sea level) merits only a short visit (maybe time for a below-sea-level swim), and Salton City is a noncity of subdivisions and utility poles; so you probably won't hang around long before driving back across the moonscape to your comfortable Casa for a taste of Polynesia—steak teriyaki or mahi mahi.

NAME: La Casa del Zorro

INNKEEPER: Donald P. Gillette

ADDRESS: Borrego Springs, Calif. 92004

DIRECTIONS: From Los Angeles, take the new Montezuma Road via Warner Springs; from San Diego, State Highway 78 via Santa Ysabel; from Palm Springs and points east, State Highways 86 (south) and 78 (west).

TELEPHONE: (714) 767-5323

ROOMS: 16 rooms, 18 cottages

RATES 1978: EP, $20 to $25 for rooms, from $30 for cottages in summer; $30 to $35 for rooms, from $45 for cottages from October 1 through May 31; plus 6% tax on rooms, 5% on food and bar bills.

MEALS AND ENTERTAINMENT: Breakfast 7:30–11, lunch 11:30–2, dinner 6:30–9 (approx. $12 to $15 for two); room service; jackets for dinner.

DIVERSIONS: Large heated outdoor pool, tennis (2 lighted courts), putting green, badminton, paddle tennis, shuffleboard; golf 8 miles away.

Furnace Creek Inn and Ranch Resort
Death Valley, Calif.

Natural waterfalls tumble over rocks into a tropical garden of ferns and palms (and one intrepid rose bush); the big swimming pool is filled with spring water, naturally heated to 87 degrees; in the evening, you can dine off fig glacée and chicken breast with artichoke hearts, prepared by a Swiss chef and served in the dining salon of a Spanish *palacio*. That may not be the way you picture Death Valley, but that's the way it is in the oasis known as Furnace Creek Inn. Don't let the word "furnace" fool you: it has nothing to do with the temperature outside, but refers rather to the old ore smelting furnaces built here in the 1800s. In fact, don't let the valley's

ominous name fool you either; death it may have inflicted on early settlers trying to walk across the borax-covered floor of the valley, but during the season when the inn is open—fall through spring—the temperature *at midday* averages only 80 degrees, and guests sunning themselves by the pool can look across the valley to snow gleaming on the peaks of the Panamints.

The inn itself is right on sea level, a granitelike palacio with red-tile roofs; its solidly furnished rooms are cooled by air conditioning (at night you may need a blanket, though), and many of them have patios or balconies with views across the Valley. The ranch is lower (two hundred feet *below* sea level, in a grove of date palms), with 164 of its rooms in new two-story, motel-type wings adjoining "the only 18-hole grass fairway course below sea level"; it's good value, and it remains open throughout the summer. Both are operated by the Fred Harvey Organization.

Plan to spend at least three days here because there are so many things to see in Death Valley—Scotty's Castle, Twenty-Mule Team Canyon, ghost towns, fourteen square miles of sand dunes (magical at sunset), Badwater (at 272 feet below sea level the lowest point in America), to say nothing of secluded picnic spots among the juniper and piñon; and you will also want to leave some time for enjoying the tropical garden and the spring-fed swimming pool.

NAME: Furnace Creek Inn and Ranch Resort
INNKEEPER: Toby Allen
ADDRESS: Death Valley, Calif. 92328
DIRECTIONS: Just over two hours by car from Las Vegas (via U.S. 95 and State Highways 29, 127, and 190); from Los Angeles via Mojave and Olancha (290 miles via State Highways 14 and 190); by private plane, or charters from Las Vegas, to the landing strip at the ranch.
TELEPHONE: (714) 786-2345; out-of-state toll free (800) 227-4700; in California, (800) 622-0838
ROOMS: 69 rooms in the inn (plus 225 in the ranch, of which 164 are new and appropriate for readers of this guide)
RATES 1978: AP only in the inn, from $68 to $85 (open only from November 1 through April 30); EP at the ranch, from $22 to $38 (open all year); plus 6% tax on total bill.
MEALS AND ENTERTAINMENT: Breakfast 8–9, lunch 12–1:30, dinner 6–8; some cookouts; separate hours (and modest prices) at the ranch restaurants; room service during dining-room hours (inn only); jackets at dinner (inn only); trio 7 nights a week in inn supperclub.
DIVERSIONS: Outdoor pool, table tennis, badminton, movies, bingo, tennis (4 courts with lights); additional pool, tennis courts, golf (18 holes, $8 per round), horseback riding ($8 for two hours) at the ranch.

Rancho Bernardo Inn
Rancho Bernardo (San Diego), Calif.

The first owner of this Spanish land grant was an English sea captain, Joseph Seven Oaks, who retired from the sea to the life of a Spanish grandee—with the name Don José Francisco Snook. Snook's nook was all hills and vales with a smattering of trees; now it has 40,000 trees, 20,000 inhabitants, shopping centers, riding stables, and a golf course. And right in the middle of it all—the inn.

Hardly the most *idyllic* spot for a hideaway, but if you plan to play golf or tennis together, or ride horses along hilly trails, you'll find the Rancho Bernardo Inn one of the most convenient places in the Southwest.

The inn is girdled by forty-three holes of championship golf (including an Executive Course with no par fives), driving range, practice trap and putting green. (The green fee is only $8 a day for inn guests, and they get priority on starting times.)

The inn's Trails and Saddle Club is five minutes up the road, on the edge of the town, with mile after mile of unspoiled trail beginning right at the hitching posts. (Horses rent for $6 an hour.)

The inn also has two heated swimming pools, and you can rent bikes, but its most famous sporting facility is probably its tennis college. The college consists of four courts (two lighted), videotape instruction, and practice machines; its two-day crash course keeps you thinking tennis, playing tennis, and watching tennis from nine in the morning to nine at night. Exhausting. Better plan on following through with a two-day crash course in love.

OVERSIZE ROOMS, OVERSIZE BEDS. The 150 rooms are said to have Spanish decor. They're as Spanish as Don José Francisco Snook. However, they *are* spacious, and they do have two oversize beds (plenty of space for post-tennis back-rubbing), private decks or patios, double washbasins, and a few nice little touches, like color TV sets concealed in handsome armoires, and heat lamps in the bathroom. The rooms overlook the golf course, swimming pool, tennis courts, or parking lot: ask for second-floor rooms in the 400 and 500 wings, with a view of the fairways.

NAME: Rancho Bernardo Inn

INNKEEPER: B. A. Coleman

ADDRESS: 17550 Bernardo Oaks Drive, San Diego, Calif. 92128

DIRECTIONS: Take U.S. 395 from San Diego to the Rancho Bernardo exit (about 25 minutes from downtown San Diego, 30 minutes from San Diego airport); from Los Angeles (2 hours), by Interstate 5 south to Oceanside, then Calif. 78 east to Escondido, and from there south on U.S. 395.

TELEPHONE: (714) 487-1611

ROOMS: 150 rooms, 7 suites

RATES 1978: EP, from $45 to $53 all year; plus 6% tax on total bill.

MEALS AND ENTERTAINMENT: Breakfast 7–11, lunch 11:30–2:30, dinner 5–10 (approx. $15 to $25 for two); room service 6:30 a.m. to 10 p.m.; dress optional; live music and dancing.

DIVERSIONS: 2 outdoor pools, hiking trails, badminton, table tennis, shuffleboard; tennis (16 courts, $6.50 per hour per court, 2 with lights, pro, ball machines, clinics), golf (18 holes, $8 per round), bikes for rent, horseback riding ($6 an hour); skiing, sailing, waterskiing nearby.

P.S. Busiest in summer, but the weather's perfect for tennis, golf, and horseback riding all year.

La Valencia Hotel
La Jolla, Calif.

Groucho Marx used to skulk behind the pillars in the lobby and leer at startled ladies. Charles Laughton visited the bar every afternoon in summer to order "a pot of real hot tea, please." Evangelist Aimee Semple McPherson used to slip off here for weeks at a time with her current boy friend ("She was a grand woman," says a long-time member of the staff, "but oversexed"). Those were the days when everyone who was anyone in Hollywood went to La Valencia to get away from it all—Greta Garbo, John Gilbert, Ramon Navarro, Joan Crawford, David Niven, Gregory Peck, Audrey Hepburn—the whole gang.

La Jolla is no longer the unspoiled little seaside village it was in Hollywood's heyday, and the Valencia Hotel now competes with bulky condominiums, but they're by no means has-beens.

La Valencia is still, as it has been since it opened its doors in 1926, *the* place to go in La Jolla. Its Mediterranean entrance is still shaded by jungly podacarpus; little old ladies still have luncheon in the mosaic courtyard; and a jigsaw puzzle still waits on the table for someone to drop in the magic piece.

TERRACES, TILES, AND POTTED PLANTS. The hotel sits on a bluff above a bluff above La Jolla's famous rocky cove. Its gardens terrace down the hillside, then sweep around the swimming pool to the street and the park by the edge of the ocean. Pictorial tiles jostle with clumps of flowers for the chance to beguile your eye, and create petaled nooks if you want to be alone. The hotel itself is eleven stories of pink stucco, Spanish style, with a pink tower. Beyond its leafy patio you enter a cool lobby leading to the big-windowed lounge overlooking the ocean—an impressive room with Spanish tiles, potted plants, a golden piano, tiled fountain, and a hand-painted ceiling. This, you feel, is how a hotel in California should look.

The decor in the guest rooms is understated and graceful, with richly striped wallpapers, handwoven Portuguese bedspreads, beamed ceilings, and elegant sofas and armchairs from England, Italy, Spain, and France. The corner rooms on the eleventh floor ($55 at the height of the season) also have small sun decks. There are also a couple of unusual rooms in a bungalow in the garden, if you want extra privacy, but they're not quite "La Valencia": Room #3 has an attic ceiling, white walls and furnishings, and a king-size bed, and #2 downstairs is a suite with a fireplace. The hitherto conventional new West Wing has been redone in Ficks Reed and McGuirre South California seaside style.

OUTDOOR AND TOWER-TOP DINING. For a hotel its size, La Valencia presents you with plenty of options when it comes to dining. You may be tempted to stay a few days longer so that you can sample a different eating spot at each meal. Say, lunch on the patio and dinner in the elegant ocean-view Surf Room (steak au poivre, rack of lamb persillade for two, veal Oscar). Second day, lunch in the Skyroom on the tenth floor, with windows on three sides (and a grandstand view of migrating whales if your timing is right); then dinner on the patio beneath the moon. Third day, lunch on the patio and dinner in the Café la Rue, next to the Whaling Bar. The Whaling Bar itself is one of La Jolla's favorite watering spots—a shuttered, leather-boothed room with authentic harpoons, New Bedford lanterns, pewter candles, and paintings of whaling scenes. And, all the posh notwithstanding, you never have to wear a jacket and tie at La Jolla.

SUN, SURF, AND SNORKELING. The hotel's free-form swimming pool is one of the more placid spots in La Jolla for working up a tan. A few steps from the garden entrance, though, and you can be taking a dip in the surf, or floating off with a snorkel to discover some of the region's unusually prolific underwater life. You never know what's going to pop out from behind a rock and leer at you.

NAME: La Valencia Hotel
INNKEEPER: Richard P. Irwin
ADDRESS: 1132 Prospect Road, La Jolla, Calif. 92037
DIRECTIONS: 14 miles north of San Diego; get off Interstate 5 at the San Clemente Canyon Road cloverleaf and follow Ardath Road to and around the waterfront.
TELEPHONE: (714) 454-0771
ROOMS: 95 rooms, 10 suites
RATES 1978: EP, from $35 to $46 in spring and fall, from $42 to $55 in summer; plus 6% tax on total bill.
MEALS AND ENTERTAINMENT: Breakfast 7:30–10:30, lunch 12–2:30, dinner 5–10:30 (approx. $12 to $20 for two); room service during meal hours; dress optional; piano in bar.

DIVERSIONS: Heated outdoor pool, therapy pool, sauna, exercise room, ocean beach across the street; tennis, golf, bicycles, sailing, waterskiing nearby.

P.S. Busiest in summer, but beautiful any time of the year (average temperatures vary only about 10 degrees between winter and summer).

The Inn at Rancho Santa Fe
Rancho Santa Fe, Calif.

It was raining outside and mystery-writer Helen MacInnes was standing in the lobby armed with a golf umbrella. We discussed the weather, traded accents, and discovered we came from the same rain-haunted part of Scotland. Then, this being California rather than Scotland, the rain stopped, and she went striding off through the garden, no doubt concocting some intricate new plot for her next best-seller.

When you think of it, the Inn at Rancho Santa Fe is the perfect setting for a thriller—secluded, unhurried, slightly mysterious. This Santa Fe is only twenty-seven miles north of San Diego, but it's a cousin of its New Mexico namesake through the Atcheson, Topeka and Santa Fe Railroad. Apparently, at the turn of the century, an ATSFRR bigwig went off to the antipodes, brought back eucalyptus trees from Australia and New Zealand, and planted them on this old Mexican land grant. His intention was to create an endless supply of railroad ties for his company, but the plan didn't take root. The trees, however, did. They grew and grew and grew into a languid grove. In the twenties the ranch was transformed into one of the country's first planned communities (although it doesn't *look* regimented) and the inn was built in 1924.

It's an enclave of adobe cottages adding up to seventy-five rooms, but if you didn't know it was there you'd drive

past it. The inn's six gardeners (six gardeners to only seventy-five rooms—remarkable) seem to feel it's their duty to
disguise the inn, to hide it behind a proliferation of eucalyptus, Brazilian peppers, acacia, strawberry trees, avocado
trees, and bougainvillea. They've certainly created one of the
most fragrant hideaways in the West.

MULTILEVEL GARDEN. The gardens and cottages are on
several levels, and as you weave among the foliage to your
room it's easy to forget that you're in an inn. All the rooms
have views of the gardens, the trees, or the mountains
beyond. All have showers, all but five have baths; and a third
of them have fireplaces and kitchens. The decor is as varied
as the flora and fauna. My own favorite is #221, with period
decor and wallpaper and a large sun deck overlooking the
dell at the rear; room #38 has a window alcove, armchairs,
french doors on to a terrace, a concealed wet bar; and #35
has hideaway beds and huge windows overlooking the terrace and lawn, a pullman kitchen, and a eucalyptus-burning
fireplace.

Even the menu is remarkably varied for an inn this size,
serving everything from snacks to continental dishes. It's
surprisingly inexpensive, too—say, Bayshore combination
seafood plate (tutuava, shrimp, scallops, bluepoint oysters)
for $4.50, stuffed crepes with bay shrimp for $4, steaks and
roast beef from $8, with a wine list to match. You can enjoy
your meal in the sunny Garden Room overlooking the pool,
the leather-and-wood-paneled Vintage Room, the Patio
Courtyard and, in summertime, by the pool.

BARONIAL LOUNGE, 4000-VOLUME LIBRARY. The Inn at
Rancho Santa Fe is essentially a place for relaxing, for lounging by the pool, with maybe an occasional game of tennis on
the inn's three courts (free), or a round of golf over one of the
three courses nearby (green fees from $9). In summer you
can drive four miles to Del Mar, where the inn has a beach
bungalow (they'll also make up picnic lunches for you). Between swims and games, you can retire to the peace and

quiet of the inn's baronial lounge, with its raftered ceiling, big open fire, voluminous sofas, Chinese screens, and models of sailing boats. A comfy, clubby place for a pre-dinner sherry or after-dinner brandy. You can also browse for an hour or two in the inn's 4000-book library. Maybe you'll pick up a thriller you won't be able to put down—which is as good a way as any of spending a rainy afternoon, next to writing one.

NAME: The Inn at Rancho Santa Fe
INNKEEPER: Dan Royce
ADDRESS: Box 869, Rancho Santa Fe, Calif. 92067
DIRECTIONS: From Interstate 5 take the Encinitas Boulevard or Lomas Santa Fe exits (from the north), the Via De La Valle exit (from the south); the Inn's limousine will pick you up at the airport in San Diego ($20 per trip for two); by Amtrak to Del Mar.
TELEPHONE: (714) 756-1131
ROOMS: 70 rooms, 5 two- or three-bedroom villas
RATES 1978: EP, from $22 to $95 all year; plus 6% tax on total bill.
MEALS AND ENTERTAINMENT: Breakfast 7:30–10, lunch 12–2:30, dinner 6:30–9 (approx. $15 to $20 for two); room service during dining-room hours; jackets at dinner in Vintage Room, optional but preferred in Garden Room; live music and dancing on patio during summer ($2 per person cover charge).
DIVERSIONS: Pool, putting green, beach cottage at Del Mar, tennis (3 courts, no charge); bikes for rent; golf, horseback riding nearby.

Beverly Hills Hotel
Beverly Hills, Calif.

"Daddy, this is such a beautiful hotel, and we love it so, I wish you'd buy it for us." So Daddy did, Daddy being Detroit lawyer and financier Ben Silberstein. Daughter Muriel was eighteen at the time she dropped the hint, and the Beverly Hills Hotel was a trifling $5¼ million. Today, it's worth $20 million. Maybe more.

Long before there was a Beverly Hills there was a Beverly Hills Hotel. When it opened in 1912, Sunset Boulevard was a bridle path, and the new pink-and-green stucco structure was surrounded by bean fields. Its original function was to attract people to the area so that they'd buy land and build homes. And buy and build they did—the Pickfords, Tom Mix, Harold Lloyd, W. C. Fields.

Today the Beverly Hills Hotel sits among broad avenues lined by royal palms and million-dollar homes, screened from the world by twelve acres of lawns and jungly gardens of banana trees, ginger plants, oleander, and jacarandas, a haven for celebrities and nonentities alike.

The haven consists of 325 rooms, all individually designed, most of them in the main building. The remainder are in bungalows tucked away among the jacarandas and date palms and bougainvillea—perfect spots for trysting lovers and bashful movie stars because you can get to them through the foliage, without ever showing your face in the lobby. Renting a bungalow is like having your own home in posh Beverly Hills; each one has one to four bedrooms (you can rent them separately), plus parlors, wood-burning fireplaces, dining alcoves, kitchens, wet bars, and garden patios. They're all luxuriously decorated—even the single rooms come with a small refrigerator.

The bungalows are expensive ($60 a bedroom, $200 or more for the lot), but they're still the most popular accommodations in the hotel. Except, perhaps, for suite #486 on the top floor of the main building—a sumptuous peach-colored $215-a-night suite with gold faucets, marble tubs, and a wet bar with a hundred glasses in case you're planning a little get-together. In recent years, this suite has hosted Prince Philip, Johnny Carson, Princess Grace and her prince. Big names, but then the history of the Beverly Hills Hotel is an anthology of anecdotes about the great and famous. Like the time Katharine Hepburn walked from the tennis courts to the pool, climbed the diving board and performed a perfect back-flip—still in her tennis togs and shoes. Or the day cartoonist George McManus unscrewed a button marked "Press" from a urinal in the men's room, stuck it in his lapel, and gate-crashed a party as a newspaperman.

BEAR STEAK FOR DINNER, CHAMPAGNE FOR BREAKFAST. To keep its guests happy, the Beverly Hills has an army of 400 reception clerks, bellhops, waiters, chambermaids, and chefs waiting to show you a thing or two about personal service. If you've been here before and made it known that you prefer a room at the rear, you'll get a room at the rear without asking; if you're the oil tycoon who has a penchant for bear steaks, a special order has already gone through to Alaska and your bear steak is waiting for you in the freezer; and if you're Brigitte Bardot you'll find the customary bottle of champagne on your breakfast tray. The hotel keeps track of these facts with a huge revolving card index system that records the basic facts plus the whims, foibles, and preferences of every guest who has signed in during the past five years; and special briefing cards are issued to key personnel, who are also expected to add to the list of foibles. The first test of Beverly Hills service is to pick up your telephone the minute you enter your room, and one of the hotel's forty operators will address you by name. (Or should. Last time I stayed there, she didn't, but maybe she didn't know how to pronounce it, and was too polite to guess.)

HAMBURGERS WITH ROSES. If you want an excuse to telephone, call room service. This is another of the hotel's fortes.

Obviously, if a big oil tycoon wants bear steak, he gets it. How about ordinary mortals? Try ordering a hamburger. It will arrive within twenty minutes on a silver tray, with your beer in an ice bucket and one perfect red rose in a bud vase. (There are roses everywhere; the hotel goes through a hundred dozen roses a week.)

You can also look forward to a rose with breakfast in bed, but here's another suggestion. Enjoy a whole gardenful of flowers with your muffins and coffee—in the Italian Garden, just beyond the fabled Polo Lounge, a patio built around an aging Brazilian pepper tree with pink azaleas dripping from its branches. The edge of the patio is scalloped with little alcoves of white brick, surrounded by hibiscus, camellias, birds of paradise, pituporum, and night-blooming jasmine, where you can linger over your fresh strawberries and cream and listen to the birdsongs. It's a lyrical way to begin a day. There are, to be sure, some people who find the Beverly Hills Hotel less than lyrical. Some people think it's overpriced (and cubic foot for cubic foot it probably is, if you're interested in cubic feet). Some find the plumbing intrusive. Some people get fidgety waiting for the valet to bring their car round from the parking lot (a rather noisy production number in the evening, so demand a room at the rear), and others think that a $3 cab ride from downtown Hollywood is $3 too far. But for its loyal fan club, it's a matter of "Daddy, this is such a beautiful hotel, and we love it so, we hope you won't sell it." Even for $20 million.

NAME: Beverly Hills Hotel
INNKEEPER: Freeman W. Hill, Jr.
ADDRESS: 9641 Sunset Boulevard, Beverly Hills, Calif. 90210
DIRECTIONS: The simplest way, probably, is to get onto the San Diego Freeway (Interstate 405), get off at the Sunset Boulevard ramp, and drive east until you come to a big pink-and-green building sticking up above the palm trees.
TELEPHONE: (213) 276-2251
ROOMS: 325 rooms, 50 suites, 20 bungalows

RATES 1978: EP, from $56 to $90 year round; plus 6% tax on total bill.

MEALS AND ENTERTAINMENT: Breakfast 7–11, lunch 12–3, dinner 6:30–10 (anything from a few dollars to a hundred); room service 6:30 a.m. to 1 a.m.; jackets at dinner.

DIVERSIONS: Heated outdoor pool; 2 tennis courts ($2.50 per person per hour); Pacific Ocean 10 minutes away.

P.S. Busy all year round—but one of the few hotels in this guide that's *less* crowded on weekends; no need to worry about conventioneers ever (the hotel won't even allow name tags), but forget about staying here on Emmy Awards night and so on, unless you want to book now for 1984.

Beverly Wilshire Hotel
Beverly Hills, Calif.

You enter through iron portals that seem grander than the Great Gate of Kiev. And if you're driving anything humbler than a Mercedes, you can be made to feel like an absolute rube. Even the doormen here have class—and they want you to know it.

It's right smack on the main drag in Beverly Hills, not one but two hotels, in fact, divided by a cobbled street named El Camino Real. The beautiful people (or however they think of themselves these days) are on the go all day and all night. Which is not to say the place is noisy. It isn't. And yes, it is expensive. But if you're the kind who flushes with pleasure at the very thought of rolling out of bed and into Tiffany or Gucci, the Beverly Wilshire is the place for you.

The rooms are quite nice in terms of size and decor, the suites are stunning (in some cases even startling), but if you write home about anything, it will be the bathrooms. They are marvels—cunningly designed into three staging areas so each of you can go about your morning *toilette* in privacy. No secrets unexpectedly exposed. Bravo for the bathrooms.

PERFECT ROSE, TONY SHOPS. Room service is swift. The breakfast table arrives about fifteen minutes after your call. (Juice, coffee, croissants, butter and jam for two: $9.22. Not very thrifty, but convenient if one of you is still trying to find his or her way around the bathroom.) The breakfast tray is accompanied by one perfect rose. Or perfect tulip. Or perfect whatever.

The toniest shops in this most tony of neighborhoods are right at the front door of the Beverly Wilshire. And if you still enjoy star gazing, just linger by the cobblestones to see who's driving through the Great Gate of Kiev in all those Rolls Royces, Lotuses, Alfas, and Mercedes Benzes. *Mooo*vie people, that's who. They seem to have money to burn. And so must you—but you'll probably enjoy every glamorous minute of it.

                                                                    R. E. S.

NAME: Beverly Wilshire Hotel

OWNER/INNKEEPER: Hernando Courtright

ADDRESS: 9500 Wilshire Boulevard, Beverly Hills, Calif. 90212

DIRECTIONS: On Wilshire, between Rodeo Drive and Beverly Drive.

TELEPHONE: (213) 275-4282; or toll free (800) 323-7500, (800) 942-7400 in Illinois, (800) 261-6353 in Canada

ROOMS: 450 rooms and suites

RATES 1978: EP from $70 to $125 for rooms, $145 to $200 for 1-bedroom suites, all year; rooms in the new, or Beverly Wing, are the most expensive, but they're the ones you want; plus 6% tax on total bill.

MEALS AND ENTERTAINMENT: You can eat from 7 a.m. to 2 a.m., in a variety of restaurants and coffee shops, at a variety of prices; room service 6:30 a.m. to 12:30 a.m.; dress casual or jacket and tie depending on the room; live music and dancing.

DIVERSIONS: Pool, sun deck, sauna, health spa; tennis and golf nearby.

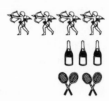

Bel-Air Hotel
Westwood Village, Los Angeles, Calif.

Truman Capote calls it "the greatest hotel in the world." Hotel? It's a magic bird cage in an enchanted garden. The first sights you see are an arched stone bridge, a white wrought-iron chair at one end, and masses of flowers everywhere. Walk across the bridge and you look down through the foliage to a lake with swans, and pathways winding to nowhere. Al Peiler and his team of gardeners have created a wonderland with pampas grass, jade plants, candytuft, tree ferns, tulip trees, red azaleas, ginger plants, coral trees, rose vines climbing stucco walls to tiled roofs, two sturdy oaks, and a rare silk floss tree, or *chorisia speciosa,* which is famous in horticultural circles. Opossum and deer often come down from the canyon to feed on the lawn.

EXERCISE RING, HORSE HOSPITAL. Actually the hotel's beginnings were earthy—it was once a stable. The estate known as Bel-Air, hideaway of the upper echelon of show business, was founded by Alphonso E. Bell, a man of the cloth who happened to strike oil on his dairy farm and put his blessing into real estate. To attract the right type of resident he built a stable, with exercise ring, milk shed, and horse hospital. A stable it remained from the 1920s to 1944, when it was converted into a hotel. Very skillfully, too—you'd never suspect that room #109 was once a horse hospital. The hotel is now owned by financier Joseph Drown, who wanted a hotel that is "relatively small, typically Californian in looks, built among gardens, around patios." He wanted, he got.

Bel-Air's shangri-la has a cloisterlike look, with Spanish arches, courtyards, patios, fountains, white and pink corridors linking white stucco bungalows with clay-tiled roofs—sandwiched between the garden and the sheer green wall of the canyon.

WOOD-BURNING FIREPLACES, GARDEN PATIOS. All the guest rooms are different (except for an unexpected paper wrapper round the toilet seat announcing "Sanitized for your protection"). Each room in its individual way is a classic of refined elegance. Or elegant refinement. Most of them have wood-burning fireplaces and garden patios. Some, like suite #160, have a marble fireplace, a small refrigerator, and a patio the size of most people's homes; suite #122 has a carved *wooden* fireplace, and harmonized wallpapers, drapes, upholstery, and bedspreads that change hue discreetly from parlor to bedroom. The most fairytale of the rooms is #240, halfway up a moss-topped tower, with a bay window and love seat overlooking Swan Lake. It's a tiny world all its own. It even has a small patio where you can have breakfast or sun-bathe.

The Bel-Air is the ideal little hideaway. You don't even have to go through the lobby, which doesn't look like a lobby anyway, more like a mansion lounge, with a large log-burning fireplace; in one corner is a tiny office, where assistant manager Phil Landon sits with a jar of jelly beans on his desk, and quietly caters to the erratic tastes of the rich and the distinguished—princesses, movie stars, society (like the multimillionaires who used to arrive with their own bed linen and toilet tissue), performers, and people so famous they need only one name. Some stable.

Ironically, you have to leave the stable if you want to go horseback riding. The only sports facilities are an egg-shaped pool and sun terrace. That's it. The Bel-Air is definitely a place for dalliance. Enjoy the garden. Enjoy the pool. Enjoy each other. Linger over dinner. The romantic atmosphere in the dining room is kindled by soft candlelight, cozy booths, and a fireplace carved into the canyon rock and surrounded by Hawaiian-style greenery; here Chef Horst Joenk serves up the sort of meal you want to spend an entire evening with— local fare with a Continental flavor, like Catalina sanddabs sauté belle meunière, broiled salmon Mirabeau, roast rack of lamb boulangerie or medaillons de veau Veronese. Even when you've added vegetables and wine and all the trimmings you can still come out for under $40 for two.

The problem is—even if it means going over $40—in an atmosphere like this it's almost blasphemy not to order champagne.

NAME: Bel-Air Hotel

INNKEEPER: James H. Checkman

ADDRESS: 701 Stone Canyon Road, Los Angeles, Calif. 90024

DIRECTIONS: Drive east on Sunset Boulevard from San Diego Freeway to Stone Canyon Road, then turn left to Calif. 701; if coming from Hollywood, drive west on Sunset to Stone Canyon Road (which dead-ends into Sunset Boulevard) and turn right. Stone Canyon is located almost at the center of UCLA facing Sunset Boulevard on the south.

TELEPHONE: (213) 472-1211

ROOMS: 46 rooms plus 22 suites

RATES 1978: EP from $48 to $75 for rooms, from $90 to $190 for one-bedroom suites, all year; plus 6% tax on total bill.

MEALS AND ENTERTAINMENT: Breakfast 7:30–noon, lunch noon–3, dinner 6–11 (approx. $35 to $50 for two); room service from 7:30 a.m. to 9:30 p.m.; jacket and tie at dinner; pianist and vocalist in lounge, after dinner.

DIVERSIONS: Heated outdoor pool, walks to the reservoir.
P.S. Busy at any time of the year, but you never have to worry
about conventions—they're not allowed over the bridge.

Marriott's Santa Barbara Biltmore
Santa Barbara, Calif.

The beamed ceilings and waxed flagstone floors, the panels
of antique Mexican tiles and the immense bowl of fresh chry-
santhemums give you your first clue about what to expect at
the Biltmore. Just step through the arched door and you can
tell you're going to find a lot of low-key luxury. And you do.

Each of the 176 rooms is different. Each has a distinctly
well-bred look—the kind you see only in fine houses or good
country clubs. The bedspreads and draperies, for instance,
aren't shiny. They look like Fortuny fabrics (perhaps they're
copies), but the bed linens are indeed Wamsutta supercales.
Three sheets per bed. The bath is well appointed, too: after
your bath, you can wrap yourselves up in a Fieldcrest Royal
Velvet towel—all twenty-seven-by-fifty inches of it. The beds,
too, are outsized (perhaps because the fifty-year-old Biltmore
was the dream child of a lanky cowboy, the late Robert
Odell). Ask for an extra-wide or an extra-long one—or both.
In either case, the mattress will be a bouncy Beautyrest or a
Serta Perfect Sleeper.

And where do you find ice? In your armoire, of course.
In a concealed refrigerator. (The inevitable TV set, however,
is in full unsightly view.) Most of the rooms also have window seats, upholstered settees, or sofas, and many of them
have fireplaces (burning, alas, gas and not wood, but the ef-
fect is still quite beguiling, especially when you're shrouded
in your twenty-seven-by-fifty towels).

CHILLED OYSTERS, BIRDS OF PARADISE. At teatime, guests
with unflagging spirits can stoke up on shrimp or chilled oys-

ters. (What true lover would ever pass the chance of lunging into some nice oysters, particularly just after a siesta?) At night, outdoor torches are ablaze for dining al fresco, so you can still admire the Biltmore's hibiscus, bougainvillea, and birds of paradise—and the fresh flowers on your table, grown not in some distant hothouse but right here on the grounds. Which are considerable—some twenty-one acres of prime land by the very edge of the Pacific. There, by the grace of you know who, you'll be seeing some startling scarlet sunsets. They're just about the most ostentatious touches tolerated around this lovely low-key place.

R.E.S.

NAME: Marriott's Santa Barbara Biltmore

INNKEEPER: Tom Gowman

ADDRESS: 1260 Channel Drive, Santa Barbara, Calif. 93108

DIRECTIONS: Take Calif. 101 to the Olive Mill Road exit, a few miles south of Santa Barbara, then follow the road to the shore and Channel Drive; 1½ hours from Los Angeles, 6½ from San Francisco; by air, to Santa Barbara Airport (limousine service); by Amtrak, the Coast Starlight.

TELEPHONE: (805) 969-2261

ROOMS: 176 rooms, 15 suites, 11 cottages

RATES 1978: EP from $48 to $83, all year; plus 15% gratuity on food and drinks, 6% tax on total bill.

MEALS AND ENTERTAINMENT: Breakfast 7–11, lunch 12–3, dinner 6–10 (approx. $15 to $25 for two); room service 7 a.m. to 10 p.m.; jackets for gentlemen after six; live music and dancing (plus harpist and fashion show on Thursday).

DIVERSIONS: Two heated freshwater pools, bikes for rent; golf, tennis, horseback riding nearby.

P.S. Basically a summer resort, but with this climate you can come at any time; some groups.

Alisal Guest Ranch
Solvang, Calif.

Solvang, of course, is that Danish-type village with windmills and tourists, bakeries and tourists, cheese shops and tourists, but if you come to The Alisal you won't be stampeded, because the ranch is three miles farther along the valley—one of the greenest, serenest valleys in these parts.

The ranch itself is part of a real working cattle ranch, lying in the bottom of the valley surrounded by sycamores, giant oaks, a river, a golf course, and stables. It's first and foremost a place for horseback riding, but even if you just want someplace placid and an occasional game of tennis or golf, you'll find it worth the shuffle through Solvang.

Its undulating golf course is less forbidding than, say, Pebble Beach, but it's still a challenging 6434 yards. (For guests only, green fee $8). The seven tennis courts are in tip-top condition (and free). There's a free-form heated swimming pool surrounded by a sun terrace, loungers, and beds of flowers; and if you want a dip in the surf, the Pacific is just fifteen minutes by car from the ranch.

But it's really the riding that corrals the guests, and ten thousand acres sprawling over the Santa Ynes Mountains, with sixty beautiful trails winding through the mountains (but you can ride only in the company of the wrangler).

The guest rooms are in small cottages scattered among the flower beds and lawns; they're not luxurious, but much more comfortable than you might expect on a ranch. No roughing it here. And when the sun goes down and the cattle come home, the ranch has two handsome restaurants serving Western food to take care of ranch-size appetites.

A real escape. A place to lie on the grass and look up at the sky until it's time to take a moonlight hayride and look up at the stars.

NAME: Alisal Guest Ranch

INNKEEPER: W. E. (Bill) White

ADDRESS: P. O. Box 26, Solvang, Calif. 93463

DIRECTIONS: The Ranch is six miles east of U.S. 101. If you're arriving from the south, watch for a sign saying Solvang-Nojoqui Falls, which is a short cut to the Ranch; from the north, turn left at Buellton, drive 3 miles to Solvang and pick up the Alisal Road, then go right and drive 3 miles to the Ranch.

TELEPHONE: (805) 688-6411

ROOMS: 60

RATES 1978: MAP only, from $80 to $92 all year; plus 6% state and 6% county bed tax.

MEALS AND ENTERTAINMENT: Breakfast 8–9:45, no lunch, dinner 7–8; room service during dining room hours; jackets at dinner; some live music and dancing in the lounge.

DIVERSIONS: Heated outdoor pool, tennis (7 courts, no charge), golf (18 holes, $8 per round), horseback riding ($9 for 2 hours), plus fishing and sailing in summer.

P.S. Busiest season is summer; some groups at other times.

SAN FRANCISCO AND ITS NEIGHBORS

And when the west is red
With the sunset embers,
The lover lingers and sings
And the maid remembers . . .
ROBERT LOUIS STEVENSON

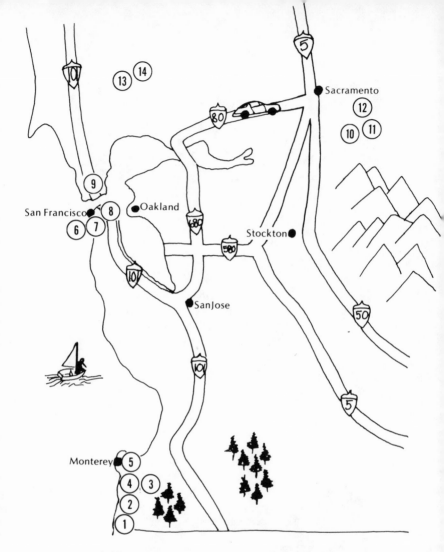

1. Ventana
2. Highlands Inn
3. Quail Lodge
4. The Sandpiper Inn
5. Del Monte Lodge
6. Miyako Hotel
7. The Stanford Court
8. The Mansion
9. Alta Mira Hotel
10. Sutter Creek Inn
11. Hotel Leger
12. The Mine House
13. The Magnolia Hotel
14. Burgundy House

Ventana
Big Sur, Calif.

If you'd like a preview of your entry into Valhalla, walk out along the enormous concrete deck of Ventana, and watch a big cloud bank come drifting in over the Pacific (look *down*, the ocean's way below you). Now you know what it's like to be sitting on top of the world. The Ventana is not short on mortal pleasures either. Management pretends to know nothing of the group therapy sessions that go in the Japanese therapy pools and saunas during the wee hours. But love, and lust, always find a way, don't they? There has already been one wedding amidst the poppies here, and more are inevitable—the place is that romantic. Ask any couple sitting around the pool sipping Chablis. They hoot if you happen to wonder where you go for tennis. "Nobody comes to Ventana to be competitive, you come to share with one another."

Only forty-eight people get to share at one time. Most of the twenty-four guest rooms have ocean views (cloud banks and morning mist permitting), others face the Santa Lucia Mountains and the redwoods. All are simply and beautifully decorated. Wicker, rush, caning, natural wood—these are the substances that give Ventana such a terrific look. The homemade quilts from Nova Scotia, Franklin stoves, and hand-painted and hand-carved headboards don't hurt either.

Continental breakfast is served in your room or by the open hearth in the guest den. (You also have a wet bar in your room, in case you want to hoard juices or wines.) For your other meals you walk or drive to the real showplace of this superb establishment, the ocean-view restaurant. Have lunch outdoors, on the deck, and drink in the forty-mile panorama of Big Sur coastline and Pacific Ocean. In the evening, enjoy dinner by candlelight in the beamed and timbered dining room. The napery is soft lilac, the music is Mozart, and, wonder of wonders, the food is excellent. If Chef Jeremiah Towers has his poached salmon on the menu, leap at it. Next night, try the tender-pink roast leg of lamb. And for dessert, *demand* the pear tart with almonds. You can swim it all off tomorrow. Or steam it all off tonight. In the sauna, that is.

R.E.S.

NAME: Ventana

INNKEEPER: Betty Burleigh

ADDRESS: Ventana Village, Big Sur, Calif. 93920

DIRECTIONS: 28 miles south of Carmel, on the coastal highway; Shell Station at entrance.

TELEPHONE: (408) 667-2331

ROOMS: 22 rooms, 2 suites

RATES 1978: EP (with continental breakfast) from $57 to $87 all year; plus 6% tax on total bill.

MEALS AND ENTERTAINMENT: Continental breakfast 8:30–10:30, lunch 11–4, dinner 6–10 (approx. $20 to $24 for two); room service for breakfast only; informal dress; live classical guitar music.

DIVERSIONS: Heated outdoor pool, therapy pool, sauna, hiking trails.

Highlands Inn
Carmel Highlands, Calif.

The cocktail lounge is called the Sunset Room and looks toward the Bird Rocks of Point Lobos (one of the most unspoiled, unusual peninsulas along the entire California coast); the dining room overlooks Yankee Point and its dramatic cedar-sided homes and crashing surf. Highlands Inn is a nest high on the granite cliffs above a cove, and as if the natural setting weren't enough, Robert Ramsey ("I'm a frustrated horticulturist") has transformed his fourteen-acre hillside

into a botanical garden with rare plants from New Zealand, Japan, Australia, Peru, South Africa, Japan, and Ethiopia—two thousand varieties of flowers from California lilac and Ponderosa lemons to heather and cypress.

CREDENZAS AND CHICKERINGS. The inn's lobby is a depository of antiques, including a cherry-wood credenza said to have been carpentered by Mormon Brigham Young for his sixteen-year-old fourth wife, a huge court cupboard belonging to the Emperor Franz Josef, and the first Chickering grand piano in California. The original guest rooms are Hansel-and-Gretel cottages secluded among the foliage and flowers; quiet, secluded, comfy, they strike the right note between rustic and modern. Not all of them have the views of the ocean and that's why the more functional lanai rooms are most popular.

Some of the lanais are quite luxurious. Room F4, for example, has a superb view, with a large balcony overlooking

Yankee Point, a tiled lanai with wrought-iron furniture, white rough-hewn pine walls, and king-size bed; and there are several rooms with balconies or patios to make the most of the sun—breakfast on the patio by the pool, dinner on the balcony overlooking the ocean. Lanai 24 is a suite with an enormous patio for sunning and dining, acres of window, a pink scatter rug in front of a fire, a red/white/blue bedroom with his and hers closets. In other words, among the inn's 105 rooms is something to suit every taste.

Your room rates include a six-course dinner, and there's an extraordinary wine list that ranges from humble Californians at $3.50 a bottle to an aristocratic Château Lafite Rothschild at $75. How's that for an elegant way to celebrate the sunset?

NAME: Highlands Inn
INNKEEPER: Paul C. Reed
ADDRESS: P. O. Box 1700, Carmel-by-the-Sea, Calif. 93921
DIRECTIONS: In Carmel Highlands, four miles south of Carmel, on scenic Highway 1, up a very steep hill.
TELEPHONE: (408) 624-3801
ROOMS: 103 rooms, 2 suites
RATES 1978: MAP only, from $72 to $145 all year; plus 6% tax.
MEALS AND ENTERTAINMENT: Breakfast 7–9, lunch 12–2, dinner 6:30–9 Sunday through Thursday, 6–10 Friday and Saturday; room service; jacket and tie at dinner; live music in the lounge.
DIVERSIONS: Heated outdoor pool; golf, tennis, horseback riding, bicycles, boating nearby.
P.S. Busiest in summer, but the view is spectacular at any time of the year; some groups in the off season.

Quail Lodge
Carmel Valley, Calif.

Someone went to a lot of trouble and expense here to create a perfect nest for lovers. A split of private-label champagne welcomes you to a room of muted colors, Ficks Reed furniture, Swedish string lamps, Fieldcrest towels, custom-made soap, rockstone tiles in the bathroom, electric percolator, *ground* coffee and ceramic mugs.

There are ninety-six of these rooms in beautifully designed board-on-board redwood cottages, some overlooking a lagoon with a Japanese bridge, others overlooking the golf course. They all have patios (but if you plan to spend much time on your patio, choose the rooms overlooking the golf course—they're farther from the highway).

DUCKS ON THE FAIRWAYS, DOVES IN THE LOBBY. Quail Lodge is part of the Carmel Valley Golf and Country Club, where the valley pushes aside the hills and spreads down to the sea. Most of the floor of the valley is the golf course, which golfers share with ducks, deer, opossums, and raccoons. The clubhouse is a handsome white building surrounded by flowers and flowering plum trees, and with a big white wrought-iron cage of temple doves in the foyer. The club facilities are available to the lodge's guests.

But isn't it only fair that since someone took all that trouble with color schemes and fabrics, you should spend a lot of time in your room?

NAME: Quail Lodge
INNKEEPER: Hoby J. Hooker
ADDRESS: 8205 Valley Green Drive, Carmel, Calif. 93923
DIRECTIONS: Four miles along Carmel Valley Road, east of
    Calif. 1—that is, 5 minutes from Carmel-by-the-Sea; by

air to Monterey Airport, and from there by airport limousine.

TELEPHONE: (408) 624-1581

ROOMS: 96, including 12 suites

RATES 1978: EP, $64 to $68 all year; plus 15% service charge in the clubhouse (none at lodge) and 6% tax on room.

MEALS AND ENTERTAINMENT: Breakfast 7:30–11:30, lunch 11:30–2:30, dinner 6:30–10 (approx. $18 to $30 for two); room service 7:30–11:30 for breakfast, 8 a.m. to midnight for liquor; jackets in Covey dining room; live music weekends.

DIVERSIONS: Outdoor heated pool, sauna (for men), hot tub; tennis (4 courts, pro, $5 per hour), golf (18 holes, $15 per round), bicycles for rent; hiking trails, horseback riding, sailing, and boating nearby.

P.S. Busiest in summer, but you can play golf or tennis any time of the year.

The Sandpiper Inn
Carmel-by-the-Sea, Calif.

Innkeeper Graeme Mackenzie was watering his roses as new guests arrived at The Sandpiper, and his warm greeting tipped them off to the general cordiality to be found during a stay at this small inn.

Irene Mackenzie is in the midst of redecorating all fifteen rooms, from the bottom up. The old beds were the first to go. Every room now has a brand-new Serta Perfect Sleeper (king or queen size), and Mackenzie antiques from Scotland and the Orient. Homey as the inn looks, it has recently been brought totally up to date in one convenience: private baths in every room.

Feel free to make tea, or chill your Riesling, in the Sandpiper kitchen; soft drinks are stored in the big refrigerator, and you pay for them on the honor system. Continental breakfast is served by the big open fireplace in the living room. Guests socialize here, and plan their days. What is there to do? The beach is a mere half-block away. (There was a sand-castle contest going on during our visit on a coolish October weekend.) Or you can hire a bike—the Mackenzies have everything from ten-speeders to bicycles-built-for-two for wheeling into town to shop or tour the two-hundred-year-old Mission San Carlos Borromeo. The Mackenzies can also advise you of the specialties at all the restaurants in the area. (Graeme Mackenzie is president of the Carmel Innkeepers Association, so he has connections, if you want to make a reservation.) Likewise, if you want to make arrangements for golf or tennis, he's the man to ask.

But maybe the thing to do is just sit around the fire and mingle with the other guests. The Mackenzies are well known in international circles, and their guest list shows names from fifty-three countries.

It's quiet here, too. The only buildings in the neighborhood are private houses. Strict zoning laws prevent any commercial encroachments. Your luck. It's like living in a pleasant private home in a jealously guarded enclave of privacy—and rose gardens.

R.E.S.

NAME: The Sandpiper Inn
OWNERS/INNKEEPERS: Graeme and Irene Mackenzie
ADDRESS: 2408 Bayview Avenue at Martin Way, Carmel-by-the-Sea, Calif. 93923
DIRECTIONS: From Highway 1, go down Ocean Avenue to the stop sign at the beginning of the village; turn left then second right into 8th Avenue, go all the way to the beach, turn left, drive along Scenic Avenue to the large stop sign in the middle of the road; next left is Martin Way, and the inn is 50 yards up on the right.

TELEPHONE: (408) 624-6433

ROOMS: 15, including two Carmel Cottage rooms

RATES 1978: EP (with continental breakfast), $22 to $40 from June 1 through October 31, probably less in the fall and winter; plus 6% tax on room.

MEALS AND ENTERTAINMENT: Continental breakfast 8–10; no other meals, but guests have use of the kitchen for storing wines and cheese, or making a pot of tea or coffee; room service for breakfast after 9; dress casual at all times.

DIVERSIONS: 10-speed bikes for hire, tandem free, backgammon, bridge, chess; the Pacific, golf, tennis, horseback riding, hill walking, mountaineering, surfing, scuba diving, polo, etc. nearby.

P.S. No children under 10.

Del Monte Lodge
Pebble Beach, Calif.

You wake up in the morning and step out onto the balcony and there spread out before you is a sight that will open wide the bleariest love-hooded eye: the eighteenth fairway of the Pebble Beach course running alongside the surfy Pacific, a flock of mudhens pecking the grass, the whole scene set in a curve of bay with rocks and pounding waves and pine and cypress trees. "A monument to the blessing nature can bestow on a golf course," as golf writer Pat Ward-Thomas called it. Even if you're not a golfer you'll probably still concede that a golf course is prettier to wake up to than a baseball diamond.

Golf made Pebble Beach famous, but you don't have to play the game to wallow in the good life.

PRIVATE FOREST, SEVENTEEN-MILE DRIVE. The present-day

Del Monte Lodge is a white, gleaming structure of slightly classical proportions, surrounded by two-story villas housing 135 rooms with views of the golf course or the ocean or both. It's on the famous Seventeen-Mile Drive around the Monterey Peninsula, which means it's part of the Del Monte Forest, a private estate decked out with some of the loveliest mansions you've ever squinted at behind fences and hedgerows—a setting of almost unalloyed peace, even in August, when Carmel itself is awash in Bermuda shorts. The guest rooms have big windows, big closets, big balconies, big beds; color TV, refrigerators, and log-burning fireplaces; and they've all been gingered up from ceiling to underfelt in the past few years, part of a rejuvenating program under manager Tom Oliver, a product of London's Ritz and Dorchester hotels. Since the rooms are all alike, more or less, the main difference is the view, and for my money the best views are from the rooms in the villas known as Colton, Alvarado, and Portola.

The main dining room, one floor above the fairway level, overlooks the ocean, and (nice touch) the tables that are not next to the window are turned to face the view. Up here, the table d'hôte menu offers you a choice of six entrées—such dishes as poached salmon sauce riche, chicken sautéed in champagne sauce, pork loin grandmère; downstairs in the Club XIX, you have a slightly fancier menu—poulardine fine champagne, côte d'agneau vert-pré, and filet de boeuf en croute.

One problem with a dining room that serves good food is that it becomes popular with the locals, and on weekends you have to reserve a table—and sometimes you can't get a reservation. In this case, who needs it? Just call room service and have them set up your meal in front of the log fire, or out on the balcony where you can listen to the surf as you sip your Pommard.

NAME: Del Monte Lodge
INNKEEPER: Tom Oliver
ADDRESS: Pebble Beach, Calif. 93953

DIRECTIONS: Take Calif. 101 to Carmel or Monterey, then
    follow the signs to Seventeen-Mile Drive; the Lodge lim-
    ousine can also pick you up at Monterey Peninsula Air-
    port ($8 per couple, one way).

TELEPHONE: (408) 624-3811

ROOMS: 135 rooms and suites

RATES 1978: EP, $80 to $90 for rooms, $100 to $145, all year;
    plus 10% service charge for gratuities, and 6% tax.

MEALS AND ENTERTAINMENT: Breakfast 7–11, lunch 12–2,
    dinner 7–10 (approx. $30 and up for two); room service
    7 a.m. to 10 p.m.; jacket and tie in the dining room; trio
    and dancing on weekends.

DIVERSIONS: Heated freshwater pool, saunas, walking, jog-
    ging, tennis (13 courts, $3 per person per 1½ hours, pro
    shop), golf (3 18-hole championship courses, $12 to $20
    a round, priority tee times for Lodge guests), horseback
    riding (100 miles of trails), trap and skeet shooting;
    sightseeing on Monterey Peninsula.

P.S. May, September, and October are the big months, but
    the climate is springlike year round; avoid the weeks of
    the Bing Crosby Pro-Am and other tournaments; some
    seminars and groups throughout year.

Miyako Hotel
San Francisco, Calif.

What do you say to a sauna for two without leaving the privacy of your own room? Voluptuous? Then reserve one of the
fourteen suites with sauna baths.

Or sample an oriental evening in one of the two Japanese *riyokan* rooms, with *tatami* mats and those voluminous
quilts known as *futons,* which are spread on the floor to
become beds. Have your dinner brought up, eat it cross-
legged on the floor, and then when you're finished simply roll

over onto bed. Soft lights glow in an indoor bamboo garden to add a moonlight-over-Fujiyama touch to your frolics on the futon.

Even the ordinary rooms at the Miyako let you indulge in a delicious Japanese tradition—the sunken tub made for two, complete with low stool and bucket for sloshing each other with cold water between bouts in the hot tub. The hotel thoughtfully supplies a specially imported perfumed powder that brings California's public utility water to the proper color and fragrance. In your subsequent state of euphoria, you may not notice the other features of the room—the delicate gold-brown-yellow decor of Japan, a *tokonoma* (the niche for flowers or Buddhas), *shoji* screens, brocade quilts, and chairs covered with Japan's traditional chrysanthemum motif. There's also color TV—a Japanese make, of course.

Now why on earth would you want to stay in a Japanese hotel in San Francisco? Apart from saturnalian plumbing, none—except that Nihonmachi, the Japanese equivalent of Chinatown, is one of the oldest parts of the city the Japanese call Soho. Plus the fact that you have less chance in this 208-room hotel of being swamped by a convention, which is a possibility in all the other top hotels.

MISO-SHIRU, SASHIMI, AND TEMPURA. You can also enjoy Japanese food here—in the hotel or in the restaurants of Nihonmachi. The room service has a few Japanese dishes among the regular occidental delicacies like club sandwiches and teriyakiburgers, but if you speak nicely to the maitre d' in the dining room, you can order up a meal from the regular menu—miso-shiru (soy bean soup), sashimi (raw fresh tuna or sea bass from Fisherman's Wharf, thinly sliced), and tempura (butterly shrimps and vegetables deep fried in a special batter).

And if you really want to pamper yourselves, pick up the telephone and order room-service massage.

NAME: Miyako Hotel
INNKEEPER: Gerald D. Wolsborn

ADDRESS: 1625 Post Street, San Francisco, Calif. 94115
DIRECTIONS: Ask for the Japanese Trade Center, or look for
    its peaked Peace Pagoda; a 5-minute cab ride from Nob
    Hill, about 10 minutes from Fisherman's Wharf.
TELEPHONE: (415) 922-3200
ROOMS: 208, 14 suites
RATES 1978: EP, $49 to $57 in spring, $50 to $58 in summer
    and fall; plus 8% local tax on total bill.
MEALS AND ENTERTAINMENT: Breakfast 6:30–11:30, lunch
    11:30–5, Sunday brunch 11:30–2:30, dinner 5–11 (ap-
    prox. $14 to $30 for two); room service 6:30 a.m. to 11
    p.m.; dress optional; live music and dancing.
DIVERSIONS: Japanese tubs—what more do you want?

The Stanford Court
San Francisco, Calif.

You don't really need the two chocolate bonbons left on your
pillow every night. You don't really need the little marvel that
warms your bath towels. And heaven knows you don't need
a second TV in the bathroom. But you're going to feel so cos-
seted once you've had them that you won't give a damn that
your room rate sounds more like a donation to a fund-raising
dinner. But then these are not everyday hotel rooms—they
were decorated and furnished for a cool $43,000 per room.

Walk through the carriage courtyard, beneath the
vaulted glass dome, past the Beaux Arts fountain, into the
subdued, antique-filled lobby and you'll find it hard to believe
that you're in a hotel opened as recently as 1972. The whole
place has such a look of noble dignity about it you'd swear its
feeling for the grand hotel tradition began in an earlier era;
but it looks and feels that way partly because it does indeed
have an architectural heritage. No jerry-built glass-and-steel
box this. It dates back to 1912, when it was opened as an

eight-story luxury apartment complex, high on Nob Hill, on the site of an enormous mansion owned by Leland Stanford. When the house was converted to a hotel each room was designed individually by one of the city's top decorators; rooms, lobby, and hallways were enriched with tapestries and marble, here an antique clock from the Rothschild estate, there a Baccarat chandelier from the château of Chambord. A French chef, groomed in Monte Carlo's Hotel de Paris and Paris's Hotel Crillon, was called in to take charge of the stylish restaurant, Fournou's Ovens. It's highly acclaimed and appropriately expensive; but The Stanford Court is an easy walk to a number of less costly three- and four-star restaurants. Daytime sightseeing is a cinch too: *two* cable-car lines go past the front door. If you're early-to-bedders, ask for a room facing the court (no view, but very quiet) or Pine Street (good view, yet still no sound of the cable cars). For the best view, check into a room on the California Street side, if the clang, clang wòn't bother you (in any case, the cable cars return to their barn somewhere between eleven and midnight). Incidentally, we have no idea how they keep the place so quiet. You won't hear a peep from the hallways. Not the maids. Not the breakfast carts. Not even the television in the bathroom next door.

R.E.S.

NAME: The Stanford Court
INNKEEPERS: James A. Nassikas (president), William F. Wilkinson (vice-president and general manager)
ADDRESS: Nob Hill, San Francisco, Calif. 94108
DIRECTIONS: At the corner of California and Powell streets, 5 minutes from Union Square, 10 minutes from Fisherman's Wharf.
TELEPHONE: (415) 989-3500
ROOMS: 402 rooms and suites
RATES 1978: EP, from $68 to $104 for rooms, $125 to $235 for suites, all year; plus 6% tax on room.
MEALS AND ENTERTAINMENT: Breakfast from 7 a.m., lunch to 6, high tea 4, dinner 5:30–11 in Fournou's Ovens ($35

and up for two); room service 7 a.m. to midnight; jacket
and tie in Fournou's Ovens.

P.S. Primarily a business executives' hotel, but romantic nevertheless; no conventions, only a few small seminar-type
groups, and name tags and that sort of thing are not en-
couraged.

The Mansion
San Francisco, Calif.

Nothing in the staid surroundings of Pacific Heights quite
prepares you for the drollery of The Mansion. Its Queen
Anne Revival facade, all buff and rust and white, signals
from its perch above a terraced flower garden. You walk up
two flights of masonry steps, past four monumental sculptures by Erskine Bufano, through a big oak door and into the
grand foyer. Bach drifts through from one of the parlors; a
wraparound mural dramatizes some highlights in the social
history of the city, but before you have a chance to figure it
all out, a young manservant in white alpaca jacket takes your
luggage and leads you up an elegant stairway, past man-
nequins in turn-of-the-century garb, to your room. He will
reappear a few minutes later proffering a tray with glasses of
wine to ease the chore of unpacking. The bedchambers are all
different sizes, but even the former maids' quarters are larger
than the average motel room. Each is outfitted with furnishings of the period circa 1890 to circa 1940—marble-
topped night stands, white ironstone ewers and basins, chairs
upholstered in tufted purple velveteen. Beds have brass or
carved-wood headboards, with sachets of fragrant potpourri
on the pillows; bedside reading might be anything from *How
to Win Friends and Influence People* to *Learning to Sail* to
Everything You Never Wanted to Know About Sex. The
bathrooms (all but one are semiprivate) are floored with the
original octagonal white tiles, augmented by tiny oriental

rugs to keep your toes warm. The conversation piece of each room is a full-length mural depicting the San Francisco worthy for whom each room is named—Emperor Norton, Sunny Jim Rolf, et al.

More murals: in the parlor, wildflowers and butterflies, a stag and unicorn folicking by a stream, a winged pig with a beatific smile flying above a meadow. More pigs: in the kitchen-cum-pantry, murals extoll the pig—pigs eating grapes, pigs playing musical instruments, pigs serenading pigs, all confirming owner Bob Pritikin's view that life should be one big "pignic." In addition to being boss of a local ad agency, Bob Pritikin is a music lover and organizes evening concerts around a baby grand adorned, need it be noted, with more pigs; and should the evening become too solemn, he is likely, as the resident virtuoso on carpenter's saw, to turn the *soirée musicale* into a *sawrée musicale* by rasping out his rendition of "I left my heart in Sawn Francisco." As another of the city's leading admen remarked: "The Mansion is a grand place for lovers who want to giggle as well as sigh."

NAME: The Mansion

INNKEEPER: Edward L. Stackhouse

ADDRESS: 2220 Sacramento Street, San Francisco, Calif. 94109

DIRECTIONS: In Pacific Heights, one of the city's prestigious residential neighborhoods; between Laguna and Buchanan streets. About 2 miles from the financial district, 10 blocks from Union Street.

TELEPHONE: (415) 929-9444

ROOMS: 16

RATES 1978: EP, $35 to $55, all year; plus 6% tax on room.

MEALS AND ENTERTAINMENT: Breakfast only, juice, croissants, and coffee served in bed from 7–10 weekdays, 7–11 weekends; no other meals, but dozens of fine restaurants nearby; room service 7 a.m. to 11 p.m. for beverages and snacks; taped Bach, occasional live recitals or chamber music.

DIVERSIONS: Backgammon and chess in the library; tennis in Lafayette Park, 2 blocks away.

Alta Mira Hotel
Sausalito, Calif.

Translated, Alta Mira means the High View. You'll find it halfway up the precipitous hill behind Sausalito—a town that likes to think of itself as very Mediterranean. Up here on the terrace, beneath the sun umbrellas with their floral print, surrounded by vivacious people enjoying life, you could almost be on the Mediterranean. But Sausalito's high view is probably more dramatic—across the bay to Alcatraz, the Bay Bridge, and the skyline of San Francisco.

This hotel is popular with visiting advertising and television types, which says a lot for it because staying there means they have to drive twenty minutes to and from their appointments across the Golden Gate Bridge, or take the ferry boat across the Bay. The Alta Mira is a combination Spanish villa and Swiss chalet, a group of cottages in a hilly garden. Fourteen of its thirty-five rooms are in the main lodge. No two rooms are alike. Rooms #11 and #8 are probably your best bets; #22 is a cottage all to itself, with two bedrooms, if you want to splurge in the interests of privacy; #26 has a fireplace and porch, and #16 is a suite with fire, kitchen and a view of Alcatraz. No air conditioning (you don't need it), no television. The most popular feature of the inn, though, is the terrace restaurant with its sun umbrellas. It has an adjectival menu—"sumptuous," "colossal," "sensational"—but you can enjoy a fine dinner of abalone steak, veal parmigiana, butterfly prawns, and so on. The prices are almost as steep as the hill up to the inn—$5.50 for breast of capon, $7.50 for the abalone steak. But then, someone has to pay for the adjectives—and the *alta mira*.

NAME: Alta Mira Hotel
OWNER/INNKEEPER: William Wachter
ADDRESS: Sausalito, Calif. 94965

DIRECTIONS: Coming from the Golden Gate Bridge, cut off on Alexander Avenue; in town, turn left at the traffic signal, then keep going up the hill until you see the signs.

TELEPHONE: (415) 332-1350

ROOMS: 20 rooms, 15 suites in cottages

RATES 1978: EP $25 to $50 (the price of most of the rooms mentioned above) all year; plus 6% tax on food and bar.

MEALS AND ENTERTAINMENT: Breakfast 7–1, lunch 11–4, dinner 5–11 (approx. $20 to $30 for two); room service all day; dress optional.

P.S. Open all year, busy all year.

Sutter Creek Inn
Sutter Creek, Calif.

Swinging couples you've heard of, but swinging *beds?* This pendulous experience is something you can look forward to in "The Hideaway" or "The Patio." The beds are suspended (securely, unless you have in mind something very peculiar) from the ceiling by sturdy old chains from ghost mines, which is only natural since this is the heart of the Mother Lode Country.

The Inn itself is a 115-year-old house, the former home of a California senator, and became an inn only a few years ago when Jane Way happened to be passing by and fell in love with it. It wasn't for sale, so she waited until it was (or maybe she willed it—she's that kind of lady). Having acquired the house, and with no more experience of running an inn than any other housewife who has reared a family, she then set about transforming it into one of the most delightful country inns on either side of the Great Divide.

And ingeniously, too. She scoured the antique shops and auctions for cranberry scoops that became toilet paper holders, old washtubs for shower stalls, a sled for a magazine rack, a portable bidet for a coffee table. The rooms are now stuffed with canopy beds, handpainted chairs, rockers, and other antiques and curios.

There are now sixteen rooms in the main cottage and in a cluster of smaller cottages in the garden. Take your pick. Some suggestions: The Hideaway, The Patio, The Cellar (which has a fireplace, patio, and pencil post bed), the Lower Washhouse, The Canopy Room (canopied twin beds, but slightly cramped), and The Library (a comfy room, but unfortunately on the ground floor between the kitchen and the parlor; if you don't want to embarrass the other guests, or be disturbed, you can while away the minutes until they've all gone to bed by reading something from the shelves—say, *Design for Steam Boilers and Pressure Vessels, New Patterns in Sex Teaching* or *What the Bible Is All About*).

SHERRY ON THE HOUSE, BRANDY IN THE COFFEE. Jane Way has also filled her inn with friendly little touches, like strategically located decanters of sherry; when you feel like a snort you simply help yourself. And if you're astir before breakfast, you can help yourself to coffee with a dash of brandy "to get you ready for an afternoon nap." Breakfast is taken family style in the brass-and-copper colonial kitchen. After breakfast, you're on your own. There's nothing to do here—no pool, no television—but just enjoy yourself. You can lounge in the hammock or laze in the garden in the shade of the flowering quince, willows, and daphne. You can play chess or Parcheesi in the pale-green parlor. Or settle into one of the deeply upholstered sofas by the fire and read *Punch*.

Otherwise, take a stroll down the arcaded main street of Sutter Creek, and check out the antique stores. Or go for a drive through the foothills of the Sierras and discover the relics of Mother Lode and all her little nuggets—abandoned mine shafts, the tumbledown shacks of Forty-niners, cemeteries where simple headstones mark the graves of young men who died old deaths. You can even try your hand panning for gold (the best time is spring, when the snows melt).

NAME: Sutter Creek Inn

INNKEEPER: Jane Way

ADDRESS: 75 Main Street, Sutter Creek, Calif. 95685

DIRECTIONS: About 50 miles southeast of Sacramento via Calif. 16, heading for Jackson; or via Calif. 88 out of Stockton, again heading in the direction of Jackson, which is 4 miles south of Sutter Creek on Calif. 49.

TELEPHONE: (209) 267-5606

ROOMS: 17

RATES 1978: EP, including hot breakfast, all year, $24 to $32 weekdays, $28 to $42 weekends (minimum stay two days on weekends, reductions for stays of 2 days or more midweek); plus 6% tax on room.

MEALS AND ENTERTAINMENT: Breakfast only (see above); for dinner, Jane Way recommends The Palace across the street; no room service, no entertainment, unless someone plays the piano.

DIVERSIONS: Pool; tennis, golf nearby.

P.S. "No children under 15, no pets, no cigars." Jane Way is something of an expert on reading palms and analyzing handwriting.

Hotel Leger
Mokelumne Hill, Calif.

It looks exactly like an authentic hotel of the Wild West, with a two-storied pillar-and-rail veranda for pushing bandits over, and when it began life as a tent beer hall in 1851, the Leger probably had its share of authentic fisticuffs and gunfights.

(In its heyday, "Moke Hill" managed to squeeze seventeen murders into one hell-bent weekend.)

The place is never that boisterous these days, even with all the saloon's amplifying equipment going full tilt. The saloon/restaurant is the most interesting part of the hotel, a medley of potted plants, striped wallpapers, and Franklin stoves—Gold Rush days with a dash of Greenwich Village. You won't find motel-modern conveniences upstairs, but the guest rooms have all been refurbished in more or less the manner of the days when Forty-niners came to town to whoop it up—or be wiped out. If the panning was good they splurged on one of the parlor suites (now $34.25); if they blew their nuggets on a poker game they had to settle for a room with semiprivate bath (now an inexpensive $19.25 double). There's a small pool in a grove of orange trees at the rear of the hotel.

NAME: Hotel Leger

INNKEEPER: Mary Sauble Churluck

ADDRESS: P. O. Box 50, Mokelumne Hill, Calif. 95245

DIRECTIONS: 7 miles southeast of Jackson, off the old Highway #49, where it meets Calif. 26.

TELEPHONE: (209) 286-1312

ROOMS: 13

RATES 1978: EP all year, $19.25 to $34.25 (tax included).

MEALS AND ENTERTAINMENT: No breakfast, no lunch, dinner 6–9 (approx. $12 to $25 for two); no room service; dress optional; live music weekends in the Golden Eagle Saloon, the Frog Park Players in the Court House Theatre on Saturdays in summer (in a theater that dates back to 1900).

DIVERSIONS: Small pool; golf, hiking, horseback riding, antiquing, sightseeing nearby.

The Mine House
Amador City, Calif.

¢

The Old Keystone Consolidated Mining Company put up this building a hundred years ago to house its head office. Now the office is one of the oddest little hotels in California.

Its eight rooms have preserved as many as possible of the original fixtures. The Retort Room, for example, has a shower stall in the arch that supports the bullion vault above (over the years, more than $23½ million worth of the stuff); the Keystone Room still has a dumbwaiter that used to carry the bullion to the vault; and the Vault Room still has the big safe that stored the bullion before it was shipped by Wells Fargo to San Francisco. The orthodox bedroom fixtures are genuine Victorian. The hotel has a small pool, but no coffee shop or restaurant; when you wake up in the morning and feel like breakfast, simply press a button and the Daubenspecks will bring over your complimentary tray of orange juice and coffee. It may not be the *plushest* spot around, but there are not too many inns in these parts that offer Victorian antiques, air conditioning, a pool, *and* coffee and juice served in your room every morning.

NAME: The Mine House
OWNER/INNKEEPER: Peter Daubenspeck III
ADDRESS: P.O. Box 226, Amador City, Calif. 95601
DIRECTIONS: On Calif. 49, 6 miles north of Jackson (again, of course, in the Mother Lode country).
TELEPHONE: (209) 267-5900
ROOMS: 8
RATES 1978: EP, $21 to $25, all year; no tax.
MEALS AND ENTERTAINMENT: Coffee or tea and juice served in room 7:30–9; no other meals.
DIVERSIONS: Outdoor pool; free lighted tennis courts within 2 miles, golf 20 minutes away, bikes, hiking trails, horseback riding nearby.

The Magnolia Hotel
Yountville, Calif.

There's a triple enticement awaiting you at this very small hotel in the Napa Valley. First, the wine cellar of some three thousand bottles being laid down by new owners Bruce and Bonnie Locken. The second lure is a bake shop, just a waddle away—and if you can resist an afternoon detour for tortes, Napoleons or lemon soufflés, you are made of stern, stern stuff.

Bad enough that you must resist the aromas wafting from the bakery all day; the Magnolia has its own dining room, its stockpot is always simmering at the back of the stove, and the cooking smells are irresistible. Dinner at the Magnolia is a one-entrée affair. But what an entrée! During our visit, it was poached salmon with hollandaise one night, roast pork Normande another. Prices are higher than you might expect in a place called Yountville, but then the food is better than you'd expect in a place called San Francisco.

The Magnolia's dining room happens to be the wine cellar as well. Banquettes are lined up along walls hewn out of solid rock and the atmosphere is joyous and convivial, becoming more joyous and more convivial as the dinner wines flow. The luckiest diners are the dozen who have reserved the few rooms in this quaint hostelry, who can stumble directly to their nearby brass beds with their crocheted bedspreads. Staying here is like a visit to Grandmother's—if Grandma was considerate enough to leave a cut glass decanter of port in every room. Will all this gustatory indulgence catch up with loving couples? It needn't. You can work some off with long swims in the Magnolia's pool, or steam it off in the hot-water spa. You can drive up to Calistoga for a taste of the local mineral water or, yet another enticement, a Calistoga mud bath.

R.E.S.

NAME: The Magnolia Hotel
OWNERS/INNKEEPERS: Bruce and Bonnie Locken
ADDRESS: 6529 Yount Street, Yountville, Calif. 94599
DIRECTIONS: In the Napa Valley, on Route 29, about 40 miles
    north of Oakland.
TELEPHONE: (707) 944-2056
ROOMS: 6
RATES 1978: EP (including full breakfast) $46 all year.
MEALS: Breakfast 9 prompt in the family dining room, no
    lunch, dinner 5:30–8 (5 courses, $28 to $32 for two);
    closed for dinner Monday and Tuesday; no room service;
    informal dress.
DIVERSIONS: Pool, hot water spa; bikes, mud baths, and win-
    eries nearby.

Burgundy House
Yountville, Calif.

All five guest rooms in this *petite auberge* were solidly booked
for eight weekends in advance when we checked the reservation list. So were the three cottages the Burgundy maintains
across the street. Week*days*, of course, would be an easier
matter. But you'll see why the place is so popular after browsing around for a bit. That baker's rack, those tea-caddy
lamps, the game table are not the commonplace bric-a-brac
you might see in any old inn. They're really old, really
French—and for sale. Hosts Mary and Bob Keenan were and
are antique dealers. They opened Burgundy House as an antique shop, and it "just sort of became an inn" because of all
the people who begged to stay over. The Keenans have lav-
ished a lot of love and good taste in making the guest rooms
beautiful too. Put in a bid for the sole room downstairs (the
only one with a private bathroom) and you also get your own
garden patio. Just waltz through your french doors and have

morning coffee under the old chestnut tree. Rooms upstairs give you a better view of what you've come to see—unending vineyards of grapes, grapes, grapes.

Bring binoculars and see if you can tell the Chardonnays from the Cabernets. Upstairs guests share the two baths, but the bathrooms are so old-timey, so leafy with ivy and ferns, you're not likely to mind. Sharing can't be all that bad, because people keep coming back to Burgundy House time and again.

Sing in the shower, if you like (make it something from *The Most Happy Fella,* which was set in this very region)— noise is no problem here, because Burgundy House walls are twenty-two inches thick. Burgundy House was built in 1879 by a Frenchman, and it still looks—well, Burgundian. Continental breakfast is served on the huge harvest table downstairs. The inn is too small to provide anything more ambitious, but you can walk down to the old pony-express station for your other meals. You'll *need* the walk if you've been on tasting tours of the local wineries all afternoon.

R.E.S.

NAME: Burgundy House
OWNERS/INNKEEPERS: Bob and Mary Keenan
ADDRESS: 6711 Washington Street, Yountville, Calif. 94599
DIRECTIONS: In the Napa Valley, on Route 29, about 40 miles north of Oakland.
TELEPHONE: (707) 944-2711
ROOMS: 5 in the inn, and 3 cottages across the street
RATES 1978: EP, $40 upstairs, $45 for the room with private bath, all year.
MEALS AND ENTERTAINMENT: Continental breakfast only.
DIVERSIONS: The countryside, the wineries.

THE PACIFIC
NORTHWEST

. . . for love is heaven, and heaven is love . . .
BYRON

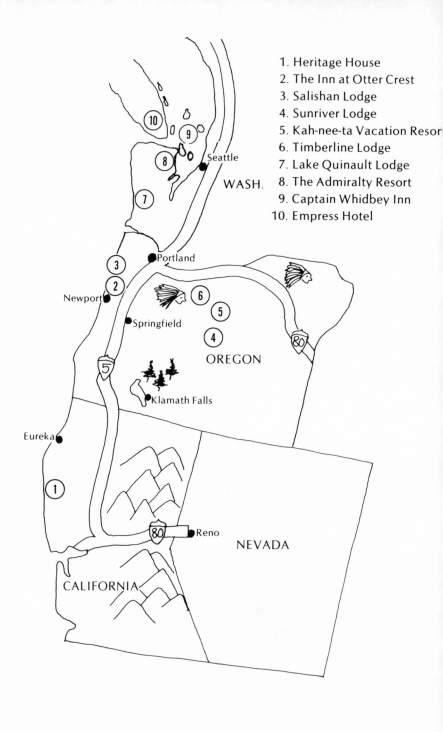

1. Heritage House
2. The Inn at Otter Crest
3. Salishan Lodge
4. Sunriver Lodge
5. Kah-nee-ta Vacation Resort
6. Timberline Lodge
7. Lake Quinault Lodge
8. The Admiralty Resort
9. Captain Whidbey Inn
10. Empress Hotel

Heritage House
Little River, Calif.

Take a walk around the cove. Sing love songs into the wind. Put your arms around each other's necks to keep the wind out. Listen to the ocean raging at the land.

A hundred years ago this site was a cove for shipping redwood ties, and for smuggling in liquor and Chinamen. The original farmhouse, dating from 1877, is now the inn's reception lobby, dining room and kitchen—a yellow clapboard building, with carriage lamps and a red door with bronze doorknobs, a refugee from New England; in fact, the whole setting looks like a picture of Maine that's been reversed, with the sun setting where it should be rising.

The Dennens spotted the old house in 1949, and decided to turn it into an inn (which is only fair, since it was built originally by Dennen's grandfather). Since then, they've added some more cottages to their hillside, and what they have now is not so much an inn as a village. The "village green" is a duck pond surrounded by elders; the gardens burgeon with azaleas, daffodils, nasturtiums, or wild blackberries; red lichen highlights the cliffs, and the Albion buoy gongs away steadily offshore.

APPLE HOUSE AND WATER TOWER. Some of the inn's fifty rooms are in new villas, but most of them are in buildings imported from other farms and sites along the coast—some of them with ingenious twists. An old apple storage house has become the inn's lounge, a clubby room with walk-in fireplace, card tables, and a bar. There are a few guest rooms upstairs—the most popular one being "Salem," mainly because

of its seventeenth-century solid cherry fourposter bed. The
most unusual room in the inn, maybe on the entire coast, is
the Water Tower—a duplex that once really was a water
tower. The bedroom is in the "tank" and a spiral staircase
swirls down to a lounge with tall windows looking across the
duck pond to the ocean. The only problem with the Water
Tower is that other guests are so intrigued, and envious, they
want to take a peek inside, and you may find yourself spending the day giving guided tours. The Firehouse Room has
lamps made from old fire hydrants; and the headboard in the
Schoolhouse is the original sign for Greenwood School 1898,
and the bedside tables are old classroom desks. No pool, no
TV, no room phones—just good innkeeping.

The presiding genius behind this inn-village, Don Dennen, learned his trade at the Clift Hotel in San Francisco. He
has since built up a loyal staff; most of them have been with
him for years, and seem to share his ideal—"Old-fashioned
hospitality," he explains, as he slides behind the wheel of his
sleek Maserati. His special brand of old-fashioned hospitality
includes nice little touches like having the waitress let the
housekeeper know when you sit down to breakfast so that

the maid can dash off to your room and fix the bed. "Just having the bed tidied up makes the place look so much neater when you get back to your room." It may not sound like much, but it makes all the difference between an average inn and a place where people care.

FRESH RHUBARB, GRANOLA, AND HOTCAKES. And when you see the gargantuan breakfast table, you might get the impression that it was created to give the maids plenty of time. Here you don't so much break your fast as shatter it. The meal begins with a buffet table groaning under a selection of juices; a choice of six fresh fruits (including rhubarb and figs); granola, porridge; followed by a choice of eggs, hotcakes, ham and bacon. You don't even have to wait for your coffee and toast: the coffee is on your table almost as soon as you sit down, and many tables have their own toasters so you can make your own toast to your own taste, from a choice of three types of bread.

All of which prepares you for a day in the open air—that walk around the cove, or a picnic in the forest where you can stand and kiss beneath a giant redwood tree. Or ride The Skunk, an old logging train that follows Pudding Creek and Noyo River for three hours and forty miles through the redwood forests.

NAME: Heritage House
INNKEEPER: L. D. Dennen
ADDRESS: Little River, Calif. 95456
DIRECTIONS: On California 1, 17 miles south of Fort Bragg; from U.S. 101 take exit marked Rte. 253 (Boonville), just south of Ukiah; then turn right when you get to the coast.
TELEPHONE: (707) 937-5885
ROOMS: 50, including 7 suites
RATES 1978: MAP only $57 to $97 February 3 to November 26; plus 6% tax on room and food.
MEALS AND ENTERTAINMENT: Breakfast 8–10, no lunch, dinner 6–8; no room service; jacket and tie requested at dinner.

DIVERSIONS: Fresh air, walking, exploring.

P.S. Closed December and January; no groups ever; for weekends reserve 6–8 weeks in advance, for Thanksgiving 3 *years* in advance.

The Inn at Otter Crest
Otter Rock, Ore.

The inspiration for the inn is one of those teetering pastel villages that decorate hillsides along Italy's Amalfi Drive. Here it's been translated into the setting of an Oregon pine forest, with weathered cedar replacing the pastel stucco, and a restless ocean replacing the placid sea.

The inn's two-story lodges are stacked higgledy-piggledy with covered walkways and stairways, with the undergrowth and tumbled timbers lying around undisturbed for a natural look. A self-operated lift takes you from the top of the inn down the hill to the top of the cliff, where you can admire a dramatic seascape: Gull Rock straight ahead, Otter Rock on the left, and Cape Foulweather—the high cliff on the right—which was given its unflattering name by Captain James Cook, who anchored offshore in 1778 when he came searching for a harbor and found instead high winds, high seas, and high cliffs.

There are 272 rooms in all, almost half of them with fireplaces; the decor is modern, fairly subdued, and the occasional dreary painting is overwhelmed by the cedar interiors and picture windows. Ask for one of the suites with a loft—bedroom and bathroom upstairs, kitchen and lounge downstairs.

RAZOR CLAMS AND KING SALMON. Where the cliff juts out into the sea there's a restaurant vaguely (very vaguely) modeled on the dining room of an ocean liner. It's a red-and-lilac room called The Flying Dutchman, with a wide-ranging cuisine—including seafood Wellington.

A few steps from the restaurant there are a heated pool, a therapy pool, a sauna (all open all year) and a glass-enclosed sun terrace; another few steps brings you to a pathway leading down to the beach and a state-owned marine garden.

There's not much nightlife in these parts. You can dance in the cocktail lounge or drive a few miles to Newport for dinner at Mo's, a modest harborside seafood place that became famous when it hosted Paul Newman and Bobby Kennedy.

Best of all, you can go back to your room, throw a few Prest-o-logs on the fire, open the balcony door, snuggle up on the rug and listen to the ocean snap and snarl at the base of Cape Foulweather.

NAME: The Inn at Otter Crest
INNKEEPER: Arthur F. Ream
ADDRESS: P.O. Box 50, Otter Rock, Ore. 97369
DIRECTIONS: 6 miles south of Depoe Bay, 8 miles north of Newport, on the Otter Crest Loop.
TELEPHONE: (503) 765-2111
ROOMS: 272, including 77 1-bedroom suites, 77 2-bedroom suites.
RATES 1978: EP all year, $36 to $42 for rooms, $58 for 1-bedroom suites; plus 5% room tax.
MEALS AND ENTERTAINMENT: Breakfast 8–12, lunch 12–5, champagne brunch on Sunday 8–2, dinner 5–10 weekdays, 5–11 weekends (approx. $15 to $30 for two); no room service; informal dress, live music and dancing most weekends.
DIVERSIONS: Outdoor heated pool, therapy pool, sauna, hiking trails, beachcombing, clamming, charter fishing, recreation room, and storm-watching; tennis (2 courts, no lights, $5 double); golf and sailing nearby.
P.S. Busiest in summer; groups remainder of year.

Salishan Lodge

Gleneden Beach, Ore.

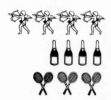

How many hotels do you know that print their own botanical guides? And tide tables? Or where every room has a leaflet extolling the habits of seagulls because the manager's favorite pastime is photographing gulls (and had been for many years before Jonathan Livingston flew on to the bestseller lists)?

Salishan is that kind of special place.

It was built by a wealthy Oregon manufacturer, John D. Gray, who used to vacation on this part of the coast and decided to build a hotel here. Something that would be a credit to Oregon, something that might also make some money. He picked a serene setting—a hill that looks over a lagoon and a promontory of beach to the ocean (but, unfortunately, across the highway); there he built what one architect has called "one of the most beautiful hotels in the world," and filled it with works of art, landscaped the grounds, tagged the plants, and hired one of the best managers in the country.

CERAMIC WALLS, 200-POUND RED OAK DOORS. John Gray and his team created a lovely lair for lovers. Ceramic walls decorate garden courtyards. Thirteen sculptured teak panels gleam on the walls of the dining room. Driftwood "sculptures" guard the driveway, and the red oak doors that welcome you weigh 200 pounds each. Even the therapy pool has a Japanese-style garden with Oregon grape, huckleberry, and vine maple. All very seductive. Enough to make you forgive any shortcomings. But you won't have to—Alex Murphy runs a tight ship, and even a faulty nozzle in the therapy pool doesn't escape his eagle eye.

Salishan's 150 guest rooms are in fifteen villas, linked by covered walkways and bridges, and constructed of Douglas

fir, hemlock, and cedar. The woodsy character is retained in the close-to-luxurious interiors. All rooms have picture windows and every window faces a treescape. But the trees have tough competition from the interiors: open fireplaces (with a well-stocked supply of, alas, Prest-o-logs, not real timber), king-size or double-double beds, club armchairs, handwoven light fixtures, floorboard electric heaters, soundproofing, TV, FM radio, individual heat controls.

INDEXED WINE LISTS. The Salishan's dining room is arranged on three levels and has lots of windows so that everyone can get a good view of Siletz Bay and the Pacific, once they've feasted their eyes on the teak sculptures. A handsome dining room is one thing, but how about the food? Chef Franz Buck, who joined the lodge in 1977, offers a seven-page menu ranging from local Tillamook Bay oysters on the half shell or salmon mousse en gelée, through a choice of nine salads to Dungeness crabmeat Pompadour and grenadines de boeuf aux morilles with cognac. (In Oregon? In Oregon.) The new Cedar Tree Room specializes in seafood and steaks cooked over "chunk charcoal processed from the mesquite tree and roots by the Yaqui Indian tribe." But wait until you see cellarmaster Phil de Vito's two wine lists. They're so comprehensive they need indexes, for scores of vintages from modest Bordeaux for $6 a bottle to a '55 Paulliac Château Lafite Rothschild for $175; a rare and welcome feature of the Salishan cellar is the range of *half*-bottles, including a Latour '64 and a La Ville Haut-Brion '62.

How do you fill your Oregon days between grapefruit juice and Haut-Brion? For starters, there are all the sports listed below (with indoor tennis and pool, Salishan is a first-rate winter choice, despite the reputation of Oregon weather). You can wander over to the beach, three miles of strand decorated with forestfuls of driftwood weathered and worn into grotesque and gruesome shapes. Or follow the old logging road up into the hills and forests, but don't forget to take along your botanical guide—here a kinnikinnick, there a salmonberry, everywhere a juniper.

NAME: Salishan Lodge

INNKEEPER: Alex Murphy

ADDRESS: P.O. Box 118, Gleneden Beach, Ore. 97388

DIRECTIONS: On U.S. 101, 20 miles north of Newport, 90 miles south of Portland; by private or charter plane to the 3000-foot runway half a mile south of the lodge.

TELEPHONE: (503) 764-2371

ROOMS: 150 rooms, 2 suites

RATES: EP, $42 and $52 in May, June, and October, $49 and $58 in July, August, and September, $38 and $48 in December, January, and February; plus 5% room tax. Special indoor tennis packages available.

MEALS AND ENTERTAINMENT: Coffee shop from 7 a.m. to 10 p.m., dinner 6–11 in Gourmet Dining Room, 8–1:30 a.m. in the Cedar Tree Restaurant (anywhere from $5 to $50 for two); room service; dress optional; live music in the lounge year round, dancing in the Cedar Tree in summer.

DIVERSIONS: Indoor pool (with hydrostatically controlled humidity to eliminate the usual damp smells), 12-nozzle therapy pool, sauna, exercise room, hiking trails; tennis (1 outdoor, 3 indoor with indirect lighting and a spectators' lounge with fireplace, $6 per court per 1¼ hour),

golf (18 holes, $10 per round); rental bikes and horse-
back riding nearby.

Sunriver Lodge
Sunriver, Ore.

This is one of the few hotels in the country with an ecologist-
in-residence and an Ecologium—a mini-natural-history museum where ecologist Jay Bowerman interprets the surrounding wildlife and nature.

And there's plenty of both. Sunriver's thousands of acres,
a lake basin formed some two thousand years ago by a lava
flow, are surrounded on three sides by a national forest with
156 lakes. This is the country of black bear, elk, and prong-
horn antelope, of bald eagles and China pheasants, where
German brown and rainbow trout outsparkle the crystal
water of mountain streams. It's a place to fill your lungs with

clean air and enjoy the wide open spaces: seventeen miles of cycle tracks (and more bikes than cars), three dozen horses champing at the bit in the stables, waiting to trot you around the meadows and forests (this is one place where twosomes can go cantering off on their own), a championship golf course. You can go canoeing on the river, bird watching in the meadow, or rock hunting among the lava beds. You never have to wear a jacket or tie. Which doesn't mean you're going to rough it: in a setting like this, most people would settle for a log shack, but up at Sunriver you enjoy wall-to-wall comfort. *You're* spoiled, not the countryside.

Sunriver is a planned community—but it looks as much like the average real estate blotch as a Rolls-Royce looks like a bulldozer. No more than one family per acre; *no* buildings on the banks of the river; all utilities underground, and so on. The man behind the project is the same John Gray who gave you Salishan Lodge, which means that the surroundings are respected and little details of design are in impeccable taste (note the direction signs, or the "sculptured" inclined sun terraces around the swimming pool).

The main lodge is an unusual timber-and-lava-stone building, a creation of the Pacific in its blend of Oregon and oriental; and the lodge condominiums dotted around the fairways have pitched roofs, sun decks, fireplaces, color TV, and in some cases kitchens. Over in the lodge you'll find sauna baths, a rumpus room to keep the teenagers out of your hair, a coffee shop, and a handsome restaurant where you can enjoy veal Cordon Bleu or chicken à la Kiev with a view of the six-hundred-acre meadow, a Japanese bridge, and the Fuji-like cone of Mount Bachelor. It's an unpolluted setting—and Jay Bowerman's there to help keep it that way.

NAME: Sunriver Lodge
INNKEEPER: Henry Hickox
ADDRESS: Sunriver, Ore. 97701
DIRECTIONS: Fifteen miles south of Bend and 2 miles west of U.S. 97; by scheduled air service to Redmond (33 miles north of Sunriver), or by private or charter flights to Sunriver's own 4500-foot strip.

TELEPHONE: (503) 593-1221

ROOMS: 300-plus in a variety of lodge condominiums

RATES 1978: EP, from $42 to $55 in spring, higher in summer (check direct with the lodge); resort homes and other condominiums from $65 to $95 in spring; plus 5% room tax.

MEALS AND ENTERTAINMENT: Breakfast 7–11, lunch 11:30–3, Sunday brunch 9:30–1, dinner 6:30–9:30/10 (approx. $18 to $25 for two); no room service; informal dress; live music and dancing in the Owl's Nest (to 2 a.m. nightly).

DIVERSIONS: Heated outdoor pool, sauna, bicycles (200 for rent, $2 an hour for tandems, 17 miles of bike trails), horseback riding (1978 rates not available), tennis (14 courts, no lights, $5 an hour for doubles, pro shop, clinics), golf (18 holes, $11 a round), boating, waterskiing, hiking trails, jogging, arts and crafts program, game room, movies; in winter, skiing, cross-country skiing (rentals), sleigh rides, ice skating.

P.S. Busiest in summer, but trying to build up winter business, small seminar-type groups throughout the year; special programs and playgrounds for children.

Kah-nee-ta Vacation Resort
Warm Springs, Ore.

At first glance, you think you've stepped into a Western: an encampment of white teepees stands beside the clear waters of the Warm Springs River; a mile away, a wedge-shaped lodge that looks like an avant-garde fort is set into the south side of an escarpment covered with sage and juniper. Indian country? Definitely. One of the most successful resorts to be built on reservation land, Kah-nee-ta is the pride of the Confederated Tribes of the Warm Springs Indian Reservation—Wascos, Warm Springs, and Paiutes.

Before the treaty of 1855, they gathered roots and berries, stockpiled a wealth of salmon from the Columbia River, and even owned slaves. William Clark wrote that they "received us with kindness," and today the Confederated Tribes are still receiving visitors with kindness—and 340 days of sunshine and the away-from-it-all calm of Kah-nee-ta.

Above the tennis courts and the eighteen green fairways of the valley, the cedar-sheathed Kah-nee-ta Lodge commands vast views of burnished hills. From up here, you could spot a smoke signal miles away. The main building is strikingly modern: the warmth of wood, vibrant color, light everywhere, a feeling of openness. Its centerpiece is a sun-filled, three-story-high lobby with a massive four-sided fireplace in the middle. One floor below, a heated pool and locust-shaded courtyard are framed by the three-story wings of guest rooms.

Each of the Kah-nee-ta's 144 rooms has a private balcony and eagle's view of the valley; each is handsomely decorated with warm orange and earth tones, bold Indian graphics, pottery lamps, the clean lines of natural pine furniture and built-in cabinets. The baths are tiny (half-size tubs) but the beds are huge. If you insist on a full-size bath, the luxurious Chief's Suite is the answer: two bedrooms and baths, living room with hi-fi, and full kitchen (and only $97 for four people).

The two levels of the Juniper Dining Room catch the last blush of the sun's rays, and the backdrop to your meal is a large painting etched into the exterior wall of the lodge. The Juniper's native American specialties include fish chowder, trout, venison steak, fresh salmon and bird baked in clay (or Cornish game hen). Best of all: the piping hot Indian fried bread with huckleberry jam. Menu prices average $8, and for a dollar or two more you can order native European dishes— chateaubriand or beef Wellington.

The lodge has on-the-doorstep pool and sauna, but you'll probably want to try the 100-degree mineral springs that give the tribe, the reservation, and the river their name. They're down in the Kah-nee-ta Village complex—three gigantic outdoor pools fed by the springs, plus separate baths for men and women. Swim, soak, have a massage. But be warned: with a trailer park, camping, eight three-unit cottages, and all those teepees, the village can sound more like a rodeo in summer. Escape on a bicycle. Go for a ride in the hills with Fred the wrangler. Or retire to your hilltop balcony and watch the sun set over those vast vistas of sage and juniper.

M.S.

NAME: Kah-nee-ta Vacation Resort

INNKEEPER: Dan Myles

ADDRESS: Warm Springs, Ore. 97761

DIRECTIONS: The Lodge is 114 miles south of Portland, 11 north of Warm Springs, off U.S. 26.

TELEPHONE: (503) 533-1112

ROOMS: 144, including 12 suites and one 2-bedroom Chief's Suite

RATES 1978: EP, $35 to $50 from March 1 through October 31, $25 to $33 from November 1 through February 28.

MEALS AND ENTERTAINMENT: Breakfast 7–11:30, lunch 11:30–5, dinner 5:30–10 weekdays and to 11 weekends (approx. $16 to $20 for two in the dining room); dress informal; no room service (mini-bars in most rooms); live music on weekends in Eagle's Nest cocktail lounge.

DIVERSIONS: Heated outdoor swimming pool, sauna at the lodge; tennis (2 courts) and golf (18 holes) in the valley; three large outdoor pools and indoor baths fed by mineral springs, at the Village; horseback riding, hiking, fishing, bicycling; Indian dancing on Sundays and holidays.

P.S. Crowded on summer weekends.

Timberline Lodge
Mount Hood, Ore.

The main door wouldn't look out of place in a medieval castle (a thousand pounds of hand-adzed planks with iron hinges and a massive iron knocker); the hexagonal lobby/lounge revolves around a ninety-two-foot-tall chimney constructed of volcanic rocks, with three huge fireplaces, flanked by six massive pillars, each one the trunk of a Ponderosa pine sculpted by one man with a broad-blade axe. Look around you, at the stair newels hand-carved from old telephone poles and the andirons hand-wrought from old railroads, and you know you're in no ordinary inn.

In fact, there is no other hotel in the country like Timberline Lodge, a gray stone-and-cedar V with a soaring roofline to match the mountain peak five thousand feet above; and for anyone who enjoys unusual hotels, the good news from Mount Hood is that this splendid specimen of Americana is being renovated, and by the time you get there, most of the woodwork will be sanded and varnished, the unique furnishings (strap-iron construction in true pioneer style) will be almost like new. Most of the rooms you're likely to prefer (they're known as standard, deluxe standard, corner, or deluxe fireplace) are one of a kind, with carved headboards, patchwork quilts, hooked rugs. (Deluxe in the context of Timberline means not so much plushness as extra floor space and a television set in the room; and you should also remember if you are here in winter to reserve a room on the upper floors, otherwise you might find yourselves looking out at a solid bank of snow.)

One of the deluxe rooms, the Roosevelt Suite, is named for the man who is usually credited with getting the Lodge off the ground in the first place. This was one of FDR's WPA projects, built by some five hundred unemployed men and women during the Depression; they performed so beautifully their handiwork is now a National Historic Monument. But is it *romantic?* Even a Howard Johnson's could be romantic in such a setting—on the timberline, six thousand feet up a rugged mountain, with glacier-covered peaks above you, rolling pine-clad hills disappearing into the haze a hundred miles to the south.

NAME: Timberline Lodge

INNKEEPER: Tad Michel

ADDRESS: Timberline, Ore. 97082

DIRECTIONS: 60 miles east of Portland, 6000 feet up Mt. Hood. Go east on Highway 80N from Portland, turn right at Wood Village, then go east on Highway 26; an hour later you'll see the signs for Timberline.

TELEPHONE: (503) 226-7979

ROOMS: 60 (8 with fireplaces)

RATES 1978: EP all year, from $30 to $50 (but you'll probably prefer the rooms costing $36 and up), with special packages for weekends and skiing; no taxes.

MEALS AND ENTERTAINMENT: Breakfast 8–9:30, lunch 12–2 (snackbar to 5), dinner 6:30–8:30 (approx. $20 to $25 for two); no room service ("well, sort of"); informal dress; occasional musical events (folk, bluegrass, sometimes yodeling in the dining room at lunchtime).

DIVERSIONS: Heated pool and heated deck (open to 11 p.m.), sauna, hiking trails (up and down and around the mountain); skiing all year (they've just built a new lift to get you up to the summer snows) and night skiing.

P.S. For your information: "Regrettably the builders of this beautiful lodge had paid scant attention to sound proofing. The wooden walls are not paper-thin but they can seem so at times. Please be considerate of others."

Lake Quinault Lodge
Lake Quinault, Ore.

Turn left when you leave the driveway and drive for half an hour (mostly unpaved road) through tall stands of fir and pine until you come to an authentic rain forest. It may not be as spectacular as the Hoh Rain Forest, a few miles up the coast, but this one is less crowded. Just you and the deer grazing on the banks of the Quinault River, beside the tumbled tree trunks. Great place for a picnic, and the lodge itself is the nicest overnight spot in these parts. It forms a cedar-shingle U, shrouded by spruce and cedar, above a lawn that sweeps down to the lake. The lobby/lounge has rafters with hand-painted beams, the dining room has a few Indian artifacts, but the guest rooms upstairs in the main lodge (about half the total) have fairly basic country-inn decor. There are a few more rustic rooms in the adjoining Lakeside Inn, a one-story annex with a big veranda, but be careful here because the kiddies' playground is right at the door, the parking lot at the rear. The spacious Fireplace Rooms, in a new wing facing lawn and lake, are the most comfortable, each with a corner fireplace (gas-powered) and sliding glass doors leading to a patio or balcony. The decor here is Oklahoma Sophisticated, but switch off the lights, light up the fire, and you won't even notice.

NAME: Lake Quinault Lodge
INNKEEPERS: Marge and Larry Lesley
ADDRESS: Quinault, Wash. 98575
DIRECTIONS: Follow U.S. 101 around the Olympic Peninsula to a point 40 miles north of Aberdeen/Hoquiam; when you spot the "Lake Quinault" signs, make sure you go east at the *South* Shore Recreation Area exit. Stay on the South Shore Road for a couple of miles.

TELEPHONE: (206) 288-2571
ROOMS: 54
RATES 1978: EP $26 to $35 all year (3 nights for the price of
2 Sunday through Thursday between November 1 and
April 1); plus 5.4% tax.
MEALS AND ENTERTAINMENT: Breakfast 7–11, lunch 11–5,
dinner 5–9 (approx. $15 to $20 for two); informal dress.
DIVERSIONS: Lake swimming (brrrr), indoor heated pool, hy-
drotherapy pool, rowboats, canoes, pool, table tennis,
putting green, hiking trails; horseback riding nearby.

The Admiralty Resort
Port Ludlow (Olympic Peninsula), Wash.

Admiralty Inlet is a mile-long cove covered with trees—
forests of fir, pine, and alder reaching right down to the
crystal-clear water. At the head of the inlet a great pile of logs
waits to be floated out to Puget Sound, reminding us that this
is lumber country. All this land, all these trees, have been
chopped down and reseeded for the past hundred years by a
company called Pope and Talbot, which has now moved into
the residential community and resort business. To keep
things in the family, most of the houses, condominiums, and
the inn buildings are constructed from local timber—wood in
all its forms from tree-trunk pillars to Prest-o-logs in the fireplaces. The resort consists of trees and clusters of condominiums, each with a view of greenery or water, each with
a private entrance. The most romantic rooms are the Loft
Suites, with bed and bath on a gallery above a luxurious sitting room with a tall stone fireplace and floor-to-ceiling windows leading to a sun deck. The Beach Club (beside "shoreline" rather than a sandy beach) is a complex of Olympic-size

pool, sauna, hydrotherapy pool, games room, and two of the development's seven courts, and if you follow the shore a hundred yards or so you come to the marina and lagoon. The Harbormaster Restaurant, focal point of the resort, has cathedral ceilings trailing chandeliers borne on iron chains, and panoramic windows looking beyond the marina to the spiky peaks of Mount Olympus. The Harbormaster features local seafood in original forms—like tournedos Dungeness (slices of filet mignon with Dungeness crab) and tournedos Ludlow (slices of filet mignon with Canterbury oysters).

With such hearty fare awaiting you, The Admiralty Resort is an ideal winter hideaway (winter temperatures seldom fall below freezing, and the rainfall, they're quick to point out in these parts, is considerably less than in Seattle), and a perfect base for touring the Olympic Peninsula and Puget Sound at any time of the year.

Pope and Talbot apparently discovered that running a resort was not the same thing as running a lumber mill, so they turned the management over to the Aircoa Corporation. Clay James, the new man at the helm, is an alumnus of Rockresorts, so The Admiralty seems to be on the right course.

NAME: The Admiralty Resort
INNKEEPER: Clay James
ADDRESS: Port Ludlow, Wash. 98365
DIRECTIONS: Port Ludlow is on the northeast tip of the Olympic Peninsula, an hour's drive from Port Angeles, 2 hours by car and ferry from Seattle; signposts on Highway 101 will guide you for the last few miles.
TELEPHONE: (206) 437-2222
ROOMS: 212 rooms, including 66 suites (all with fireplaces)
RATES 1978: EP, $28 to $36 from November 1 through April 30, $32 to $41 remainder of year (suites for two a few dollars higher); plus 5.1% tax.
MEALS AND ENTERTAINMENT: Breakfast 7–11, lunch 11–3, dinner 5–10 (approx. $15 to $25 for two); no room ser-

vice; informal dress; live music in the lounge (beneath the dining room) 5 nights a week.

DIVERSIONS: Heated Olympic-sized pool, saltwater lagoon, saunas, pool table, table tennis, tennis (7 courts, no lights, in various locations on the estate)—all without charge; 18-hole golf course ($8 weekdays, $10 weekends, free transportation from the hotel, open all year), bikes for rent, horseback riding and hayrides nearby, sailboats and ketch with crew for rent.

Captain Whidbey Inn
Coupeville, Whidbey Island, Wash.

Captain Whidbey sailed with Captain George Vancouver, RN, when they scouted the Pacific Northwest at the end of the eighteenth century, but the inn bearing his name was built by a judge at the beginning of the twentieth. Its two stories of rugged madrona logs stand watch by the edge of Penn Cove, in a grove of fir trees. Across the choppy water, you can see the hamlet of San de Fuca, and off in the distance the snowy tip of Mount Baker. The entrance to the log cabin is guarded by Barney the golden Labrador, and once you get his sleepy nod of approval you enter a friendly lobby with armchairs and sofas pulled up around a big beachstone fireplace; beyond that is a rustic dining room decorated with nautical antiques, then a rustic bar festooned with empty bottles and calling cards, in honor of some seventy years of conviviality. The nine guest rooms on the second floor are mini-log-cabins, each with its own washbasin and sharing a couple of bathrooms in the hallway. They're the most popular rooms in the inn (especially the rooms on either end), although the newer wing beside the lagoon (rooms here have private baths and occasional antiques) probably offer more quiet and privacy.

Peace and quiet are presumably what you have come here for, because other than a few excursions through the San Juan Islands and maybe a shopping trip to tiny Coupeville, there's little to do here. There is one bonus, and as good a reason as any for spending an extra day here—the Captain Whidbey wine list, pride and joy of young John Stone, who has taken over day-to-day operations from his father. Your choices include Puligny Montrachet "Clavoillon" 1974, Vosne Romanée Larronde Freres 1971, Pauillac Château Mouton Rothschild 1967, to say nothing of a collection of moderately priced California and Beaujolais vintages. Drain the bottle, and leave it hanging from the rafters as a souvenir of your idyll.

NAME: Captain Whidbey Inn

INNKEEPER: John Stone

ADDRESS: Route 1, Box 43, Coupeville, Wash. 98239

DIRECTIONS: About 90 miles from Seattle, 3 miles north of Coupeville on Whidbey Island, via ferry from Mukilteo to Columbia Beach; by air (Harbor Airlines) from Seattle to Whidbey Island airport, 30–45 minutes from the inn (free ride, if you let them know in advance).

TELEPHONE: (206) OR8-4097

ROOMS: 25, including 9 upstairs (sharing bathrooms), 4 in cabins, and 12 overlooking a lagoon

RATES 1978: EP all year, $20 in the inn, $30 by the lagoon, $32 in the cabins; plus 5.1% tax.

MEALS AND ENTERTAINMENT: Breakfast 8–11, lunch 12–2, dinner 5–10 summer, 6–8 winter (approx. $15 to $22 for two); no room service; informal dress.

DIVERSIONS: 2 rowboats (help yourselves), walking trails through woods; tennis, golf, sailboats, and scuba nearby.

Empress Hotel
Victoria, B. C., Canada

Empress by name and Empress by nature. Majestically she dominates the harbor, her venerable ivy-covered walls rising to an array of Victorian pinnacles and turrets. The oak-paneled Library Lounge is a clublike bar with armorial ceiling, and the main dining room could well be an exile from Buckingham Palace. Upstairs, the corridors are almost wide enough to accommodate the railroad cars of its owner, Canadian Pacific; the rooms have lofty ceilings, brass door fittings and, in some cases, period bath fixtures, but the decor is gracious and, in the case of the Vice-Regal Suite, palatial. If you decide to forgo the Vice-Regal Suite, ask for one of the rooms facing the harbor, the interior transformed into a tiny bower by the sunlight filtering through the ivy that frames the windows.

Like any empress, however, this one is plagued by celebrity seekers and the inquisitive, expecially on weekends in summer. One of the famed attractions here is afternoon tea ($4.50 for scones, muffins, cakes, and tea served in large silver pots on silver trays), a normally genteel ritual, but here the muffin masses turn the elegant lobby/lounge into a company cafeteria. It's as if you went to Lord's for a cricket match and found a baseball game instead. No problem, of course, if you have checked into the Empress: just nip off to your room and have your tea and scones served in your ivy-framed bower.

NAME: Empress Hotel
INNKEEPER: E. G. Balderson
ADDRESS: 721 Government Street, Victoria, B.C. V8W 1W5
DIRECTIONS: The easiest route is by ferry from Port Angeles, Washington, which deposits you almost at the Empress's feet.

TELEPHONE: (604) 384-8111

ROOMS: 416

RATES 1978: EP, from $48 to $64 from May 20 through September 30, lower rates remainder of year; plus 5% room tax.

MEALS AND ENTERTAINMENT: Breakfast 7:30–11:30, lunch 11:30–2:30, afternoon tea 2:30–5:30, dinner 5:30–10 (approx. $15 to $25 for two in the main dining room); room service to 11:30 p.m.; jackets "recommended" at dinner; pianist at teatime, disco in the basement.

DIVERSIONS: Victoria.

ADDED ATTRACTIONS

Herewith a few hotels, inns, and resorts which did not, due mainly to reasons of deadlines, make the guide proper; plus a few others which were in the first edition but have now been relegated to these pages because a) they no longer quite measure up, or b) they were too tardy in supplying updated data. However, they may fill in a few gaps in your itineraries. They're arranged alphabetically by state, with summer rates for 1978.

ARIZONA

Rio Rico Resort, Rio Rico

From the Santa Cruz Valley it looks promising, shimmering in the sun high on a mesa, a white pueblo with modern lines. On closer inspection, it turns out to be another cluster of terrace townhouses around a plaza and pool. The rooms are comfortable (some are equipped with kitchens); the dining room has a sweeping view of the countryside and the Robert Trent Jones golf course. There are also tennis courts on the mesatop and stables in the valley.

If you're bound for Mexico, keep Rio Rico in mind: it's only twelve miles from Nogales, and the most interesting stopover for miles around. 160 rooms, EP $30 to $35. *Rio*

Rico Resort, P. O. Box 2050, Nogales, Ariz. 85621 (telephone 602-287-5601).

CALIFORNIA

Rancho La Costa Resort Hotel & Spa, Rancho La Costa

This must be the Cecil B. DeMille of resorts: four swimming pools, thirteen tennis courts, twenty-one miles of riding trails, a visiting palmist, its own post office, a movie theater, three restaurants, two snackbars, and a health spa with rock steam baths, sitz baths, colonic baths, roman baths, salt glows, and a Swiss shower with seventeen shower heads that zap alternating hot and cold water on your tingling flesh. It's not the coziest or the friendliest place, but you'd be surprised at the number of renowned anatomies that have suffered through that fiendish Swiss shower. Rancho La Costa is only sixty miles by limousine from Los Angeles and thirty from San Diego, so it's a convenient place for the beautiful people to nip off to for a few days to make themselves more beautiful between movies, tournaments and big deals. The guest rooms are plush (pile carpeting, double drapes, color TV with bedside controls); some have wet bars, others bookshelves stacked with reading material, pullman kitchens and electric beds that disappear into the wall. If you want to get away from the mainstream, ask for a room in one of the cottages facing the fairways. The ranch covers something like five thousand acres, most of which seem to be taken up with new or about-to-be-built homes and condominiums, and you really have to work at solitude here, unless you do what most of the movie biggies do: check into the health spa and stay there, surviving on special calorie-conscious diets, enjoying group classes with intriguing titles like Costa Curves and Costa Capers, tingling in the Swiss shower, glistening in the salt glow. Think what all this will do for you in bed: you'll sleep like a baby. The Rancho doesn't want to be included in this guide (odd, since it doesn't cost them a penny) so they won't supply updated information—but you can be sure it's expensive. *Rancho La Costa Resort Hotel & Spa, Costa del Mar Road, Rancho La Costa, Calif. 92008 (telephone 714-729-9111).*

Rio Bravo Tennis Ranch & Lodge, Bakersfield

One of the newest of the species, this tennis ranch has spacious rooms, deep-pile comfort, modern decor, two pools, whirlpool, and a stable with a score of horses nearby. Cole Porter's personal chef heads up the kitchen, but the service in the dining room is as erratic as my service on court. Since the scenery is hardly worth a second glance, the only reason to come here is tennis—there are plenty of courts to go around, all Plexi-paved, all lighted. 55 rooms, $35 EP. *Rio Bravo Tennis Ranch & Lodge, P. O. Box 9128, Bakersfield, Calif. 93309 (telephone 805-366-3251).*

Sausalito Inn, Sausalito

Feeling heroic? Spend a night in General Grant's bed—a hulking construction with a victoriously carved headboard so tall it would go right through the roof of a motel. But this is a rather unusual inn. You enter through a modest enough doorway and climb a narrow stairway to a tiny lobby with bold blue wallpaper and potted plants. There are only fifteen rooms, all different, but each one a valentine of Victoriana: the prizes are the Marquess of Queensberry (Grant's bed, a corner fireplace, velvet sofas and chairs, campaign chests) and the Queen Victoria (corner room, bay window, golden drapes, potted plants). Both the Marquess and the Queen rate private bathrooms, most of the others have washbasins only, and you have to walk down the hallway to the toilet. But why not? The charm of Sausalito is said to be its "Europeanness." The inn is right smack in the middle of town, between the main street and the waterfront—but Anita Bryant wouldn't be at ease here. Rates for 1978 not available, but they are relatively inexpensive. *Sausalito Inn, 12 El Portal, Sausalito, Calif. 94965 (telephone 415-332-0577).*

Timber Cove Inn, near Jenner

The shower stalls here (or at least some of them) have floor-to-ceiling windows looking out to the ocean, and you can stand and scrub each other's backs while you watch the gulls and the surf. Timber Cove is about as close as you'll ever come to the perfect blending of inn and setting: on one side the ocean, on the other the inn, but since this is timber country, the inn looks almost as if Paul Bunyan's son had built a matchstick house on top of a cliff. The timbers still look like *trees*, and the inn seems to grow naturally out of a rocky garden. The lobby is a cavernous hall of glass, with timber pillars, a walk-in fireplace, an art gallery, and a bar/lounge. The forty-seven guest rooms maintain the rustic atmosphere (even the bases of the bedside lamps are rough-hewn timber, and the decorations are hunks of driftwood), and about half of them have Franklin stoves. No telephones or TV, just simple log-cabin comfort. Alas, many readers have written to report poor service and poorer housekeeping; a new manager has been installed, and although it's too early to predict results, keep your fingers crossed. 47 rooms, EP $43 to $69. *Timber Cove Inn, North Coast Highway, Jenner, Calif. 95450 (telephone 707-847-3231).*

Sea Ranch Lodge, near Jenner

Here's another spectacular clifftop location on the Sonoma Coast, but completely different from its neighbor fourteen miles down the coast at Timber Cove. Its contemporary redwood design encloses custom-made furniture in natural woods, canvas roman blinds, chunky fabrics, timber coffee tables and headboards, tiled bathrooms, picture windows. No TV or telephone, but some rooms have fireplaces. Part of Rancho de Herman (one of the last great Mexican land grants), it's now a real estate project, a place for enjoying the zesty pleasures of nature. Moderately priced (but several requests for 1978 rates went unanswered). *Sea Ranch Lodge, P. O. Box 44, The Sea Ranch, Calif. 95497 (telephone 707-785-2371).*

Little River Inn, Little River

Silas Coombs built this Maine-style mansion when he settled in these parts a hundred years ago and made a fortune in lumber and shipbuilding. Now his great-granddaughter and her husband run the old home as an inn, but its Victorian lobby still looks like the entrance to a prosperous home. The most interesting rooms are the attics, brightly decorated in early Californian style, with shower stalls added. Unfortunately, there are only half a dozen of these rooms, and the remaining forty-four are in a motel-like wing and cottages behind the eucalyptus trees—clean, comfy, but nothing special. There's a dining room serving steaks, seafoods, and home-baked breads; and the wood-paneled bar keeps special hours "for the benefit of early morning risers and golfers." Inexpensive-to-moderate rates (requests for 1978 rates went unanswered). *Little River Inn, Little River, Calif. 95456 (telephone 707-937-5942).*

COLORADO

Far View Lodge, Mesa Verde National Park

You can scout high and low but you'll be hard pressed to find a love nest in a more dramatic location: on top of the mesa, a tortuous forty-five-minute drive from the park entrance, on an elevation looking across 125 miles of wilderness to Shiprock, the Carrizo Mountains, and most of the thirty-two canyons that slice the mesa. This is Nature at its most shuddery spectacular; by day, it's mellowed by gardens of serviceberry and rabbit brush, but in the evening, when the day-trippers have wiggled their way back to the highway, you're on top of the world, alone with the stars and the coyotes that holler at each other across the canyons, and you'd better be in love with each other. The main lodge is inspired by an Indian *kiva,* or ceremonial chamber, and decorated with Navajo sand paintings and rugs. The tri-level dining room has acres of windows so that you don't have to forgo the view when you settle down to dine. The menu tries to reflect the Indian heritage, but with the Food and Drug Administration and the Department of Health breathing down the chefs' necks, this is more of a token gesture. Rates are moderate, but unfortunately the Lodge did not supply new figures in time for this edition. Maybe it has slipped off the mesa. *Far View Lodge, Mesa Verde National Park, Colo. 81330 (telephone 303-529-4421).*

CONNECTICUT

Stonehenge, Ridgefield

A flotilla of swans patrols the pond, pathways lead off into the woods, and three pines as old as the U.S.A. stand guard at the front door of this trim white Colonial-style mansion. Swiss chef Ans Benderer reigns over the kitchen, smokehouse, and the trout tank under the waterfall. A complete dinner here costs $15.95 and it's one of the best values in the Northeast. Stonehenge is for gourmets rather than lovers; the guest rooms (two in the inn, six in motel-style cabins) are less sumptuous than the dining, but there's a tray of wine and cheese and an apple to greet you when you check into your room. And after dinner, it's so much nicer to jump into bed than into a car. Rates for 1978: $35 and $45, with continental breakfast, served in the room. *Stonehenge, Route 7, Ridgefield, Conn. 06877 (telephone 203-438-6511).*

Mayflower Inn, Washington Village

The shingle-sided, steep-roofed Mayflower crowns a knoll on thirty acres of gardens and woodlands, a pleasant place to idle away a few days among maples and pines and beechnut trees. You have a choice of rooms in the main lodge or in a couple of cottages in the garden, all with period furniture and private bathrooms. It used to be a wonderful place in the fall, to return after a tramp among the foliage to a welcoming fireplace; but on a recent visit, the fires were dead and a giant TV set provided the only glow. New owners, but no new up-to-date data. *Mayflower Inn, Washington, Conn. 06793 (telephone 203-868-7411)*.

MAINE

Pentagöet Inn, Castine

"The place where the waters meet," Pentagöet, the Indians called it, and if you walk down to the end of Castine's elm-and-clapboard–lined main street and board a boat, you can lose yourselves in scores of inlets and coves. The guest house is a newcomer, although the house itself was erected in 1894; the veranda and potted plants recreate its Victorian ancestry, and the fourteen dainty and spotless rooms (four with private bath) are decorated with pencil post beds and hooked rugs. No meals (you can dine in the Castine Inn across the street), but Julia Radford and Marilyn Michaels serve breakfasts with homemade muffins, afternoon tea with scones and cucumber sandwiches. $20 to $26, including breakfast. *Pentagöet Inn, Castine, Me. 04421 (telephone 207-326-8616)*.

MASSACHUSETTS

The Village Inn, Lenox

Yet another listing for that inn-endowed Berkshire village, this one sits well back from the main road, its long screened porch facing a garden with maple trees. You can have breakfast or lunch in this porch in summer, or an after-concert nightcap during the Tanglewood Festival season. Of the twenty-five rooms, eight have air conditioning, half have pri-

vate baths, and the remainder share bathrooms in the ratio of
two rooms to one bath. The Village Inn is a shade less expensive than other Lenox inns in this guide ($21 to $24 EP most
of the year), but in July and August it's a hefty $29 to $42.
*The Village Inn, 16 Church Street, Lenox, Mass. 01240 (tele-
phone 413-637-0020).*

MINNESOTA

Lowell Inn, Stillwater

Stillwater is a small town outside Minneapolis-St. Paul, and
the Lowell is a place to keep in mind if you're driving cross-
country on Interstate 94. Its thirteen-pillared veranda gives it
something of the air of Mount Vernon, and the George Washington dining room carries the image one stage further with
Williamsburg ladderback chairs, Dresden china, Capo di
Monte porcelain and other items from the Palmer family's
private collection. The Matterhorn Room, on the other hand,
honors the Palmers' Swiss ancestry with custom-carved
woodwork that includes a life-size eagle. The twenty-five
guest rooms, on the two upper floors, feature mostly Williamsburg reproductions. EP $29 to $69. *Lowell Inn, 102
North Second Street, Stillwater, Minn. 55082 (telephone 612-
439-1100).*

NEW HAMPSHIRE

Christmas Farm Inn, Jackson

Sydna and Bill Zeliff from Pennsylvania took over this small
inn a few years ago, and their friendly welcome makes it
Christmas all year round. You'll find a hillside setting with
panoramas of the White Mountains almost every way you
turn, a small swimming pool across the roadway (not much
traffic), and all the sports attractions of the area a short drive
away. The main lodge dates from the eighteenth century,

and it's been added to ever since (including an abandoned church that was eased down the hill and ingeniously transformed into deluxe guest rooms). Rooms vary considerably in size and comforts, depending on whether you're in the Log Cabin, the Sugar House, the main house or the church. The pleasant dining room is in Colonial style. 22 rooms, from $42 MAP (without private bath) to $60 MAP (with private bath). *Christmas Farm Inn, Route 16B, Box 176, Jackson, N.H. 03846 (telephone 603-383-4313).*

The Dana Place Inn, Pinkham Notch

The forte here is food, served in a rustic-chic garden patio with floor-to-ceiling windows, but having come so far you might as well stay the night. Originally a farmhouse, the inn dates from the late 1800s, and for the past four years it's been owned and upgraded by Mal and Betty Jennings. Rooms vary in size, style, and decor, but put in a bid for numbers 6 or 14 or the Honeymoon Suite, a frilly, dainty room on the second floor. The swimming pool is screened by the apple orchard, the tennis courts are a short walk through the trees, and there's plenty of lawn for lounging and listening to the birds. (That is, if the traffic will allow, because Highway 16, though narrow and winding, is a popular route for Canada-bound tourists.) 14 rooms, EP $26 to $30 (sharing bath), $32 to $36 (private bath), all with full country breakfast. *The Dana Place Inn, Pinkham Notch, Jackson, N.H. 03846 (telephone 603-383-6822).*

Dexter's Inn & Tennis Club, Sunapee

The panoramas of lakes and wooded hills, the three tennis courts, and the cross-country ski trails will keep you busy all day. In the evening, you can draw up a chair beside the fireplace in the library and browse among some of the inn's five hundred books. Dexter's has been an inn only since 1948, but its trim rooms are decorated in traditional country style. 25 rooms, MAP $47.50 to $60 in summer. *Dexter's Inn,*

Stagecoach Road, Sunapee, N.H. 03782 (telephone 603-763-5571).

Sugar Hill Inn, Franconia

Sugar, the hill, is a mere lump compared to the peaks all around; Sugar Hill, the inn, is a friendly little spot with fireplaces in the lounge and Pewter Tavern, and the cheerful dining room has views all the way across the valley to Franconia Notch and lofty Lafayette. There's a swimming pool on the grounds, and tennis and golf are nearby. 11 rooms (5 in the inn, 6 in a motel unit in the garden), $52 MAP. *Sugar Hill Inn, Franconia, N.H. 03580 (telephone 603-823-5621).*

NEW MEXICO

The Inn of the Mountain Gods, Mescalero

You're seven thousand feet up here, among the gods and bald eagles, on a 460,000-acre reservation belonging to the Mescalero Apache tribe. Owners and operators of this unique deluxe resort, the Apaches allow no billboards or neon to spoil the views of mountain peaks, forests, and man-made lake. The entrance, via a bridge, waterfall, and stream, leads to a lobby dominated by a three-story copper-sheathed fireplace and a "chandelier" with 2,400 bulbs. Outdoors, there's boating on the lake, skiing at nearby Sierra Blanca, and tennis, golf, and swimming on the reservation. 134 rooms, EP $42 to $50. *The Inn of the Mountain Gods, Mescalero, N.M. 88340 (telephone 505-257-5141).*

Hotel Edelweiss, Taos Ski Valley

Taos Ski Valley is the brainchild of a champion called Ernie Blake, and it's reputed to have some of the toughest ski runs in the world. That may be; right now we're considering the valley as a nice place to go in summer and fall. It's tucked away, nineteen miles deep within a steep-sided canyon, and speckled with half a dozen hotels and lodges, pools, sauna, tennis courts, stables, and a choice of hearty restaurants. The Edelweiss is a pleasant base camp for walks through the forest or hikes up the mountain (the hotel will supply box lunches). Dinner is served family style at 6:30, but stay on the EP and you can dine whenever you like at one of the restaurants in the valley—or in Taos itself. Occasional entertainment includes chamber music and folk singing. 16 rooms, EP $40 in summer, EP $44 in winter. *Hotel Edelweiss, P. O. Box 83, Taos Ski Valley, N.M. 87571 (telephone 505-776-2301).*

OREGON

The Inn of the 7th Mountain, Bend

The name is romantic enough. Ditto the setting: among the tall pines, red-barked manzanitas and blue sage of Oregon's High Country, surrounded by forest trails, rivers, and waterfalls, with Mount Bachelor popping its almost-perfect cone above the pines. 7th Mountain *should* be Seventh Heaven, but it falls short (say, Fifth Heaven), probably because it's primarily a condominium development and the emphasis is on real estate rather than traditional innkeeping. But keep it in mind in case nearby Sunriver Lodge is full. In winter, 7th Mountain is a ski resort; for the remainder of the year it's a mountain playground with tennis, ice skating, outdoor chess with hand-carved three-foot-high pieces, raft trips down the rapids, sailing and rowing on the lake, two heated pools, a therapeutic pool, two saunas, horseback riding, golf. The two hundred guest rooms are in rows of cedar-sided villas around the perimeter, so that *all* the picture windows look out onto views of lake, forest, and mountain; they all have fireplaces, contemporary decor and furniture, color TV, tiled bathrooms, and thermostatically controlled temperatures. Updated data for 1978 not supplied by Inn, but 1977 rates were $24 to $78 EP. *The Inn of the 7th Mountain, P. O. Box 1207, Bend, Ore. 97701 (telephone 503-382-8711).*

PENNSYLVANIA

Toftrees Country Club and Lodge, State College

There's a university nearby (Penn State) but Toftrees is a quiet enclave insulated from the groves of academe by the groves of trees lining the fairways and forest trails. In addition to golf and walking trails, Toftrees offers platform tennis (day and night, year round), tennis, swimming pool, saunas, and in-room movies. "Luxurious resort accommodations at regular motel rates" is what Toftrees promises—and delivers. 78 rooms, EP $40 in summer. *Toftrees Country Club and Lodge, 1 Country Club Lane, Toftrees, State College, Pa. 16801 (telephone 814-237-5311).*

SOUTH CAROLINA

Fripp Island, Fripp Island

Here's another barrier island, like nearby Hilton Head, with all the right ingredients—beautiful expanse of beach, groves of live oak and loblolly pine, crabbing dock, tennis center, golf course, glossy brochure. But in this case, although the ingredients are right, the mix is wrong, and Fripp has only a hint of the flair and personality of its competitors. In fact, the rooms in the Beach Club, the so-called Sun Suites, are so dreary you might decide the place should be called Frump Island. However, some of the beachside villas are attractive, and the resort is quieter than Hilton Head. Requests for 1978 rates went unanswered, but the figures for summer 1977 were EP $40 poolside, $43 oceanside in the Beach Club. *Fripp Island, Fripp Island, S.C. 24920 (telephone 803-838-2411).*

POSTSCRIPT

If you'd like to share your experiences with other people who enjoy special places, please send me your comments, criticisms, and suggestions. Your reports can be invaluable in keeping track of the performance of individual inns. Also, if you'd be interested in subscribing to a quarterly newsletter featuring additional special places, in the U.S.A. and elsewhere, please let me know; if enough people are interested, I'll send you details at a later date.
Please address your letters:

Ian Keown
c/o Macmillan Publishing Company, Inc.
866 Third Avenue
New York, N.Y. 10022